# A Companion to British-Jewish Theatre since the 1950s

**Methuen Drama Engage** offers original reflections about key practitioners, movements and genres in the fields of modern theatre and performance. Each volume in the series seeks to challenge mainstream critical thought through original and interdisciplinary perspectives on the body of work under examination. By questioning existing critical paradigms, it is hoped that each volume will open up fresh approaches and suggest avenues for further exploration.

**Series Editors**
Mark Taylor-Batty
University of Leeds, UK
Enoch Brater
University of Michigan, USA

**Titles**
*Brecht and Post-1990s British Drama*
Anja Hartl
ISBN 978-1-3501-7278-4

*Drag Histories, Herstories and Hairstories: Drag in a Changing Scene Volume 2*
Edited by Mark Edward and Stephen Farrier
ISBN 978-1-3501-0436-5

*Contemporary Drag Practices and Performers: Drag in a Changing Scene Volume 1*
Edited by Mark Edward and Stephen Farrier
ISBN 978-1-3500-8294-6

*Performing the Unstageable: Success, Imagination, Failure*
Karen Quigley
ISBN 978-1-3500-5545-2

*Drama and Digital Arts Cultures*
David Cameron, Michael Anderson and Rebecca Wotzko
ISBN 978-1-472-59219-4

*Social and Political Theatre in 21st-Century Britain: Staging Crisis*
Vicky Angelaki
ISBN 978-1-474-21316-5

*Watching War on the Twenty-First-Century Stage: Spectacles of Conflict*
Clare Finburgh
ISBN 978-1-472-59866-0

*Fiery Temporalities in Theatre and Performance: The Initiation of History*
Maurya Wickstrom
ISBN 978-1-4742-8169-0

For a complete listing, please visit
https://www.bloomsbury.com/series/methuen-drama-engage/

# A Companion to British-Jewish Theatre since the 1950s

Edited by
Jeanette R. Malkin, Eckart Voigts and
Sarah Jane Ablett

*Series Editors: Mark Taylor-Batty and Enoch Brater*

*methuen* | drama
LONDON • NEW YORK • OXFORD • NEW DELHI • SYDNEY

METHUEN DRAMA
Bloomsbury Publishing Plc
50 Bedford Square, London, WC1B 3DP, UK
1385 Broadway, New York, NY 10018, USA
29 Earlsfort Terrace, Dublin 2, Ireland

BLOOMSBURY, METHUEN DRAMA and the Methuen Drama logo are trademarks of Bloomsbury Publishing Plc

First published in Great Britain 2021
This paperback edition published 2022

Copyright © Jeanette R. Malkin, Eckart Voigts and
Sarah Jane Ablett and contributors, 2021

Jeanette R. Malkin, Eckart Voigts and Sarah Jane Ablett have asserted their right under the Copyright, Designs and Patents Act, 1988, to be identified as editors of this work.

For legal purposes the Acknowledgements on p. x constitute an extension of this copyright page.

Series design by Louise Dugdale
Cover image © SWD

All rights reserved. No part of this publication may be reproduced or transmitted in any form or by any means, electronic or mechanical, including photocopying, recording, or any information storage or retrieval system, without prior permission in writing from the publishers.

Bloomsbury Publishing Plc does not have any control over, or responsibility for, any third-party websites referred to or in this book. All internet addresses given in this book were correct at the time of going to press. The author and publisher regret any inconvenience caused if addresses have changed or sites have ceased to exist, but can accept no responsibility for any such changes.

A catalogue record for this book is available from the British Library.

A catalog record for this book is available from the Library of Congress.

ISBN: HB: 978-1-3501-3596-3
PB: 978-1-3502-1195-7
ePDF: 978-1-3501-3597-0
ePUB: 978-1-3501-3598-7

Series: Methuen Drama Engage

Typeset by Integra Software Services Pvt. Ltd.

To find out more about our authors and books visit www.bloomsbury.com and sign up for our newsletters.

# Contents

Notes on Contributors     vii
Acknowledgements     x

1   Invisible Otherness: An Introduction to British-Jewish Theatre since the 1950s   *Eckart Voigts and Jeanette R. Malkin*     1

**Part One   The Post-War East End Scene: Pinter, Wesker, Berkoff, Kops**

2   The Theatre of Arnold Wesker: Didactic, Utopian, Biblical *Peter Lawson*     31

3   Restaging the Jewish East End: Bernard Kops and Steven Berkoff   *Jeremy Solomons*     44

4   The Theatre of Harold Pinter: Staging Indefinable and Divided 'Jewishness'   *Peter Lawson*     56

5   A Jew Who Writes: The Shadow of the Holocaust in Harold Pinter's Work   *Mark Taylor-Batty*     66

**Part Two   Force Fields and Fault Lines: The Holocaust, Antisemitism and the Israel-Palestine Conflict**

6   British Holocaust Memory and Polish Holocaust Commemoration: Eva Hoffman's Play, *The Ceremony* *Phyllis Lassner*     85

7   Dramatic Responses to the Resurgence of Antisemitism: On Trial – the Blood Libel, Arnold Wesker and Steven Berkoff *Axel Stähler*     104

8   Representing the Israel-Palestine Conflict in Contemporary British-Jewish Theatre   *Mike Witcombe*     121

## Part Three  Contemporary British-Jewish Playwrights and Theatres in Britain: Continuities and Departures

9   'Affiliation and Belonging': Contemporary British-Jewish Women Playwrights  *Eckart Voigts and Sarah Jane Ablett*   141

10  Three Ways of Being a Contemporary British-Jewish Playwright: Tom Stoppard, Patrick Marber, Ryan Craig  *Jeanette R. Malkin*   154

11  Staging Jewishness in the Twenty-First Century: Reflections on Key London Venues  *Cyrielle Garson*   172

## Part Four  Television Drama

12  British-Jewish Television Drama: Jack Rosenthal to the Present  *Sue Vice*   187

13  'It Was F***ing Biblical, Mate': The Maturing of British Television Drama  *Nathan Abrams*   201

## Part Five  Interviews with Contemporary British-Jewish Theatre Artists (2017–2018)

14  Nicholas Hytner   217

15  Julia Pascal   221

16  Patrick Marber   230

17  Ryan Craig   238

18  John Nathan   246

Index   255

# Notes on Contributors

**Sarah J. Ablett** studied English literature, philosophy and creative writing at the Universities of Hamburg, Manchester, Heidelberg, and Hildesheim, and completed her doctorate at TU Braunschweig, Germany. She has taught literary and cultural studies and was part of the research project 'Hyphenated Cultures: Contemporary British-Jewish Theatre' funded by the VolkswagenStiftung. Her latest publication is a book on *Dramatic Disgust. Aesthetic Theory and Practice from Sophocles to Sarah Kane* (2020).

**Nathan Abrams** is Professor in Film at Bangor University, UK, where he also directs the Centre for Film, Television and Screen Studies. His most recent books are *Stanley Kubrick: New York Jewish Intellectual* (2018) and (with Robert Kolker) *Eyes Wide Shut: Stanley Kubrick and the Making of His Final Film* (2019). He is currently editing *Kubrick's Mitteleuropa: The Central European Imaginary in the Films of Stanley Kubrick* with Jeremi Szaniawski; *Alien Legacies: The Evolution of a Franchise* with Greg Frame; and *New Wave, New Hollywood: Reassessment, Recovery, and Legacy* with Greg Frame.

**Cyrielle Garson** is Lecturer in Contemporary Anglophone Theatre at Avignon University, France, and a member of the Cultural Identity, Texts and Theatricality research team. She is also the Secretary of Radac (the French Society for the Study of Contemporary Theatre in English) and was one of the recipients of the CDE (The German Society for Contemporary Drama in English) biannual award in 2018 for her PhD dissertation on British verbatim theatre, which she is turning into a monograph for De Gruyter. Her current research explores VR theatre, minority theatre in Canada, as well as Anglophone theatre at the Avignon Festival.

**Phyllis Lassner** is Professor Emerita in the Crown Center for Jewish and Israel Studies at Northwestern University, USA. Her publications include *British Women Writers of World War II*, *Colonial Strangers: Women Writing the End of the British Empire*, *Anglo-Jewish Women Writing the Holocaust*, and *Espionage and Exile: Fascism and Anti-Fascism in British Spy Fiction and Film*. She co-edited the volume *Antisemitism and Philosemitism in the Twentieth and Twenty-First Centuries*, the new edition of Gisella Perl's memoir, *I Was a Doctor in Auschwitz*, and *The Palgrave Handbook of Holocaust Literature and Culture*. She was awarded the International Diamond Jubilee Fellowship

2015–17 at Southampton University, UK, for her work on Holocaust representation. Her current publications include essays on Polish post-Holocaust film, Josef Herman's art of Holocaust lamentation, Trudi Kanter's escape memoir, and boyhood in the Holocaust. She is a member of the Education and Outreach Committee of the Illinois Holocaust Museum.

**Peter Lawson** lectures on English literature and creative writing at the Open University, UK. He has written extensively on British-Jewish literature, in particular poetry, theatre and Holocaust narratives. His books include *Passionate Renewal: Jewish Poetry in Britain since 1945* (2001), *Anglo-Jewish Poetry from Isaac Rosenberg to Elaine Feinstein* (2006), and a collection of his own poems, *Senseless Hours* (2009). Peter is guest-editor for a special issue of *Humanities* on 'Contemporary British-Jewish Literature, 1970–2020'.

**Jeanette R. Malkin** is retired from the Theatre Studies Department at the Hebrew University Jerusalem, Israel. She co-edited the book *Jews and the Making of Modern German Theatre* (2010) and is the author of *Memory-Theatre and Postmodern Drama* (1999) and *Verbal Violence in Contemporary Drama: From Handke to Shepard* (1992). Her works on ethnicity and theatre culture, postmodernism and modernist German theatre have appeared in numerous academic journals and books. Malkin served as a member of the board of the Franz Rosenzweig Research Centre for German-Jewish Literature and Cultural History at the Hebrew University Jerusalem from 1998 to 2006.

**Jeremy Solomons** is Lecturer in Writing, Stonehill College, MA. Previously he was Scholar in Residence at the Elie Wiesel Center for Jewish Studies at Boston University. He is researching Post–Second World War British-Jewish theatre, applied theatre and humanities.

**Axel Stähler** is Professor of Comparative Literature at the University of Kent, UK. His research interests include modern Jewish writing and intermediality. He has published on Anglophone Jewish literature, the Holocaust, and on the convergence of Zionist, racial, and colonial discourses in early twentieth-century German-Jewish literature and culture. His most recent publications include *Zionism, the German Empire, and Africa* (2019) and the award-winning *Edinburgh Companion to Modern Jewish Fiction* (2015; co-edited with David Brauner). He is a Leverhulme Research Fellow, currently working on a book project on the representation of the destruction of Jerusalem in nineteenth-century European literature, art and music.

# Notes on Contributors

**Mark Taylor-Batty** is Senior Lecturer in Theatre Studies at the University of Leeds, UK. He has interests in modern and contemporary British and European theatre and has published books and articles on Harold Pinter, Samuel Beckett, Sarah Kane and the French director Roger Blin. His most recent publication is *The Theatre of Harold Pinter* (Methuen Drama, 2015). Most recently, he has been the principle investigator on an AHRC-funded research project *Harold Pinter: Histories and Legacies*.

**Sue Vice** is Professor of English Literature at the University of Sheffield, UK, where she teaches contemporary literature, film, television and Holocaust studies. Her most recent publications include the monograph *Textual Deceptions: False Memoirs and Literary Hoaxes in the Contemporary Era* (2014) and the co-authored study *Barry Hines: 'Kes', 'Threads' and Beyond*, with David Forrest (2017). Her latest book, *Claude Lanzmann's 'Shoah' Outtakes: Holocaust Rescue and Resistance*, will be published in 2021.

**Eckart Voigts** is Professor of English Literature at TU Braunschweig, Germany. He was President of CDE (German Society for Theatre and Drama in English, 2010–16), co-editor of *JCDE* and has written, edited and co-edited numerous books and articles, such as *Janespotting and Beyond: British Heritage Retrovisions since the Mid-1990s* (2005), *Reflecting on Darwin* (2014), *Dystopia, Science Fiction, Post-Apocalypse* (2015) and *Companion to Adaptation Studies* (2018, with Dennis Cutchins and Katja Krebs).

**Mike Witcombe** is Visiting Lecturer at Royal Holloway, University of London, UK. He is co-editor of the collection *New Voices in Jewish American Literature* (2018) and is co-editor of a forthcoming publication on the work of Naomi Alderman. His research focuses on gender and sexuality in contemporary Jewish literature. He has additional research interests in psychoanalysis, videogames and baseball fiction.

# Acknowledgements

We would like to thank the Federal State of Lower Saxony/VolkswagenStiftung for funding the three-year project 'Hyphenated Cultures: Contemporary British-Jewish Theatre' in the funding initiative Niedersächsisches Vorab: Research Cooperation Lower Saxony, Israel.

Many people have provided guidance and assistance in composing this *Companion*. We are grateful to all the writers, artists and theatre-makers willing to share their knowledge with us. Ido Telem provided invaluable assistance and companionship as researcher on this project. We are grateful to Leora Gal for her professional editing and preparation of the volume. We would also like to acknowledge the work of Luciana Tamas and the student assistants who have contributed in various ways to this research project, such as Antonie Huff, Ann-Catherine Sternberg and others.

We would like to thank everyone involved in the international conference on 'Contemporary British-Jewish Theatre' that took place in October 2018 at TU Braunschweig. Eckart Voigts and Jeanette R. Malkin wish to thank the organizers of the conference 'Shakespeare and the Jews' (London 2017) where they presented part of our work at an early stage. We would like to thank Nathan Abrams and Ruth Gilbert, the organizers of the 'British-Jewish Contemporary Cultures' conference at Bangor University, Wales, in March 2018, where we held a panel on 'Contemporary British-Jewish Theatre'. Eckart Voigts would like to thank the organizers of the conference 'Harold Pinter: Stages, Networks, Collaborations' at the University of Birmingham (April 2018) where he presented his paper '"Too Much of a Modern?" Pinter's Jewishness'.

Finally, we are grateful to our publishers Methuen Drama and to the series editors, Mark Taylor-Batty and Enoch Brater, for welcoming this *Companion* into their book series and offering thoughtful comments as well as to invaluable leads from our anonymous readers in their reader reports.

# 1

# Invisible Otherness: An Introduction to British-Jewish Theatre since the 1950s

Eckart Voigts and Jeanette R. Malkin

## Cultural Passing: The Jews Who Write

In the preface to *Two Thousand Years* (2006), Mike Leigh provides an important observation about his British-Jewish identity:

> Here's my Jewish play. I've been threatening to do it for years, but I haven't felt ready until now, when I'm well into my sixties. ... Those of us who escaped from our Jewish background have usually spent most of our adult lives keeping quiet about our Jewishness, at least. This isn't about being ashamed of one's identity, it's rather about being perceived as something you're actually not, or being cast as a stereotype role that isn't your true self. ... *Two Thousand Years* is both a Jewish play, and a play for and about everybody.
>
> (Leigh 2006: v, vii)

Leigh seems to be wary that the British perception of what it means to be a Jew will inevitably cast him in a light untrue to his self-perception. It is, after all, about 'perception': British Jews are very aware of how they are *seen* by Christian England and have long strived for invisibility. In 2003, Bryan Cheyette asked a question that in the view of Ruth Gilbert 'underpins much subsequent work in British-Jewish studies: "What is it about Britishness ... – that is so *deforming*?"' (Gilbert 2013: 3; emphasis added). Britishness and Jewishness have never been fully compatible. Linda Grant surmises that 'everyone knows that the British are tactful, decorous, well-mannered, prudent, prone to meaningful silences, and Jews are – well, the opposite' (Grant 2006b: 5). Playwright Ryan Craig, interviewed in this volume, has a similar take on British Jews. 'The Jewish personality doesn't compliment the English personality,' he says. 'The English are reserved, don't really talk about themselves too much. They don't like to brag, or push themselves forward. ... The Jewish personality ... rubs up against the English one' (Craig interview, in this volume, p. 241). Samantha Ellis felt her play *Cling to Me like Ivy* (2010) was reconnecting with 'Jewish storytelling. All the Jews I know are full of stories' (Ellis 2011).

Work by British-Jewish theatre artists which does not specifically include Jewish characters or themes has rarely been addressed as reflecting British-Jewish identities. The cultural transformations that have shaped contemporary British-Jewish theatre have never been researched, since neither from without nor from within were they perceived as particularly or significantly 'Jewish'. While there is research on key practitioners, movements and genres, we have identified the hyphenated identity of being British-Jewish as an often overlooked and underexplored ethnic dimension 'hidden in plain sight', a phrase borrowed from the title of Nathan Abrams' 2016 book on Jewishness in British film. Following the advice of Barbara Kirshenblatt-Gimblett and Jonathan Karp, 'we take Jewishness as contingent and contextual rather than definitive and presumptive' as 'no single definition of "Jewish art" can suffice' (2008: 3). As David Bial (2005: 21) reminds us, we should distinguish between Jewishness and Judaism; Jewishness is the performance of generalized cultural codes; it is more inclusive than Judaism, which is based on religion, tradition and practice, or even *Yiddishkeit*, referencing an often idealized European past. Thus, this *Companion* for contemporary British-Jewish theatre addresses the neglected dimension of Jewishness in the work of many prominent British theatre-makers while seeking to avoid simplistic essentialism that links thematic predilections or aesthetic choices to ethnic background.

The immediate post–Second World War generation of British-Jewish theatre artists were cagey about their identity. Harold Pinter, when asked, said he considered himself a Jew who writes rather than a Jewish writer (in Billington 2007: 189), yet Jewish characters and themes can be found in his plays and are especially clear in his penultimate play, *Ashes to Ashes* (1996). Like Leigh, Pinter finally turned to address his Jewishness most directly in his later years. Tom Stoppard, another key British theatre-maker of Jewish background, wrote his first 'Jewish play', *Leopoldstadt*, in 2019, at the age of 82; it opened in the West End at Wyndham's Theatre in February 2020. Stoppard, born in Czechoslovakia, was always aware of his 'outsider' roots, but apparently only learned in 1993, at the age of 56, just how Jewish he was. Even the most outspoken Jewish playwright of this generation, Arnold Wesker, easily blended into the broader discontentment of disillusioned utopias articulated by John Osborne and the angry young men so that Sally Whyte concludes: 'Although Wesker is an open and partisan Jew, very little of this is evident in the bulk of his work' (2003: 1149), a view that Peter Lawson redresses in this volume in his exploration of the dialectics of utopian Jewishness. In Wesker's generation, utopian socialist views were often conflated with deep messianic elements in the Judaic tradition, certainly in Eastern Europe and Russia.

South African-born Sir Ronald Harwood, best known for his screenplays for *The Dresser* (1983) and *The Pianist* (2002), is another example of the uneasy acculturation of the first generation of British-Jewish playwrights. Harwood anglicized his name from Horwitz after having been told by a teacher at the Royal Academy of Dramatic Arts (RADA), where he trained, that his name was too foreign and too Jewish for a British actor (Walker 2006). Harwood says simply that this decision was made to ease his career into British theatre and not as a disavowal of his Jewish origins or for fear of antisemitism (Robinson 2017). Harwood's plays and film scripts often dealt with the Nazi period, which fascinated him. Peter Shaffer, another prominent British-Jewish playwright of this generation, explored Jewish themes early in his career, long before he found international fame with his most successful plays *Equus* (1973) and *Amadeus* (1979). In *Five-Finger Exercise* (1958), Shaffer gives the young German music teacher Walter Langer both Anglophilia and an unrepentant Nazi father. His television play, *The Salt Land*, broadcast on ITV in 1955, focused on the Mayers, a German-born refugee family in Mandatory Palestine of the mid-1940s, whose two sons embody the antagonism between religious and secular Jewishness. Later, in *Shrivings* (1970), Shaffer again explores his trademark dualist antagonists by juxtaposing the sceptical, rootless Jewish-born poet Mark Askelon to the more pragmatic, self-accepting Gideon. Shaffer's successes, however, have only a tenuous thematic connection to his Jewishness. His brother Anthony, a crime writer famous for his screenplay of the movie *The Wicker Man* and his play *Sleuth*, refrained from delving into Jewishness, with the possible exception of his early play *This Savage Parade* (1963), which explored the idea of a Jewish revenge on the Nazis.

There are also British-Jewish writers of younger generations who do not engage thematically with their Jewish ancestry. These include Peter Morgan, whose father, Arthur Morgenthau, fled Germany for London in 1933. Morgan is known for his visions of Englishness (*The Queen* 2006, *The Special Relationship* 2010, *The Audience* 2013, *The Crown* 2016) and biographical speculation (*Frost/Nixon* 2006, *Bohemian Rhapsody* 2018). Stephen Poliakoff is in some ways similar to Morgan. Some of Poliakoff's thematic preoccupations, such as the discovery of clandestine histories, buried family secrets or the potential power of media documents (especially photographs and film images) to investigate an undisclosed past might speak to the

Jewish preoccupation with the past, but his plays are rarely openly Jewish-themed. Poliakoff emerged in the late 1970s as part of a new generation of left-leaning political playwrights addressing contemporary Britain during the Thatcher years, including Mike Leigh, David Hare and Howard Brenton. Poliakoff was relatively successful but drew little critical attention working at the National Theatre, with the Royal Shakespeare Company and at other prestigious writer's theatres such as the Almeida, Hampstead, Bush and Royal Court. Poliakoff began exploring his Jewishness more explicitly in his forties, such as in his 1999 play *Talk of the City*, which addresses failure of the BBC radio broadcasts to report on the full extent of Jewish persecution in Nazi Germany before the Second World War. As with Harwood, Poliakoff's acute awareness of continental European history allows him to transcend the British perspective on Europe, more particularly into Russia and Germany. Robin Nelson remarked in his study of Poliakoff's plays: 'As the descendant of Russian émigré Jews, Poliakoff is conscious of the need to be watchful lest Europe's latent totalitarian tendencies in the first half of the twentieth century erupt again' (Nelson 2011: 8).

Peter Brook and Jonathan Miller have also preferred not to stress their Jewish roots. Brook has always refused to discuss his Jewish background or its meaning for him. An ideological internationalist and a disciple of the Greek-Armenian mystic and philosopher George Gurdjieff, Brook found ethnic particularism meaningless to himself. Medical doctor, theatre actor and director Jonathan Miller, in contrast, came from a large Lithuanian Jewish family and struggled to play down his Jewishness. Miller's character in *Beyond the Fringe* once announced, 'I'm not really a Jew, you know, just Jew-*ish*,' a painful witticism that Miller often repeated in interviews (Bassett 2012: 31). Miller's biographer Kate Bassett notes that Judaism was an important part of his background, as was his wariness of antisemitism (Bassett 2012: 32). Miller admitted in an interview with Dick Cavett in 1980 that had he lived in New York, where there are many open and proud Jewish intellectuals, he too might have been more open about being a Jew. Most of these Jewish theatre people were acculturated in London but some came from Manchester, Liverpool or Leeds, such as Miller, Poliakoff, Leigh, Hytner, Morgan and Anthony and Peter Shaffer, where there were – and still are – large Jewish communities.

Yet among those first-generation British-Jewish playwrights there were also those who wrote often about their Jewish world, such as Bernard Kops and Steven Berkoff. Berkoff has had a long and varied career in theatre and film and has written and staged numerous plays. Like Wesker, both Berkoff and Kops were and remain (both are alive and active as of this writing) open about their Jewish roots. They remain ever suspicious of antisemitism and, resisting assimilationist forces, have often articulated their East End Jewishness. As the other examples above make clear, most British-Jewish artists have been conditioned for decades by social pressure towards cultural passing, learning to keep a low profile and not to highlight their ethnic or religious identity. Identity, however, sometimes finds more discrete markers. In her book *Transferring to America: Jewish Interpretations of American Dreams*, Rael Meyerowitz contends that in some Jewish-cultured artists and critics, 'a certain Jewishness ... provides a discernible subtext for all their work, that comes to the surface at significant moments, and that, whether latent or manifest, is fundamental to the desires and anxieties that they deal with and express' (1995: 3). These subtexts and anxieties must be decoded and opened for interpretation, as they are in the chapters of this book.

We may, therefore, distinguish two phases of British-Jewish theatre in England: a first phase when British-Jewish theatre was often (but not always) passing and often (but not always) a medium for transferring European culture. In this phase, British-Jewish theatre is often noted for its connection to European theatre innovations, transported by émigré directors and writers or playwrights predominantly from European-Ashkenazi families, such as Peter Brook, Tom Stoppard, Harold Pinter, Arnold Wesker, Steven Berkoff, Bernard Kops and others. While their Jewish identities may have been well known in theatre circles, their Jewishness has never been a subject of public debate. If there was otherness in most Jewish theatre writing, it was largely invisible. The second phase, in which British-Jewish theatre artists began to bring their identity more clearly to the emerging multi-ethnic metropolitan mix, began with the new wave of the 1990s, but was most clearly articulated after the turn of the millennium, as one new voice among the 'flowering of various sensibilities, a whole new variety of voices' (Sierz 2011: 26).

## Invisible Otherness: Defining British-Jewish Theatre

The term 'British-Jewish' links a transnational ethnicity and a problematically ill-defined national dimension. Our definition of British-Jewish is seemingly straightforward: British theatre artists who also identify as belonging to the Jewish 'tribe'. But are British-Jewish artists who have not created anything recognizably Jewish in terms of characters, settings and themes still relevant to our endeavour? Ezra Mendelsohn defines Jewish art as 'work by artists of Jewish descent that not only depicts Jewish life but may also advance a Jewish agenda' (Kirshenblatt-Gimblett and Karp 2008: 3). Yet Jewish agendas such as debates on Israel or antisemitism are rarely present before Wesker's *The Merchant* (1973, later renamed *Shylock* 1976) which fervently rewrites the most infamous British-Jewish character with a definite agenda in mind, suggesting how antisemitism turned Shylock into Shylock. One of the rare agenda plays prior to Wesker was written by the American Charles Marowitz, who worked with Peter Brook during his 'Theatre of Cruelty' season at the Royal Shakespeare Company (1964). Marowitz, originally a New York Jew, was a major figure of the London theatre fringe scene: in 1968 he founded the important Open Space Theatre with Thelma Holt on Tottenham Court Road. There he directed a range of Shakespeare plays he had adapted, including *The Merchant of Venice*, set in pre-Israel Palestine in 1948 with Shylock the leader of a Jewish Zionist organization that targets the British administrators in Mandatory Palestine, mirroring the historical bombing of the King David Hotel in Jerusalem by the Irgun (see Malkin and Voigts 2018). Shylock is a heroic figure in this version and, in fact, shoots the entire British hotel staff while reciting his revenge speech 'Hath a Jew not eyes?'

American émigré writers such as Marowitz and Ed Berman brought the American-Jewish avant-garde to the attention of the British theatre scene. From 1968, the Pip Simmons Theatre Group brought American-Jewish alternative theatre techniques to Britain. American writer Martin Sherman has worked in London since 1980 and Nancy Meckler has American roots. Meckler's early work was heavily influenced by Joe Chaikin and Richard Schechner.[1] Key American-Jewish playwrights from Arthur Miller and David Mamet to Tony Kushner are a staple on British stages. Clearly, Patrick Marber has been influenced by American-Jewish playwright David Mamet, while Ryan Craig is often compared to Arthur Miller. Other American-born or American-influenced Jewish playwrights in Britain include, among the new generation, Stephen Laughton and Elyse Dodgson. Activist-playwright Anders Lustgarten is of Hungarian Jewish ancestry; he was brought up in Oxford by American immigrant parents and began writing plays while teaching in St Quentin prison, California. In reverse, British-Jewish directors, playwrights and actors have been successful in the United States, chief among them are directors Sam Mendes and Stephen Frears, comedian Sacha Baron Cohen, and actors and actresses from Elizabeth Taylor and Sam Wanamaker to Daniel Day-Lewis, Helena Bonham Carter, Daniel Radcliffe and Rachel Weisz.

Matthew Baigell and Milly Heyd write of Jewish art as including 'art created by Jewish artists in which one can find some aspect of the Jewish experience, whether religious, cultural, social, or personal' (2001: xiv). Yet the case of Nicholas Wright raises the question of whether ethnic or religious boundaries are always necessary. While Wright is neither ethnically nor religiously Jewish, his play *Travelling Light* (2012) is a frequent reference point to this subject. The play is a tribute to the Eastern European Jewish immigrants who established themselves as influential personalities in Hollywood's golden age. It premiered at the National Theatre in January 2012, directed by Nicholas Hytner and starring Antony Sher, both Jewish, and was a great success. The definition 'art created by Jewish artists in which one can find some aspect of the Jewish experience' also poses the question of why 'Jewish experience' must include Jewish content. Most of Wesker's plays don't have explicitly Jewish characters but are still part of the world of a Jewish, socialist *tikkun olam* (Hebrew, repairing the world). In this volume, theatre critic John Nathan makes the point that argumentativeness is a particularly Jewish trait, adding that 'to my mind, theatre is almost a form of Jewish expression' because, 'if argument is, as we already discussed, a particularly Jewish characteristic, then you can bring those characteristics to the stage ... Because drama is about conflict'. Patrick Marber, who in interview with John Nathan in the *Jewish Chronicle* stated that he considers himself 'a Jew first and Englishman second' (Nathan 2015b), has written only one play with explicit Jewish characters, *Howard Katz*, whose theme is redemption – hardly a specifically Jewish subject of interest. Marber's other plays, such as *Dealer's Choice* (1995) or *Closer* (1997), were far more successful yet only hint at Jewish characters. An interested Jewish viewer might pick up on the 'Jewishness' of characters such as Stephen in *Dealer's Choice* or Daniel Woolf in *Closer*, but this character aspect cannot be regarded as essential for the plays. On the other hand, the rhythm of these plays, of their debates and arguments, can be seen as a Jewish undertone.

## Background: Doing Jewishness

Jews in Britain are a minority disproportionately represented in the arts. As the examples above suggest, many British-Jewish writers are well integrated into the mainstream of British theatre, much more so than other minority writers. According to recent data, between 266,740 and 284,000 Jewish people live in the UK, around two-thirds of whom live in London, representing approximately 0.5 per cent of the UK population.

British Jews were expelled from Britain in 1290 after being accused of ritual murder, persecuted and rioted against; they were only officially readmitted in 1656, a mere 365 years ago. After gradual legal and cultural emancipation, British-Jewish literary writing emerged in the nineteenth century. We have thus to consider that Anglo-Jewish history 'is well researched in historiographical terms ... but remains marginal to the UK's cultural memory and a minor reference point on 20th century and early 21st century discourses of religious and ethnic diversity' (Sternberg 2009: 3).

Based on the 2011 census figures, the UK has the fifth largest Jewish population in the world, and the second largest population in Europe, after France.[2] It is clear, however, that both the number of Jewish practitioners in the arts and their cultural and aesthetic impact are much larger than 0.5 per cent. And then, there is the problematic category of BAME, which stands for Black, Asian and minority ethnic. BAME has replaced the categories Black or non-white, after sociologist Tariq Modood and others criticized the fuzzy concept of 'Blackness' – a very different concept from the American-heritage-based differentiation among African American, Jewish American, Italian American and so forth. Latent antisemitism, assimilationist pressures and the fact that UK 'citizenship has not as warmly embraced the notion of the hyphenate identity as in the United States' (Abrams 2010: 59) are decidedly factors in Britain, whereas the identity of being American and Jewish does not seem to be contradictory or problematic.[3]

Coming to a substantial extent out of the transnational European-Jewish diaspora, we could address British-Jewish writers simply as experts in extraterritoriality, given that most of their families have a background of migration, or as Sicher and Winehouse write, 'as veteran diaspora globetrotters who have borne racism and entered their host cultures as migrants and outsiders' (Sicher and Weinhouse 2012: 14). Across aesthetic and generational chasms, experiences of homelessness, migration and extraterritoriality feed into the British-Jewish identity from Harold Pinter and Tom Stoppard to Ryan Craig and Patrick Marber, from Deborah Levy and Diane Samuels to Julia Pascal. Jewish writers are in a clearly different situation from that experienced by people of colour where anti-Muslim or anti-Black racism is much more pronounced and which may to some extent have replaced traditional antisemitic sentiments (Reitz 1998: 25–6). Julia Pascal refers to the special multicultural position of Jews in Britain: 'In Britain, there is a culture of multiculturalism, which does not include Jews. 'Cause Jews are considered white, privileged and rich. It's never said, because the British won't say it, but that's the subtext' (Pascal quoted in Behlau and Reitz 2004: 301). While many British Jews have indeed reached social prominence and are often highly visible members of the scene in arts, commerce and politics, in terms of numbers most of the British Jews are Haredi, a sect of ultra-orthodox fundamentalists which has increased both in number and in its cultural impact over the last decades. These communities traditionally have large families and often little income and have only recently begun to become culturally visible, largely through Netflix series such as *Shtisel* (Israel 2013–16) and *Unorthodox* (Germany 2020). Carol Gerson argues that British-Jewish writers write 'from a colony within a colony, looking backward to continental Europe, forward to Israel, and sideways at the United States, the current homeland of English-language Jewish culture' (Gerson 1982: 104).[4]

Yet Anglo Jewry is far from homogeneous. Claudia Sternberg warns that '[a]nother potential fallacy is to speak of the Jews in Britain without qualification, glossing over significant intra-communal differences based on migratory backgrounds (Sephardi or Ashkenazi, Western, Eastern or non-European, historical or recent), orthodox, progressive and secular lifestyles, degree of assimilation, class and ultimately the social status and recognition afforded by all of these' (Sternberg 2009: 3). While the eastern European or middle European Ashkenazi diaspora prevails in the family backgrounds of most British-Jewish theatre-makers discussed so far, there are also British-Jewish theatre-makers of Sephardic and Mizrahi descent such as Samantha Ellis, Shelley Silas and Laughton. In general, migratory backgrounds are varied. Some still have family in mainland Europe or Israel, and many have family ties to South Africa (Antony Sher, Ronald Harwood, Gail Louw, Gillian Slovo), India (Shelley Silas) or Australia (Miriam Margolyes). All of the playwrights we encountered are secular so that we can conclude that the British-Jewish theatre identity is not predominantly religious. True, many of our interviewees described religious practices in their parents' homes and many continue some of these traditions, but invariably they relegate religion to the almost subconscious background of a non-believing urban intelligentsia. Most would agree with Peter Brook, who reported about his father: 'Jewishness to him had to do with religion and rabbis, and he was a modern assimilated Englishman' (Croyden 2009: 295). Brook echoes the stance taken by Harwood and others about a smooth transitioning between the poles of the hyphenated British-Jewish identity: 'In the milieu in which we lived, there was never, at any point in my life, any friction' (Croyden 2009: 296). In his autobiography, Brook recalls that 'I had learned as a child that I was Jewish and Russian, but these words were abstract concepts to me; my impressions were deeply conditioned by England: a house was an English house, a tree was an English tree, a river was an English river' (Brook [1998] 2007). It is worth noting that Brook's wife, Natasha Parry, was also Jewish and far more assertive on the subject. Similarly, Jonathan Miller described his own Jewishness as prophylactic in keeping him away from Christianity; his son remembers 'an amphibious relationship with his Jewish origins ..., half in and half out of Jewish water' (Bassett 2012: 33).

David Herman has argued that European locations, biographical vagaries, disguises and unrest as themes in Tom Stoppard's work can be related to an implicitly Jewish experience (Herman 2015: 193) that has finally come to the fore in *Leopoldstadt*. Similarly, Linda Grant found Jewish themes in Mike Leigh's work that can be traced to his Jewishness even before *Two Thousand Years*, such as the focus on families and sibling rivalry, thwarted idealism, diaspora and tragicomedy in the work of 'this most English of playwrights and film-makers' (Grant 2006a). Peter Brook has articulated that unrest is the key to identify Jewishness with a theatre identity. In fact, Brook himself is the global theatre-maker who in transitioning from London to Paris via Africa most effortlessly transcends the narrow confines of an insular British or English theatre. We can, thus, argue that Jewishness is one element of otherness that is key in making contemporary British theatre polyglot and cosmopolitan. In the attempt to unify universalism and cultural differences, Kwame Anthony Appiah stresses the mobility of cultural practices and objects. In *Cosmopolitanism: Ethics in a World of Strangers* (2006: 4) Appiah highlights the ethical obligations among human beings, praising 'the recognition that human beings are different and that we can learn from each other's differences'. Furthermore, Judith Butler has made otherness and alterity key terms in her refutation of the tendency to equate Jewishness and Zionism: 'the distinctive trait of Jewish identity is that it is interrupted by alterity' (Butler 2012: 6). In the Butlerian sense one cannot *be* Jewish, but one can *do* Jewishness.

Theatre critics John Nathan (2015a), David Jays (2000) and Michael Billington (2012) have argued that Jewish identities bring an outsider's identity and outside (often European) perspectives to British theatre. Billington, in a journalistic essay, wondered 'how much an inherited sense of exile, loss and isolation offers a key to [British-Jewish dramatist's] work. Is there, in fact, such a thing as a Jewish theatrical identity?' (2012). Billington here taps into a much-contested debate – from the universalist claim of Harold Bloom that Jewishness is a 'paradigm for humanity' to George Steiner on the insistence of the singularity of the religious and racial past and the Jews' experience of extraterritoriality (see Brauner 2001: 2). With some trepidation, Bryan Cheyette has remarked on 'the protean instability of "the Jew"' as a 'tenacious signifier' (1993: 8), and David Brauner concluded by bringing the dualisms together: 'For some ... Jewishness is an innate, inalienable property, for others a learned tradition; for some, a belief system, for others a cultural construct; for some a race, for others a religion; for some a nationality, for others a sensibility; for some a historical legacy, for others a metaphysical state' (Brauner 2001: 3).

Jewish culture, then, is the prototypical example of a transnational imagined community – a rather fluid 'ethnoscape' in the words of Arjun Appadurai (2003: 25). Thus, theoretical keywords for the discussion of British-Jewish theatre come from inter- and trans-culturalism (Knowles 2010; Pavis 1996), ideas of cultural transformation and adaptation, as well as intersectionality – the study of interrelations in cultural discrimination (Gilman 2001; Ginsberg 1996). How, then, is British-Jewish theatre continuously reimagined from within and without and how can there be a sense of shared trajectories within the group of Jewish writers currently active?

## 'Central but Unidentified': Existing Research

In 2013 Axel Stähler claimed that '[d]rama has remained a conspicuous absence in the critical engagement with Jewish cultural production in Britain' (Stähler 2013: 320), and David Jays suggested the urgency of our project: 'Jewish theatre artists have been central but often unidentified' (Jays 2019). The blatant gap in research on British-Jewish theatre is surprising, considering British theatre critic Michael Billington's claim in 2012 of 'modern theatre's heavy dependence on Jewish writers'. How do we account for this paucity of research into British-Jewish theatre-making? Playwright and director Julia Pascal believes that British-Jewish artists' reluctance to openly examine their Jewish heritage is due to still prevalent stereotypes and exposure to 'constant low-level anti-Semitism that filters through British Society' (in Quinn 2009). In her opinion, this prejudice is also reflected in the subsidization of ethnic minorities by the Arts Council, from which Jewish minorities have received little support. In her Ph.D. thesis, Pascal (2016) bemoans the scarcity of Jewish stage characters who are invariably reduced to a set of stereotypes rooted in English literature, such as Shylock, Barabas and Fagin. Pascal also notes British theatre's almost complete omission of Jewish women, with the possible exception of Anne Frank (Pascal 2016: 64). She maintains that when Jewish women are portrayed at all, they tend to be redeemed by conversion to Christianity (Pascal 2016: 33). Pascal's examples are Jessica in *The Merchant of Venice* from 1605 and Eva in Diane Samuels' 1993 play *Kindertransport*.

There are various studies of national hyphenated identities: German-Jewish theatre artists and culture have been well researched (most recently by Malkin and Rokem 2010), as have American-Jewish theatrical relations (Alexander 2001; Bial 2005; Novick 2008). In the field of British-Jewish theatre, however, there are only very few dissertations and monographs. Notable work is focused on the role of memory in British-Jewish drama since 1945 (Behlau-Dengler 2011; Lassner 2014) and includes Julia Pascal's account of the lack of representation of Jewish women on the British stage since 1945 (Pascal 2016). We have also found some scattered studies of individual dramatists or sections on dramatists in studies and anthologies devoted more generally to Jewish cultural life in Britain (Behlau and Reitz 2004; Cesarani 1990; Cheyette 1998; Lawson 2011; Neumeier 1998; Sicher 1985; Valman 2014) or Jewish theatre more generally (Nahshon 2009; Rozik 2013). In terms of individual dramatists, the focus is very much on the first wave of male British post-war dramatists, and while the burgeoning literature on Harold Pinter and Tom Stoppard is hard to fathom, rarely do studies discuss their Jewishness. There is a stream of studies on Arnold

Wesker, Peter Shaffer (Gianakaris 1992) and a few notable biographical studies on Bernard Kops (Baker and Shumaker 2014), Ronald Harwood (Robinson 2017), Steven Berkoff (Cross 2004), Stephen Poliakoff (Nelson 2011) and Peter Barnes (Dukore 1981). Significant actor-writers such as Steven Berkoff (1993, 1996, 2000, 2020) or Antony Sher (2001, 2004, 2005, 2018) have left a flourishing trail of autobiographical texts, diaries and memoirs.

There are also some studies of British-Jewish directors' work at key theatre venues, their methods and institutional anchoring. Peter Brook, whose approach in *The Empty Space* was revelatory and revolutionary for the theatre and practice of world theatre in 1968, and, to a somewhat lesser degree, Jonathan Miller have been discussed at great length (Bassett 2012; Brook 1998; Croyden 2009; Kustow 2006; Romain 1992). Jonathan Miller's polymath interests, which took him from student comedy and a medical degree to the artistic directorship at the Old Vic and beyond to television, film and opera, mirror Brook's polyglot engagement with the world. Other significant theatre-makers are Mike Alfreds, who founded the influential ensemble Shared Experience in 1975, and David Aukin. The generation of powerful Jewish directors of the 1990s is discussed in (auto)biographical texts: Nicholas Hytner at the National Theatre and the Bridge Theatre (*Balancing Acts*, 2017), David Lan at the Young Vic (*As If by Chance*, 2020), Dominic Cooke at the Royal Court and the National Theatre, and Sam Mendes at the Royal Shakespeare Company and the Donmar Warehouse (Leipacher 2011; Wolf 2004) have also left their indelible mark on the history of British theatre. Mendes' epic *The Lehman Trilogy* (National Theatre, adapted by Ben Power from Stefano Massini's original play), on the failures of capitalism, was a high-profile success in 2018.

Thus, while the Man Booker Prize win of Howard Jacobson's *The Finkler Question* (2010) may have provided impetus for studies of British-Jewish novelists such as Jacobson, Clive Sinclair, Anita Brookner, Stephen Fry, Jenny Diski or Will Self, and while we have seen first approaches to British-Jewish poetry (Lawson 2006), TV productions (cf. Abrams 2010) and popular culture (Abrams 2016), studies of British-Jewish theatre to this date remain partial and rare.

The differing positions on the current situation of Jewish people in Britain are marked by conflicting statements in the interviews we conducted as part of our research project, some of which are appendixed to this volume. The former head of the National Theatre, Nicholas Hytner, while admitting that antisemitism has been on the rise recently, told us that anti-Jewish sentiments have only played a minor role in his career:

Speaking as a sixty-year-old gay man, no comparison. It was agony in the sixties and the seventies – to grow up then and try to come to terms with being gay. That was awful, to get to the other side of it. Being Jewish? It didn't matter. Really, truly. Being gay was tough; being Jewish was not tough. That's my experience.

(Hytner interview in this volume, p. 219)

Hytner's statement brings up the question of intersectionality: how does being a woman, or being gay or lesbian, or being Black, or coming from Kolkata, shape writers' identities in addition to being Jewish? Julia Pascal's view on how anti-Jewish sentiments have shaped arts and theatre policies in Britain articulates a probable shift in the perception of antisemitism:

The Left, who run the arts and the theatre, is profoundly anti-Israel, therefore anything a writer produces or anything that is said in public, ... or whether support is given or not given to BDS,[5] affects whether work is commissioned. Many British Jews are frightened. To be a Jew in England has always been, and is, a state of low-level anxiety. ... Being a Jew does not place a person in a fashionable minority. ... If you go to the Arts Council to put on a play that touches Jewish history in any complex way, you're very unlikely to get support because Jews are perceived to be rich and can look after themselves.

(Pascal in this volume, p. 223)

## New Jewish Plays for the Twenty-First Century

The recent generation of playwrights has seemingly moved away from the acculturated, assimilated stance of their forefathers and is tackling contemporary identity issues more directly. As ethnic diversification increases in the urban theatre centres, Jewish theatre-makers have ceased to be amalgamated into a mainstream yet are increasingly challenged to demarcate their identities. That is, British-Jewish theatre artists today will largely be positioned (and position themselves) as expressing a hyphenated British-Jewish identity, rather than merely the work of 'Jews who happen to write', to quote Harold Pinter's disavowal of Jewishness in his writing. The current British-Jewish play is smaller in scale and frequently seeks to define Jewishness as one ethnic node within the network of diverse ethnic theatres in contemporary urban Britain (and this frequently still means London), as well as a more diverse perspective on gender identities. It is carried by theatre spaces that more directly engage with their immediate communities and are thus embedded in London's ethnic mix, which is composed of a more diversified scene of outsiders compared to the East End of the 1950s. Jewish actress and playwright Tracy Ann Oberman has commented on the practice of anglicizing names as assimilationist when doing so was suggested to her: 'I think the British Jewish voice is there but we've been ashamed of it and kept it under wraps' (in Jays 2019).

Donald Weber recounts how Mike Leigh was inspired by Kwame Kwei-Armah's *Elmira's Kitchen* in 2003 to write *Two-Thousand Years* as a Jewish 'ethnic equivalent' (Leigh in Weber 2016: 162). Maybe following the example of other multicultural cosmopolitan London writers, the twenty-first century has seen 'a rising generation of British Jewish theatre artists' who are less reticent about their Jewishness, 'getting mouthy, raising their Jewish voices unabashedly, in the process overturning the tradition of "Stay shtumm."' (Weber 2016: 159, 161). We argue that this process began even before the millennium. Prominent writers active in the first phase of this new chapter of British-Jewish writing in the 1990s include Shelley Silas, whose family descended from Sephardi Jews of Kolkata and Palestine, Diane Samuels, Julia Pascal, Ryan Craig and, above all, Patrick Marber. This coincides with an awareness of more localized British-Jewish theatres, many of them fringe venues in north and north-east London, catering to their respective liberal Jewish communities, such as the Hampstead Theatre under David Aukin, Jenny Topper and Edward Hall, Shared Experience under Mike Alfreds and Nancy Meckler et al., the Park Theatre under Jez Bond, the Tricycle/Kiln Theatre, the Arcola Theatre in Dalston, further north the Watford Palace Theatre, further west the Finborough Theatre, West Brompton and, since 2013, the Jewish cultural centre JW3 in West Hampstead. While we may thus tie British-Jewish theatre to distinct Jewish-inflected audiences, the influence of Jewish artistic directors reaches far beyond any ethnically homogeneous community. Critic John Nathan holds – with some justification – that the success of British theatre in the 2000s is linked to three significant Jewish directors: Nicholas Hytner at the National Theatre, Dominic Cooke at the Royal Court and David Lan at the Young Vic (Nathan 2015a).

While not focused on specifically Jewish themes, the success of Patrick Marber's multi-award winning *Closer* (1997), adapted by him for the high-profile film production in 2004, directed by Mike Nichols (an American Jew) and starring Julia Roberts, Natalie Portman, Clive Owen and Jude Law, may have given twenty-first-century Jewish writers an impetus to more directly address their situation in contemporary Britain. Representative examples of contemporary urban plays for metropolitan (and, in part) Jewish communities in the twenty-first century might include Samantha Ellis' *Cling to Me like Ivy*, Shelley Silas' *Calcutta Kosher*, Alexis Zegerman's *Holy Sh!t*,

Josh Azouz' *The Mikvah Project* and *Buggy Baby*, Daniel Kanaber's *Shiver*, or Stephen Laughton's *One Jewish Boy*.

Alexis Zegerman is one representative of the new generation of British-Jewish theatre artists. She started her career as an actress and is best known for her role as Zoe in Mike Leigh's Oscar-nominated comedy-drama film *Happy-Go-Lucky* (2008), for which she won a British Independent Film Award for Best Supporting Actress and a London Film Critics Award. She also played the part of Daliah Sofer in Leigh's *Storm* (2009) and in his stage play *Two Thousand Years* (2005) as well as Eva in Stoppard's *Leopoldstadt* (2020). *Holy Sh!t* opened the new Kiln Theatre (formerly the Tricycle Theatre) in 2018. Here, Zegerman explores religious and cultural issues among two middle-class couples in London, the secular Jews, journalist Simone and designer Sam Kellerman, and their Anglican best friends, Black teacher Nick and white marketing manager Juliet Obasi. The conundrum is whether to send their kids to a Catholic school, St. Mary's, considered the best school in the area. The fight for the place prompts a foul-mouthed descent of the Jewish couple into racism and of the Black and white couple into antisemitism, suggesting a dark layer of festering prejudice under a thin veneer of middle-class multiculturalism.

The success of novels such as Eve Harris' *The Marrying of Chani Kaufman* (2013) and Naomi Alderman's exploration of a lesbian relationship among Orthodox London Jews, *Disobedience* (2006, turned into a film in 2017), have led to the Haredi communities of north London becoming a theme in contemporary British-Jewish theatre. Daniel Kanaber's *Shiver* (Palace, Watford, 2014) engages (like Steven Berkoff's *Sit and Shiver* in 2004) with Jewish mourning rites in a play focused on how protagonist Mordecai should react to the loss of his wife Sadie and how to prepare for the shivah, the seven-day period of Jewish mourning. Stewart Permutt's *A Dark Night in Dalston* (Park Theatre, London, 2017) juxtaposes Haredi (ultra-Orthodox) and secular Jews, when a young Orthodox Jewish man ends up spending Friday night with a local woman because the onset of darkness prohibits him from travelling. Gail Louw's more recent and as yet unpublished two-hander *Eishes Chayill – Woman of Valour* explores the sexual mores in the Haredi community. Here, an Orthodox housewife, Chasida, must come to terms with her husband's decision to have sex with men during her 'unclean' days (*niddah*), which results in his HIV infection. Samantha Ellis' *Cling to Me like Ivy* (2010) is one of the few plays to fully explore the world of Hasidic Jewry in contemporary London. Rivka, the 21-year-old daughter of an Orthodox rabbi, escapes from an arranged marriage to David, the son of another rabbi. While this engagement remains non-sexual, discussions of Rivka's hair and, in particular her *sheitel* (wig),[6] are a metaphor for Rivka's growing exploration of sexuality through her affair with the secular, English

Patrick. Patrick is the boyfriend of her best friend Leela, who is Hindu. Ellis has explained that her play was provoked by 'Sheitel-gate' in 2004: Hindu hair used in the making of wigs for Hasidic Jewish women. In *Cling to Me like Ivy* (2010), Ellis explores the multi-ethnic, multireligious world of contemporary London.

The London-based writer and director Josh Azouz (b. 1985) also represents this younger generation of British-Jewish theatre artists in prototypical ways, and his work is equally steeped in Jewish signifiers. Emerging from writers' groups at the Royal Court and the Bush Theatre, Azouz became an associate artist for the Yard and MUJU (Muslim-Jewish Theatre Company), where he deliberately sought to cooperate with Muslim Londoners in the comedy sketch show *Come In. Sit Down!* (Tricycle Theatre, co-directed with Salman Siddiqui) in 2015. Referring to this project, Azouz said: 'I'm in my 20s, I live in London, and I don't have a Muslim friend. The problem is that if you don't know people from other communities, you make assumptions' ('Shalom, salaam and goodnight!' 2015). Both of his full-length plays are set in a contemporary multicultural London. *Buggy Baby*'s (2018) central refugee couple are fighting drug-induced horror visions of bazooka-toting rabbits triggered by the harrowing experience of raising a child after traumatic expatriation. *The Mikvah Project* (2015), revived but cancelled due to the COVID-19 pandemic at Orange Tree Theatre in 2020, is a Brechtian play ostentatiously set in a specifically Jewish site, the eponymous cleansing bath. As in British-Jewish playwright Nick Cassenbaum's most popular *Bubble Schmeisis* (2014), Azouz engages with the forgotten Jewish bath culture in London. Here, middle-aged Jewish Avi and the seventeen-year-old boy Eitan explore a potentially tragic homosexual affair within a community riddled by ambivalence and described as 'Postmodern Orthodox!' (Azouz 2018: 77). Both plays enjoyed extended sold-out runs at the Yard Theatre in East London and are typical of the Yard which itself was rejuvenated from a derelict warehouse in Hackney Wick, where the first wave of east London British-Jewish theatre artists emerged sixty-five years earlier. With artistic director Jay Miller's programming of both Josh Azouz and, more recently, Arthur Miller's *The Crucible* (2019), it seems that contemporary British-Jewish theatre has come full circle. It is now ready to usher in a new, more ethnically aware and maybe both more self-consciously and self-confidently Jewish phase of contemporary British-Jewish theatre. Azouz' work is refreshing because it is a variation on the template that has dominated British-Jewish theatre-making for a long time: formally uninventive well-made plays that feature conversations on Jewish themes at the dinner tables of middle-class families.

Stephen Laughton's play *Run*, which opened at the Vaults Festival in 2016 and went on to tour the UK until April 2017 to much critical acclaim, also addresses gay Jewishness and is exemplary of new British-Jewish theatre's interest in complexified intersectional identity. The brouhaha around Laughton's significant play *One Jewish Boy*, which premiered in December 2018 at the Old Red Lion Theatre in Islington, London, and transferred to the Trafalgar Studios in March 2020, is indicative of the increasingly contested and precarious, but at the same time more openly Jewish position of British-Jewish theatre artists as well as the persistent conflation of the Palestine-Israel conflict and the situation of Jews in contemporary Britain. *One Jewish Boy* is a two-hander that follows the relationship and marriage of Alex, a mixed-race woman from Peckham (she refers to herself as a 'Jamaican-Irish Catholic Windrush girl from a council estate', Laughton 2020), and Jesse, a middle-class Jewish man from Highgate. What sets *One Jewish Boy* off from previous discussions of cultural strife in multicultural urban centres is the directness of Jesse's confrontation with contemporary antisemitism in Britain and Europe. The play's title obviously references Caryl Churchill's *Seven Jewish Children* (2009), which caused a major upheaval and a strong reaction in British-Jewish communities. As Mike Witcombe argues in this *Companion*, the play takes issue with precisely the conflation of diaspora Jewish identity with conflicts in contemporary Israel so that its protagonist, the British Jew Jesse, argues in vain that he has 'very little … in fact nothing to do with Israeli foreign policy' (Laughton [2018] 2020). The play's resolution, which has Jesse concluding that Israel might now be seen as a safe haven for European Jews confronted with the threat of antisemitic violence, directly invokes current discourses precipitated by events in Paris, Halle or New York.[7] Yet recent data shows that the number of Israeli-born Jews in Britain is actually rising ('New figures' 2019).

## Introducing the *Companion*

This *Companion* focuses on Jewish theatre in English, a non-Jewish language. Theatre in Jewish languages – Hebrew, Aramaic, Yiddish and Ladino – did and continue to exist. In Europe, Yiddish theatre has declined as a consequence of the Shoah and assimilationist pressure, although Yiddish theatre has a rich tradition in Britain and particularly London before the Second World War. The *Companion* excludes significant writers active before the Second World War, such as Israel Zangwill. The structure of our *Companion* reflects the historical development of British-Jewish theatre after the Second World

War, beginning with an analysis of the first generation of writers that now forms the core and mainstream of post-war British drama. The second part identifies significant thematic force fields and fault lines, above all the Shoah, antisemitism and the Israel-Palestine conflict. We then focus on the new generation of British-Jewish playwrights, with special attention to women writers, the role of particular theatres as well as television drama in the development of British-Jewish theatre.

The chapters in the section on post-war British-Jewish theatre address the search for Jewish qualities, or cultural markers, as a positive and creative mark of difference, together with the more constraining effects of assimilationist pressures towards strategies of passing. Peter Lawson's chapter discusses the didacticism in 'The Wesker Trilogy', describing Wesker as a utopian and didactic British-Jewish playwright. Lawson finds both British and Jewish roots in Wesker's 'postponed utopias' and sketches their influence both on the next generation of British political writing and on the younger generation of British-Jewish writers such as Ryan Craig, Mike Leigh and Jack Rosenthal.

Post-war British-Jewish theatre came into its own in the mid-1950s as part of the traditional date of renewal that ushers in the phase of modern British theatre. First productions by Arnold Wesker, Bernard Kops and Harold Pinter appeared in 1957 (Pinter: *The Room*, Bristol; Wesker: *The Kitchen* 1957; Kops prepared *The Hamlet of Stepney Green* for the Oxford Playhouse[8]). These were followed by another set of pivotal moments in 1958, with the London debuts of Wesker's *Chicken Soup with Barley* (first produced in Coventry also in 1958) at the Royal Court and *The Hamlet of Stepney Green* at the Lyric Hammersmith on 14 and 15 July 1958, while Pinter's *The Birthday Party* was also first produced in London in 1958. The first section is dedicated to this first wave of post–Second World War playwrights, many of whom grew up in specifically Jewish environments to parents who were immigrants or first-generation British citizens.

Contemporary plays such as Ryan Craig's *Filthy Business* (2017) speak for the continuing fascination of British-Jewish playwrights with the East End. Jeremy Solomons takes a closer look at the role of the East End and in particular Whitechapel, Stepney and Hackney in the work of playwrights such as Wesker and Pinter. Yet Solomons suggests we not overlook Bernard Kops and Steven Berkoff and their uniquely British-Jewish theatre language. The towering influence and stature of Nobel Prize laureate Harold Pinter merit two chapters that explore aspects of Jewishness in his plays. Peter Lawson throws into sharp relief Pinter's Jewish-inflected East End speech rhythms and argues for an acknowledgement of Pinter's 'indefinability' and European modernism. Mark Taylor-Batty views Pinter as 'both Jewish and not Jewish', highlighting the contradictions in his work and seeing Jewishness first in the engagement with questions of 'home' and belonging and, in his final years, a more direct engagement with Nazism and the terrors of the Second World War.

The Shoah is a recurrent and relatively well-researched force field in contemporary British-Jewish playwriting (Behlau-Dengler 2011; Plunka 2009; White 1999) and its centrality in contemporary Jewish consciousness is beyond doubt. Crucial questions are how British-Jewish playwrights have responded to the challenges of representability posed by the Holocaust. Are images of the Shoah exploitative, idolatrous? Is art after Auschwitz, as Adorno claimed, 'barbaric', and 'unspeakable' in language and literature (George Steiner, see Plunka 2009: 11, 14)? Positioning English spectators as non-present witnesses to the horrors of the Shoah, many plays have dealt with these issues from the early 1990s to the first decade of the new millennium after 9/11; they most frequently discussed cases such as Diane Samuels' *Kindertransport* (1993) or Harold Pinter's *Ashes to Ashes* (1996) to, most recently, Stoppard's *Leopoldstadt* in 2020.

Memory narratives of survivors are the format of choice in many plays that tackle the Shoah. Antony Sher's *Primo* (National Theatre 2004), an adaptation of Primo Levi's Auschwitz memoir *If This Is a Man*, is exemplary in its spare aesthetics and deliberate avoidance of directly illustrating an unrepresentable horror. Sher is aided by the matter-of-fact sobriety of horrific detail in the Italian chemist's account. Similar memory narratives include one-handers such as Martin Sherman's *Rose* (National Theatre 1999) and Gail Louw's multi-award-winning *Blonde Poison* (2011). *Blonde Poison* is quite remarkable for its focus on a guilty female Jewish character, Stella Goldschlag, a Nazi collaborator. Based on the historical narrative, like Rose and Levi, Goldschlag is portrayed reminiscing on her war experience, focusing not on the suffering she caused but on the motivation and rationalization of evil. Louw's antipathy towards her character and her desire for the audience to vilify her (Louw 2015: 5), is not always fulfilled by audiences who have also empathized with Goldschlag's own suffering.

Following plays such as Peter Barnes' *Laughter!* (1978), a dark comedy on the Auschwitz bureaucracy, or C. P. Taylor's *Good* (1981), which chronicles the descent of German literature professor into Nazism, Samuels' *Kindertransport* is arguably the most successful Holocaust play by a British-Jewish playwright. It is a set text in schools and has been played in prominent UK venues. The play is steeped in biographies of the *Kinder* transported to Britain before the beginning of the Second World War and the Shoah. In successful expressionist stage techniques, Samuels opts for a *kairos* technique (Samuels 2014: 46) to express the mingling of past and present, never fully separating the past off as 'flashbacks'. The joint endeavour of *Kindertransport* and other British-Jewish plays that engage with the Shoah fill a blind spot in British collective memory. Behlau-Dengler concludes: 'Pascal, Samuels and Pinter criticise the lack of engagement with the Holocaust within British collective memory. British collective memory of the Holocaust is still focused on the memory of the Blitz and the liberation of the concentration camps. The internment of and discrimination against Jewish refugees on the Channel Islands does not have a prominent place in this context' (2011: 444).

Behlau-Dengler addresses Julia Pascal's play *Theresa*. Indeed, the differences between the approaches of Diane Samuels and Julia Pascal, who has contributed her immensely rich *The Holocaust Trilogy* (1995) to this group of memory plays, are instructive. Samuels has described her feminocentric play as intensely internal and private, in direct confrontation of the masculine public theatre world. In *Theresa*, Pascal chooses to intervene politically, tackling British collaboration with the Nazis head on. Phyllis Lassner finds that '[t]hese plays challenge those wartime myths of British identity as it was solidified in the rhetoric of the British Empire standing alone against the Axis imperial alliance while the home front muddled through with patient good humor and traditional allegiances to liberty, the law, and the community' (Lassner 2014: 176). The accusation of British collaboration combined with latent antisemitism led to *Theresa* being banned in Guernsey, where only a radio broadcast of the play could be heard (Lassner 2014: 175). The play was largely ostracized in the British theatre scene because it challenged the 'distinctiveness of the British character in contrast to those who fell victim to Hitler' (Luckhurst 2000: 147). *Theresa* explores the fate of Theresia Steiner, who was deported from Guernsey in 1942 and subsequently murdered in Auschwitz, revealing British collaboration with the Nazis on the Channel Islands. *Theresa*, as *Kindertransport*, is based on interviews, and Pascal reports she was horrified to find persistent antisemitic tropes in the Guernsey islanders' memories (Pascal 2000: 5).

In her chapter in this volume, Phyllis Lassner continues her engagement with Shoah plays that stage uncomfortable and traumatic memories, focusing on Eva Hoffman's play *The Ceremony*, performed on 21 May 2017 at London's JW3 (Jewish Cultural Center). Lassner offers a balanced analysis of Polish-Jewish relations that had by that time become politically contentious following the Polish right-wing government's unwillingness to engage with Polish responsibility – or even complicity – in the Holocaust.

We have frequently alluded to the persistence of antisemitism in Britain, which is further explored in Axel Stähler's chapter. He links Stephen Laughton's recent play *One Jewish Boy* to two earlier, thematically converging plays, *Blood Libel* (1994) by Arnold Wesker and *Ritual in Blood* (2000) by

Steven Berkoff. Stähler argues that these lesser-known plays bear witness to the resignation of their authors in the face of the persisting irrationality and calumnies of antisemitic manifestations, which seem to evade the juridical discourse in their plays.

Next, Mike Witcombe's chapter links the debate on latent antisemitism in Britain to its conflation with discussions of contemporary Israel. He argues that the simultaneous productions of Mike Leigh's *Two Thousand Years* and Ryan Craig's *What We Did to Weinstein* in 2005 mark a turning point. The controversial discussion on *My Name Is Rachel Corrie* in the same year might be another contributing factor, while positions were subsequently antagonized by the Jewish reaction to Caryl Churchill's *Seven Jewish Children* (2009). Discussing plays such as Julia Pascal's important *Crossing Jerusalem* (2003), Witcombe notes their pessimism, their shared family setting – often involving the exposition of a shattering secret and exposure of fundamental generational rebellion ignited by conflicting attitudes towards the conflict, and increased engagement with contemporary politics.

The next section, on contemporary British-Jewish playwrights and theatres in Britain, explores writers and venues that have transformed British-Jewish theatre. The first chapter by Eckart Voigts and Sarah Jane Ablett explores the work of British-Jewish women dramatists. These include Julia Pascal, Diane Samuels, Samantha Ellis, focusing on Shelley Silas and Nina Raine, whose plays explore the cultural specificity of Jewishness within British society, breaking with previous traditions such as Wesker's humanistic universalism or Pinter's modernist abstraction.

Jeanette R. Malkin's chapter examines the ways that three prominent contemporary male playwrights inscribe their Jewish identity into their plays, sometimes purposely, sometimes not. Tom Stoppard, whose 2020 *Leopoldstadt* was the most discussed Jewish play of the time, is the first playwright discussed. The next is Patrick Marber, of *Closer* fame, who directed Stoppard's *Leopoldstadt*. The third playwright is Ryan Craig who has written six well-received Jewish-themed plays. All are Londoners who have had multiple plays performed at the Royal National Theatre – and still each is a very different type of British-Jewish playwright.

The third chapter in this section, by Cyrielle Garson, addresses the role of venues in the unprecedented surge of British-Jewish theatre since 2000. Garson provides an analysis of key London venues such as the National Theatre, the Donmar, Hampstead, Tricycle and Young Vic. She also supplies a snapshot of today's landscape through the study of two new London venues, JW3 (2013) and the Bridge Theatre (2017), as well as to both the visibility and camouflage of Jewish elements in the plays produced there.

The next section is on British-Jewish television drama. While television is frequently considered a different sphere, we include this section since many theatre artists have worked for both stage and screen, and in Britain the links seem to be particularly pronounced. Sue Vice's discussion of the pivotal role of Jack Rosenthal addresses questions of agency, while Nathan Abrams addresses representation of Jews and Jewish characters in British television, pointing to a departure from cliché and suggesting a period of greater realism and maturity in British-Jewish television drama. To keep this volume manageable, we focused on writers and directors. Thus, the important histories of many Jewish actors such as Peggy Ashcroft, Felicity Kendal, Maureen Lipman, Henry Goodman, David Warner or Sophie Okonedo, comedians and TV personalities such as Stephen Fry, Simon Amstell, David Baddiel, Ben Elton or Matt Lucas, and other co-creators of theatre such as key producers Oscar Lewenstein, Michael White or Sonia Friedman will not receive due attention.

The *Companion* concludes with a selection of interviews with significant theatre practitioners: Nicholas Hytner, Julia Pascal, Patrick Marber, Ryan Craig, and John Nathan. Additional interviews and a cornucopia of biographical information can be found on our web database at https://britishjewishtheatre.org.

## Notes

1. On Jewish-American influence on British-Jewish Theatre see Weinberg (2017), who focuses on Jim Haynes, Charles Marowitz, Nancy Meckler and Ed Berman.
2. See House of Commons Home Affairs Committee (2016: 5).
3. According to Bial, Jewishness had begun to be accepted into the American mainstream since the 1960s (2005: 27).
4. In a controversial argument, Efraim Sicher and Elaine Weinhouse have even suggested that Jews have been 'silenced' in postcolonial discourse because of latent Christian resentment and easy subsumption of Apartheid as a 'Euro-Judaic' evil, while European stereotyping of Jews as non-white, arrogant, chauvinist, primitive or separatist persists (Sicher and Weinhouse 2012: 15). As evinced by the fierce debate around Camaroonian scholar Achille Mbembe, the role of antisemitism within postcolonial studies is a highly contested arena.
5. The Boycott, Divestment and Sanctions movement (BDS) is an international campaign targeting Israel's occupation policy through economic action.

6   This refers to wigs worn by orthodox Jewish women in fulfillment of religious requirement to cover womens' hair, since it is considered erotic. It is frequently used as a symbol of patriarchal oppression of women.
7   On 29 December 2019, knife-wielding Grafton Thomas attacked a Hanukkah celebration in Monsey, north of New York City.
8   With Kops' *The Hamlet of Stepney Green*, dates given vary from writing (1956/1957) to the Oxford Playhouse production directed by Frank Hauser (Meadow Players 19 May 1958) and the London production (1958). A production at the Theatre Workshop, Stratford East, never materialized.

## References

Abrams, N. (2010), 'Hidden: Jewish Film in the United Kingdom, Past and Present', *Journal of European Popular Culture*, 1 (1): 53–68.
Abrams, N., ed. (2016), *Hidden in Plain Sight. Jews and Jewishness in British Film, Television, and Popular Culture*, Evanston: Northwestern University Press.
Alexander, M. (2001), *Jazz Age Jews*, Princeton, NJ: Princeton University Press.
Appadurai, A. (2003), 'Disjuncture and Difference in the Global Economy', in J. E. Braziel and A. Mannur (eds), *Theorizing Diaspora: A Reader*, 25–48, Oxford: Blackwell.
Appiah, K. A. (2006), *Cosmopolitanism: Ethics in a World of Strangers*, New York: W. W. Norton.
Azouz, J. (2018), *Buggy Baby and the Mikvah Project. Two Plays by Josh Azouz*, London: Nick Hern Books.
Baigell, M. and M. Heyd (2001), 'Introduction', in M. Baigell and M. Heyd (eds), *Complex Identities. Jewish Consciousness and Modern Art*, xiii–xvii, New Brunswick, NJ and London: Rutgers University Press.
Baker, W. and J. R. Shumaker (2014), *Bernard Kops: Fantasist, London Jew, Apocalyptic Humorist*, Plymouth: Fairleigh Dickinson University Press.
Bassett, K. (2012), *In Two Minds. A Biography of Jonathan Miller*, London: Oberon.
Behlau, U. and B. Reitz, eds (2004), *Jewish Women Writers in the 1990s and Beyond in Great Britain and the United States*, Trier: WVT.
Behlau-Dengler, U. (2011), *Zakhor!: Remembering the British-Jewish Experience in British-Jewish Drama after 1945*, Trier: WVT.
Berkoff, S. (1993), *Theatre of Steven Berkoff*, London: Methuen Drama.
Berkoff, S. (1996), *Free Association: An Autobiography*, London: Faber and Faber.
Berkoff, S. (2000), *Graft: Tales of an Actor*, London: Oberon Books.
Berkoff, S. (2020), *A World Elsewhere*, London: Routledge.
Bial, D. (2005), *Acting Jewish. Negotiating Identity on the American Stage and Screen*, Ann Arbor, MI: University of Michigan Press.
Billington, M. (2007), *Harold Pinter*, London: Faber and Faber.

Billington, M. (2012), 'J Is for Jewish Dramatists', *The Guardian*, 14 February. Available online: https://www.theguardian.com/stage/2012/feb/14/jewish-dramatists-modern-drama (accessed 29 May 2020).

Brauner, D. (2001), *Post-War Jewish Fiction: Ambivalence, Self-Explanation and Transatlantic Connections*, Basingstoke: Palgrave.

Brook, P. ([1998] 2007), *Threads of Time. A Memoir*, London: Bloomsbury. Kindle Edition.

Butler, J. (2012), *Parting Ways. Jewishness and the Critique of Zionism*, New York: Columbia University Press.

Cesarani, D., ed. (1990), *The Making of Modern Anglo-Jewry*, Oxford: Blackwell.

Cheyette, B. (1993), *Constructions of 'the Jew' in English Literature and Society. Racial Representations, 1875–1945*, Cambridge: Cambridge University Press.

Cheyette, B., ed. (1998), *Contemporary Jewish Writing in Britain and Ireland: An Anthology*, London: Halban.

Churchill, C. (2009), *Seven Jewish Children. A Play for Gaza*, London: Nick Hern Books.

Cross, R. (2004), *Steven Berkoff and the Theatre of Self-Performance*, Manchester: Manchester University Press.

Croyden, M. (2009), *Conversations with Peter Brook 1970–2000*, New York: Theatre Communications.

Dukore, B. (1981), *The Theatre of Peter Barnes*, London: Heinemann.

Ellis, S. (2011), *Cling to Me like Ivy*, London: Nick Hern Books. Kindle Edition.

Gerson, C. (1982), 'Some Patterns of Jewish Writing of the Commonwealth', *Ariel*, 13 October: 103–14.

Gianakaris, C. J. (1992), *Modern Dramatists: Peter Shaffer*, Basingstoke: Macmillan.

Gilbert, R. (2013), *Writing Jewish: Contemporary British-Jewish Literature*, London: Palgrave Macmillan.

Gilman, S. (2001), 'R.B. Kitaj's "Good Bad" Diasporism and the Body in American Jewish Postmodern Art', in M. Baigell and M. Heyd (eds), *Complex Identities. Jewish Consciousness and Modern Art*, 223–37, New Brunswick, NJ and London: Rutgers University Press.

Ginsberg, E. K., ed. (1996), *Passing and the Fictions of Identity*, Durham, NC: Duke University Press.

Grant, L. (2006a), 'Mike Leigh Comes Out', *The Guardian*, 18 April. Available online: https://www.theguardian.com/film/2006/apr/18/theatre.religion (accessed 29 May 2020).

Grant, L. (2006b), *The People on the Street: A Writer's View of Israel*, London: Virago.

Herman, D. (2015), 'Jewish Émigré and Refugee Writers in Britain', in D. Brauner and A. Stähler (eds), *The Edinburgh Companion to Modern Jewish Fiction*, 188–98, Edinburgh: Edinburgh University Press.

House of Commons Home Affairs Committee (2016), *Antisemitism in the UK*. Available online: https://publications.parliament.uk/pa/cm201617/cmselect/cmhaff/136/136.pdf.

Hytner, N. (2017), *Balancing Acts*, London: Jonathan Cape.
Jays, D. (2000), 'Missing', *New Statesman*, 30 October. Available online: https://www.newstatesman.com/node/152277 (accessed 29 May 2020).
Jays, D. (2019), '"We've Been Ashamed of Our Voice"': The Secret History of UK Jewish Theatre', *The Guardian*, 13 March.
Kirshenblatt-Gimblett, B. and J. Karp (2008), 'Introduction', in B. Kirshenblatt-Gimblett and J. Karp (eds), *The Art of Being Jewish in Modem Times*, 1–21, Philadelphia, PA: University of Pennsylvania Press.
Knowles, R. (2010), *Theatre and Interculturalism*, London: Palgrave Macmillan.
Kustow, M. (2006), *Peter Brook. A Biography*, London: Bloomsbury.
Lan, D. (2020), *As If by Chance*, London: Faber.
Lassner, P. (2014), 'Dramatizing Britain's Holocaust Memory', in N. Valman (ed.), *Jewish Women Writers in Britain*, 74–191, Detroit: Wayne State University Press.
Laughton, S. ([2018] 2020), *One Jewish Boy*, London: Nick Hern Books.
Lawson, P. (2006), *Anglo-Jewish Poetry from Isaac Rosenberg to Elaine Finestein*, London: Vallentine Mitchell.
Lawson, P. (2011), 'Theater: Britain', in J. R. Baskin (ed.), *The Cambridge Dictionary of Judaism and Jewish Culture*, 592–3, Cambridge: Cambridge University Press.
Leigh, M. (2006), *Two Thousand Years*, London: Faber.
Leipacher, M. (2011), *Catching the Light. Sam Mendes and Simon Russell Beale*, London: Oberon.
Louw, G. (2015), *Collected Plays. Blonde Poison, Miss Dietrich Regrets, Shackleton's Carpenter, Two Sisters*, London: Oberon Books.
Luckhurst, M. (2000), 'The Case of Theresa: Guernsey, The Holocaust and Theatre Censorship in the 1990s', in I. Janicka-Swiderska and J. Jarniewicz (eds), *Jewish Themes in English and Polish Culture*, 138–48, Lodz: Wydawnictwo Uniwersytetu Lodzkiego.
Malkin, J. R. and F. Rokem, eds (2010), *Jews and the Making of Modern German Theatre*, Iowa City: University of Iowa Press.
Malkin, J. R. and E. Voigts (2018), 'Wrestling with Shylock. Contemporary British Jewish Theatre and Shakespeare's *The Merchant of Venice*', *European Judaism*, 52 (2): 175–85.
Meyerowitz, R. (1995), *Transferring to America: Jewish Interpretations of American Dreams*, New York: SUNY Press.
Miller, J. (1980), '"I Am Not Jewish" Interview on the Dick Cavett Show PBS.' Available online: https://www.youtube.com/watch?v=PLbymPBRvGk&ab_channel=AbhilashNambiar (accessed 31 May 2020).
Nahshon, E. (2009), *Jewish Theatre. A Global View*, Leiden/Boston, MA: Brill.
Nathan, J. (2015a), 'Visionary Behind the Shock of the Young Vic', *The Jewish Chronicle*, 20 April. Available online: https://www.thejc.com/culture/theatre/visionary-behind-the-shock-of-the-young-vic-1.66131 (accessed 31 May 2020).
Nathan, J. (2015b), 'Interview: Patrick Marber', *The Jewish Chronicle*, 30 July.

Nelson, R. (2011), *Stephen Poliakoff on Stage and Screen*, London: Methuen.
Neumeier, B., ed. (1998), *Jüdische Literatur und Kultur in Großbritannien und den USA nach 1945*, Wiesbaden: Hassarowitz.
'New figures show near-doubling of Israeli-born UK residents since 2001' (2019), *Jewish News*, 29 November.
Novick, J. (2008), *Beyond the Golden Door: Jewish American Drama and Jewish American Experience*, New York: Palgrave Macmillan.
Pascal, J. (2000), *Theresa; A Dead Woman on Holiday; The Dybbuk*, London: Oberon Books.
Pascal, J. (2016), 'The Absence of Female Jewish Characters on the Post-War English Stage: Thesis and Three Plays', PhD diss., University of York, York.
Pavis, P., ed. (1996), *The Intercultural Performance Reader*, London: Routledge.
Plunka, G. A. (2009), *Holocaust Drama. The Theatre of Atrocity*, Cambridge: Cambridge University Press.
Quinn, B. and T. Forward (2009), 'New Depiction of Fagin on London Stage Sparks Fears of Anti-Semitic Stereotypes: Critics Question Whether Portrayal of Jewish Street Thief Fagin in Dickens' "Oliver!" Is Acceptable', *Haaretz*, 29 January. Available online: https://www.haaretz.com/1.5069031 (accessed 31 May 2020).
Reitz, B. (1998), '"Forget Things and You'll Go to Pieces": Jüdische Identität zwischen Erinnerung und Annäherung, Utopie und Holocaust im englischen Drama der Gegenwart', in B. Neumeier (ed.), *Jüdische Literatur und Kultur in Großbritannien und den USA nach 1945*, 25–42, Wiesbaden: Harrassowitz.
Robinson, W. S. (2017), *Speak Well of Me: The Authorised Biography of Ronald Harwood*, London: Oberon Books. Kindle Edition.
Romain, M. (1992), *A Profile of Jonathan Miller*, Cambridge: Cambridge University Press.
Rozik, E. (2013), *Jewish Drama and Theatre. From Rabbinical Intolerance to Secular Liberalism*, Brighton: Sussex Academic Press.
Samuels, D. (2014), *Diane Samuels' Kindertransport. The Author's Guide to the Play*, London: Nick Hern Books.
'Shalom, salaam and goodnight! Behind the scenes of a new Muslim-Jewish comedy' (2015), *Jewish News*, 23 July. Available online: https://jewishnews.timesofisrael.com/shalom-salaam-and-goodnight-behind-the-scenes-of-a-new-muslim-jewish-comedy/.
Sher, A. (2001), *Beside Myself. An Actor's Life*, London: Hutchinson.
Sher, A. (2004), *Year of the King. An Actor's Diary*, London: Nick Hern Books.
Sher, A. (2005), *Primo Time*, London: Nick Hern Books.
Sher, A. (2018), *Year of the Mad King. The Lear Diaries*, London: Nick Hern Books.
Sicher, E. (1985), *Beyond Marginality. Anglo-Jewish Literature after the Holocaust*, Albany, NY: State University of New York Press.
Sicher, E. and L. Weinhouse (2012), *Under Postcolonial Eyes: Figuring the 'Jew' in Contemporary British Writing*, Lincoln: University of Nebraska Press,

Vidal Sassoon International Center for the Study of Antisemitism (SICSA), Hebrew University of Jerusalem.
Sierz, A. (2011), *Rewriting the Nation. British Theatre Now*, London: Methuen.
Stähler, A. (2013), Review of Ulrike Behlau-Dengler, 'Zakhor!', *Journal of Contemporary Theatre in English*, 1 (2): 320–3.
Sternberg, C. (2009), 'Introduction', *Journal for the Study of British Cultures*, 16 (1): 1–10.
Valman, N., ed. (2014), *Jewish Women Writers in Britain*, Detroit: Wayne State University Press.
Walker, T. (2006), 'In Praise of the Patriotic Playwright', *The Spectator*, 14 June.
Weber, D. (2016), 'Peckhlach. Mike Leigh's British Jewish Soul', in N. Abrams (ed.), *Hidden in Plain Sight: Jews and Jewishness in British Film, Television, and Popular Culture*, 157–79, Evanston: Northwestern University Press.
Weinberg, D. (2017), *Off-Broadway/Off-West End. American Influence on the Alternative Theatre Movement in Britain 1956–1980*, London/Hamburg: Ibidem.
White, N. J. (1999), 'In the Absence of Memory?: Jewish Fate and Dramatic Representation; Production and Critical Reception of Holocaust Drama on the London Stage 1945–1989', PhD diss., City University London, London.
Whyte, S. (2003), 'Arnold Wesker', in S. Kerbel (ed.), *Jewish Writers of the Twentieth Century*, 1146–9, New York: Fitzroy Dearborn.
Wolf, M. (2004), *Sam Mendes at the Donmar*, New York: Limelight.
Zegerman, A. (2018), *Holy Sh!t*, London: Nick Hern Books. Kindle Edition.

# Part One

# The Post-War East End Scene: Pinter, Wesker, Berkoff, Kops

2

# The Theatre of Arnold Wesker: Didactic, Utopian, Biblical

Peter Lawson

Reading Wesker (1932–2016) is an ambivalent experience. On the one hand, his early plays – *Chicken Soup with Barley*, *Roots* and *I'm Talking about Jerusalem* (known together as 'The Wesker Trilogy'; 1958-60); *The Kitchen* (1961), *Chips with Everything* (1962), and *Their Very Own and Golden City* (1965) – present a utopian impulse towards creating 'a just and beautiful society' (Wesker 1970: 110). On the other hand, Wesker's utopian and didactic plays dramatize disillusionment and the failure to realize utopia. In this chapter, I argue that Wesker dramatizes overlapping utopian and messianic visions and that both relate to his portrayal of the 'Good Jew'. The countervailing disillusionment in Wesker's plays has its roots in both secular and biblical narratives of paradise lost, whether that paradise be conceived as socialism, Eden or a world without antisemitism. Although the 'Good Jew' repeatedly finds his innocence betrayed, compromised or lost, this chapter argues that utopian aspirations remain characteristic of Wesker's didactic theatre.

Wesker was not alone among the young generation of playwrights in the 1950s to dramatize the fight for a better world following the Second World War. In his autobiography *As Much as I Dare (1932–59)* (1995), Wesker emphasizes how important John Osborne's *Look Back in Anger* (1956) was for him. He writes: 'The impact [of *Look Back in Anger*] cannot be understated [*sic*] … Six months later, on 8 October [1957], I began to write *Chicken Soup with Barley* – original title *When the Wind Blows* – finished six weeks later' (Wesker 1995: 566). The title *When the Wind Blows* possibly referred to the potential nuclear holocaust feared in the 1950s. Wesker was a member of the Campaign for Nuclear Disarmament and joined the first protest march in 1958 to the Atomic Weapons Research Establishment at RAF Aldermaston. In his autobiography, Wesker recalls marching 'in the rain, collecting blisters, and singing Blake's "Jerusalem"' (Wesker 1995: 610). Perhaps Ronnie Kahn from Wesker's trilogy can be understood as a Jewish Jimmy Porter – the leading character in *Look Back in Anger* – and another so-called Angry Young Man.[1]

Wesker writes in 'Theatre, Why?', an essay from 1967: 'I can remember the thrill of seeing *Waiting For Godot* for the first time, long before I began writing plays, and finding in it an echo of much that was preoccupying my thoughts. I experienced a similar feeling of recognition when I saw Pinter's *The Birthday Party*' (Wesker 1970: 97–8). So, we can approach Wesker as part of that generation of young British and Irish dramatists struggling to shape a new vision of society after the disaster of the Second World War. Often Wesker is grouped with such 'angrier' playwrights as Osborne, Pinter, 'John Arden and Margaretta D'Arcy, Edward Bond' and David Mercer (Ponnuswami 1998: 137). These were playwrights engaged in a 'quest for a radically reconfigured socialism' which they presented 'as a quest for survival, not only for the Left but for all humankind' (142).

Wesker's dramatic heirs might include 'Howard Brenton, David Hare, David Edgar, Trevor Griffiths, John McGrath, Caryl Churchill and the myriad of artists and groups which constituted the socialist theatre's avant-garde from the mid-1960s onwards' (Ponnuswami 1998: 138). To this eclectic cast of talents, I would add a number of British-Jewish playwrights, in particular, Ryan Craig and Mike Leigh.

Wesker, I argue, differs from other playwrights of his generation in enacting a utopia-disillusionment dialectic within an explicitly British-Jewish environment. Furthermore, he suggests other dialectics: between domestic dreams and worldly reality, and between intellectual combativeness and British-Jewish repression. To put these dialectics in some sort of theoretical framework, it is helpful to turn to the American-Jewish novelist Philip Roth. In a 1974 essay about his classic novel of repression and self-expression, *Portnoy's Complaint* (1969), Roth explains how '*Portnoy's Complaint* took shape out of the wreckage of four abandoned projects', one of which was a 'manuscript of about two hundred pages titled *The Jewboy*' (Roth 1985: 33). 'The second abandoned project', he explains, 'was a play entitled *The Nice Jewish Boy*' (34). Roth goes on to define these discursively semitic terms in the following ways: 'Jewboy', he states, 'signifies to Jew and Gentile alike ... aggression, appetite, and marginality', while 'nice Jewish boy' implies 'repression, respectability, and social acceptance' (35). According to Roth, these oppositional tropes lend themselves to different genres: the assertive 'Jewboy' to 'extremes of unmanageable fable or fantasy' and the repressed 'nice Jewish boy' to 'familiar surface realism or documentation' (37).

This 'Jewboy'-'Nice Jewish Boy' dialectic seems to apply to Wesker's drama. It can help us understand both the utopian impulse, displayed in 'extremes of unmanageable fable or fantasy', and its repression in 'familiar surface realism or documentation'. Consider 'The Wesker Trilogy'; the title of the first play,

*Chicken Soup with Barley* (1958), is redolent of Jewish domesticity. Indeed, the play is dominated by the presence of Sarah Kahn, Ronnie Kahn's mother and a committed communist. The play begins with the stage directions: 'SARAH KAHN *is in the kitchen washing up, humming to herself. She is a small, fiery woman, aged thirty-seven, Jewish, and of European origin*' (Wesker 2001: 37). While the action is confined to the Kahns' home, their debates concern the fantastic challenge of forging a utopian world. Fabulous utopia is both domesticated and repressed in Wesker's style of documentary realism. In *Chicken Soup with Barley*, the articulation of utopian dreams is confined to what Wesker categorizes as 'Jewish' and 'European' domestic space, yet these dreams cannot be realized in the non-domesticated Britain beyond this space.

According to Wesker's autobiography, his dramatic *and* utopian muse is his mother, 'Leah Wesker, née Perlmutter, born in Gyergószentmiklos, Transylvania' and 'arrived in this country aged eleven' in 1910 (Wesker 1995: 5, 7). Wesker explains the genesis of *Chicken Soup with Barley* in the following way: 'My memory of how and why I wrote the play is clear. I had quarrelled with my mother over politics, raging at her continuing adherence to communism' (599). He continues: 'On two memorable occasions, after bitter exchanges, I wrote down what she had said … I fused them into one speech … knowing with certainty when I heard it that it would become the speech to end this play' (599). This is the utopian speech with which the play climaxes, featuring the telling lines:

> If the electrician who comes to mend my fuse blows it instead, so I should stop having electricity? I should cut off my light? Socialism is my light, can you understand that? A way of life. A man *can* be beautiful. I hate ugly people – I can't bear meanness and fighting and jealousy – I've got to have light. I'm a simple person, Ronnie, and I've got to have light and love.
>
> (Wesker 2001: 76)

In a letter to his wife Dusty on 30 May 1958, Wesker writes: 'Funny that, the triumph of *Chicken Soup with Barley* is also not my triumph but my mother's. I wonder why' (Wesker 1995: 647).

My reading of this relationship is that Wesker remains essentially in love with his mother. That is to say, Wesker idealizes Leah/Sarah as his 'triumph' and the 'light' of his life. A letter from the mid-1950s, which Wesker cites in *As Much as I Dare*, gives voice to this idolization: 'My darling little mother,' it reads, 'if there is any integrity, any nobleness, any goodness and kindness, any sensitivity [in me] – it is yours … Any guts I have you had. This is what you gave him [Wesker], and you can tell them all that, and when you have told them that you can tell them to go to Hell!' (Wesker 1995: 452). In this construction of Wesker's mother, she is all goodness. Indeed, she is the ultimate 'Good Jew', reproduced in her son, and set in binary opposition to those who belong in 'Hell'. It is probably no coincidence that the opening essay of Wesker's collection *Fears of Fragmentation* (Wesker 1970) is titled 'O Mother Is It Worth It?' (1960), clearly invoking the muse-mother ('O Mother').

Here we turn to another pair of helpful discursive terms: 'Good Jew' and 'Bad Jew'. Not only are Wesker's plays replete with visions of utopia, they are also replete with 'Good Jews': Sarah Kahn, Ronnie Kahn, Monty Blatt and Dave Simmonds in 'The Wesker Trilogy', Paul in *The Kitchen* (1961) and, perhaps most notably, Shylock in *The Merchant* (1976), Wesker's reworking of Shakespeare's *The Merchant of Venice*. Such 'Good Jews' – as we have seen in Wesker's letter to his mother – have 'integrity ... nobleness ... goodness ... kindness ... sensitivity ... [and] guts'. A 'Good Jew' has utopian visions, suggestive of Jewish messianism in the titles of such plays as *I'm Talking about Jerusalem* (1960) and *Their Very Own and Golden City* (1965). Interestingly, this discursive 'Good Jew' has much in common with the repressed traits of Roth's 'Nice Jewish Boy'. The 'Good Jew' represses the 'Bad Jew' of appetite, aggression and cynicism, much as the 'Nice Jewish Boy' represses the 'Jewboy' in order to be respectable and socially accepted (Roth 1985: 35). Ronnie Kahn is referred to as 'a strong socialist' and 'a Jew boy' in *Roots* (Wesker 2001: 137), a play in which he significantly does not appear. Although Ronnie behaves badly by jilting his girlfriend, Beatie Bryant, no 'Bad Jew' makes an entrance in the play; again, the 'Bad Jew' is repressed. In eschatological terms, the 'Good Jew' and the 'Nice Jewish Boy' are both going to Heaven, while the 'Bad Jew' and the 'Jewboy' are heading straight to 'Hell'.

Throughout Wesker's plays and prose, including his only novel *Honey* (2005), there is a consistent link between idealism, innocence and 'Good Jews'. For example, the Jewish character Tamara in *Honey* says of Beatie Bryant (a protagonist resurrected from the 1959 play *Roots*): 'I like this young woman, she's innocent, naïve, fresh'; adding for good measure: 'She seemed like a modern-day Candide' (Wesker 2005: 133). Although the characters of *Their Very Own and Golden City* are not identified as Jews, the play begins with a typical 'atmosphere' of '[i]nnocence' (Wesker 2010: 88). The Jewish Tamara in *The Journalists* (1975) similarly claims her innocence: 'Between the oppressors and the fanatics there's the rest of us' (Wesker 1990: 94). What is consistently excised, or repressed, is the common discursive link between cynicism, worldliness and 'Bad Jews'.

That said, the 'Bad Jew' of semitic discourse does make an allusive appearance in Wesker's autobiography. Here Wesker quotes from a fictionalized diary of the 1950s, 'The Diary of Jon Smith':

> I rolled slightly to my right and gazed at a gargoyle that presided in miniature over an ashtray. It is a replica of one of the Notre Dame devils ... Nothing seems to disturb the hooked nose, the wide mouth and pointed chin ... Somehow that devilish face inspired a calm as if to say – I know it all and one day you will too.
>
> (Wesker 1995: 438)

Here the 'Bad Jew' of semitic discourse is domesticated as a post-Holocaust 'ashtray'. This 'Bad Jew' is so awfully bad ('devilish') that moral striving can be dismissed, inspiring 'a calm'. Yet this ugly ('gargoyle') and demonic ('devils') Jew (with 'the hooked nose, the wide mouth') may eventually take over the young innocent narrator ('one day you will [know it all] too'). Therefore, behind the protagonist's 'calm' of innocence lies the potentially opposite 'calm' of being a desperately 'Bad Jew'.

Yet the ashtray is also an inspiration. As Wesker sits down to 'write' (in 1956), the 'gargoyle ashtray with its broken wings is with me' (Wesker 1995: 492). Its 'broken wings' may remind us of what Wesker has earlier referenced as the 'broken Jews' (213) of the Holocaust who can no longer aspire to utopia since their transcendent 'wings' of poetic flight (according to Theodor Adorno) are 'broken' after Auschwitz. I would suggest that such 'broken Jews', survivors of the Shoah, may also be understood as 'Good Jews' on whose behalf Wesker feels obliged to fight.

Contemplating the nature of evil in a diary entry of 12 November 1956, Wesker concludes simply: 'Evil is the absence of fight' (Wesker 1995: 530). On the one hand, Wesker's conclusion relates to the recent memory of Nazism and echoes Enlightenment philosopher Edmund Burke's observation that the 'only thing necessary for the triumph of evil is for good men to do nothing'. On the other, it suggests the fight of the 'Good Jews' against the cynicism of the 'Bad Jews': 'I know it all and one day you will too.' Indeed, evil appears to be everywhere in Wesker's autobiography. He writes: 'Every Tom, Dick and Mary behaves meanly' (535); '[M]en are pretty lousy creatures in general' (539). This somewhat pessimistic *Weltanschauung* is, I suggest, quite different to what the utopian plays present, and may relate to the Holocaust.

For example, Wesker writes in his 1950s Paris diary:

> These last days have been a sort of crisis. I think it began when Dusty [Wesker's wife] and I visited the memorial of the Unknown Jewish Martyr

last month. An emotional excursion to a museum of photographs of Jews in concentration camps and other terrible and humiliating scenes. It left me cold and unresponsive to her, estranged me in some way. For weeks in fact.

(Wesker 1995: 543)

It seems reasonable to suppose that such 'humiliating scenes' are countered in Wesker's plays which depict the fight for human dignity. Indeed, his utopian and socialist theatre answers the Holocaust with hope.

To be sure, there are references to the Holocaust in Wesker's plays. The final scene of *I'm Talking about Jerusalem* features Dave remarking: '[E]vil and Hitler still made it, didn't they, eh? And out went six million Jews in little puffs of smoke' (Wesker 2001: 228). The play ends with Ada anxiously asking: 'Are you sure you turned the calor gas off properly?' (232). In Wesker's next play, *The Kitchen*, it is the German chef Peter who loses his temper when a waitress, Violet, calls him 'a bloody German bastard!' and – according to the stage directions – Peter 'turns to the gas-lead at which he hacks with an "auf geht's"' (Wesker 2009: 83). *The Kitchen* ends on a note of aspirational hope beyond this disaster, as the restaurant 'proprietor' (9) Marango pleads: 'I want to learn something (*To all in the kitchen.*) Is there something I don't know? ... What more do you want? Tell me, what is there more?' (85). Utopian dreams are born from the disaster of the 'bloody German bastard!' hacking at the 'gas-lead' and causing total chaos. Similarly, in *Chips with Everything,* Washington, a trainee soldier on National Service, is rebuked for being 'like an old Jew'. The corporal in command explains: '[Y]ou know what happens to Jews? They go to gas chambers' (Wesker 2010: 58). The subsequent victimization of Washington leads to him being 'broken' (73), but a type of socialist utopia follows with a vision of 'unity, unity' and the men all 'Proud! Proud!' (77). *Their Very Own and Golden City* counters 'Depression! Hitler!' (97) with Andy's vision of fighting for utopia. Andy quotes William Blake's 'I will not cease from mental strife, nor shall my sword sleep in my hand, till we have built Jerusalem in England's green and pleasant land' (111). This quotation from Blake's Preface to his poem 'Milton' links Jewish messianism with the English Protestant idea of preparing for a New Jerusalem (Dornan 1998: 69).

Of course, the world did not suddenly become utopian after the defeat of Hitler. Indeed, Wesker's essay 'Theatre, Why?' lists a veritable litany of atrocities taking place across the world in the 1960s. In this 1967 essay, Wesker lists some of the terrible things occurring such as 'the massing of Arab troops on Israel's borders' (Wesker 1970: 88) before the Six Day War, and explains how suddenly I was aware of the existence of monumental cruelty and stupidity, and of the uncontrollable forces of violence in the world and of the bigotry and demagogy that constantly inflames that violence, and to my horror I realised that I had in me a great capacity to despise human beings. I do not know how other artists are affected when they reach such a crisis, but the knowledge that I have in me this capacity to despise is a knowledge that paralyses and renders me creatively impotent. The power to despise may be the driving force behind some writing, but I cannot bring myself to expose an audience to the sterile experience of ferocious contempt.

(88–9)

Succumbing to the urge to 'despise' and feel a 'ferocious contempt' for the 'bigotry', 'demagogy' and 'violence' which seem to define the modern world would render Wesker 'creatively impotent' and 'sterile', presumably because he identifies with the victims of such 'cruelty and stupidity', as his example of 'the massing of Arab troops on Israel's borders' suggests. This may help to explain his turn towards utopianism, for empowerment and hope beyond worldly experience ('a knowledge that paralyses'). Wesker's plays counter a sense of despair in 'human beings' that, he says, sometimes 'stabs me into large silences' (1970: 89). Like Adam in *The Four Seasons* (1964), Wesker has 'a desperate need to give joy' (24).

A slightly later essay, 'Fears of Fragmentation' (1968), presents art (including theatre) as 'a desperate attempt by man to understand his own nature and the world in which that nature exists' (121). It then outlines Wesker's redeeming utopian vision, beginning – bathetically enough – in the Camden district of London:

A group of people would assemble in a district – let us suppose it is the Camden district. These people should consist of representative members of the community – teachers, students and workers' leaders who have invited artists and professors to assist them. They would agree that they have assembled in order to discover two things: how to encourage a pursuit of art and has [sic] to evolve a way of sewing the habits of intellectual inquiry in to the fabric of their daily life. They have also realised that they cannot simply make these things happen in a void. They must have a reason, a goal, to begin with at least, until such time as these activities provide their own inherent and self-perpetuating justifications. What could that goal be? I suggest it could be simply stated, even though its implications are complex and far-reaching; and they could state them thus, 'We are going to set in motion a dialogue at the end of which we hope to arrive at a newly defined concept of a just society.'

(124–5)

Wesker continues:

> Then the real problems begin and I can only hint at them. Someone must first of all face the mammoth challenge of breaking down history into manageable and unsuperficial periods and subjects. Someone must decide for performance of the best drama, poetry and music belonging to these periods; which literature reflected the thoughts of these periods.
>
> For instance: if they wanted to understand the period of the Reformation through Sir Thomas More then they might want to see the play about More by Robert Bolt; and then an investigation of Sir Thomas More might lead to a contemporary writer dramatizing More's *Utopia*. And then they would want to hear the popular songs and the religious music of the day. And all this might lead to a search for other writers in the world who had written plays or made films or written novels about utopias or against utopias; and they might want to know where in the world were utopian communities founded, and did they last, and if not then why not; and they might then want to see an exhibition of prints or drawings or photographs of what these communities looked like, and then perhaps they would want to see an exhibition by architects of how they imagine a beautiful or humane city of the future would look. For a month or six weeks the halls and public places of the district would be given over to drama, music, exhibitions, debates and lectures relating to utopias or the Reformation or whatever period or subject had been decided upon.
>
> (Wesker 1970: 126)

Such is the force of Wesker's utopian response to despair that he does not even entertain the frequently twinned concept of dystopia; rather, he recommends texts 'about utopias or against utopias'. It is probably worth emphasizing that the essay in which these passages appear was written in 1968, a time of revolutionary optimism for socialists in Britain and the wider world. Indeed, 'Fears of Fragmentation' ends with the hope 'that tomorrow's revolution will not be an ugly but a noble one' (Wesker 1970: 128). Interestingly, the contrast between 'ugly' and 'noble' echoes Wesker's discursive opposition between the 'Bad Jew' and the 'Good Jew'.

Affiliating with the Jewish matriarch as a 'Good Jew', Wesker's characters are often domesticated, feminized and innocent. For example, 'Cohen' (known as Dodger)[2] in *Chips with Everything*, 'owns a pram shop' (Wesker 2010: 13). He explains: 'Every time I see pregnant women I get all maternal. You can have your women's breasts all you want and her legs. *Me*, only one spot interests me – one big belly and we've made a sale' (31). Again, the title of *The Kitchen* suggests a feminine domestic space; at least, it would have when first performed in 1959. As Wesker explains in his autobiography: 'Had not some of my most delightful memories been of the Weald Square kitchen, helping my mother ... a small, cosy space, she and I talking, sharing a sardonic tongue-in-cheek view of life?' (Wesker 1995: 394). It is probably no coincidence that Wesker was training to be a chef before he became a playwright: 'The future was a kitchen,' he writes, 'my role in life' (394).

Furthermore, the act of writing is feminized and affiliated with the maternal. Wesker writes about conceiving his first play, *Chicken Soup with Barley*, in the following terms: '[He] wrote to his mother high and pregnant with something' (Wesker 1995: 395). Eventually, the play is born: 'I thought so long and intensely about the play [*Chicken Soup with Barley*] that it came out in a rush, with ease, a swift if imperfect delivery ... I came out of my room bursting to read the play to my mother' (602). To be fair, Wesker was a young man in his twenties living with his parents. Still, his parturient language suggests that the maternal and creative were inextricably linked in his imagination from the beginning.

For Wesker, Jewish maternity is not only a model for creativity. It also is a model for innocence, the 'Good Jew', or what Wesker repeatedly terms *sweetness*. His autobiography ends with this word 'sweet' (Wesker 1995: 694) to encapsulate Leah, Wesker's mother. The novel *Honey* features beekeeping as a vivid symbol of cultivating such sweetness. Indeed, *Honey* evokes the 'Good Jew' in terms of the *mensch*, who is raised to be a 'sweet-natured' and 'Nice Jewish Boy':

> I [Manfred] could hear the father [of David] telling his friends: 'We brought up a well-mannered boy, believe me. Taught him to be thoughtful and considerate of others. Taught him to be a mensch.'
>
> It's an interesting word, this Yiddish word mensch. Although its literal translation is 'man' it is applied to both men and women. It means not only honourable and trustworthy, but carries within it a sense of grace, compassion, pity. A mensch is someone you can trust, someone who is neither mean nor petty. It is not always easy to live with a mensch. Their honourable nature can be a judgement of our own. Most, however, are sweet-natured and comfortable to be with.
>
> (Wesker 2005: 200)

The *mensch* stays sweet, not succumbing to the sourness which experience might suggest as a logical response to the world. In British-Jewish terms, such sweetness is a rebuff to mean-spirited English sourness. Wesker relates in *As Much as I Dare* how his wife's cookery book 'was sourly reviewed – the

English were uncomfortable with the spirit of abundance suffusing her entertaining' (Wesker 1995: 346). The implication is that British Jews, domestic, matriarchal and at home in the kitchen, represent a sweet 'abundance' which is quite foreign to the gentile English.

Needless to say, the *mensch* also stays sweet in the face of antisemitism, rather than succumbing to bitterness. Wesker comes close to such bitterness in his autobiography (and in such plays as *When God Wanted a Son* (1986)) when he evokes the novelist Kingsley Amis' 'English whippet nastiness parading as the truth of things' (Wesker 1995: 401) and continues: 'We [Kingsley and I] were very different animals, it seemed. He wasn't Jewish for a start and, though, no doubt, some of his best friends were Jews, I must have given out a literary smell that curled his poor nostrils' (403).

Certainly, one Jew who stays sweet under antisemitic duress is Wesker's Shylock in *The Merchant* (1976), which eventually became simply *Shylock* (1989, Wesker 1990). This character consistently treats the Venetian Christians as family and friends, despite everything: 'The Jew is the Christian's parent. Difficult, I know. Parent-children relationships, always difficult, and even worse when murder is involved within the family. But what can we do? It *is* the family! Not only *would* I be your friend but I *have* to be your friend. Don't scowl, Signor sweet Christian. For life. Old Shylock, Jew of Venice. For ever!' (225). The keyword here is 'sweet', although some might find the depiction of Shylock saccharine and even kitsch. As Malkin and Voigts argue, in attributing 'unambiguous "nobility of purpose"' to Shylock, Wesker 'divests the play of its dramatic tension as well as its moral ambiguity' (Malkin and Voigts 2018: 179). For Wesker's Shylock is another wholly 'Good Jew' and perhaps therefore a casualty of the playwright's propensity to create didactic characters who can seem unconvincing caricatures. Wesker appears to recognize this possibility in his 'Note to Actors and Producers' for *Roots*, where he protests: 'My people are not caricatures' (2001: 82).

Wesker's Shylock becomes a Zionist in order to flee antisemitism. He ultimately decides that 'now is the time to make that journey to Jerusalem', while Portia cancels Jessica's marriage to Lorenzo and provides for Jessica to follow her father to the Holy Land (1990: 259–60). Rather than messianic or utopian, Shylock's turn to Israel is pragmatic in the face of persecution. Zionist traces appear too in *I'm Talking about Jerusalem*, where Ronnie, according to the stage directions, '[s]tarts doing a Zanny Hora on his own' (Wesker 2001: 224). As Ronnie explains: 'Isn't it all terribly, terribly sad. (*Suddenly.*) Let's do an Israeli dance before we go – come on, let's dance' (224). Here Israel is associated with joy, whereas the diaspora remains 'terribly, terribly sad', which does suggest a utopian Zionist perspective.

Indeed, Wesker has a long association with support for both communist and Zionist utopias. As he states in his autobiography, his early political canvassing was for 'the Young Communist League and the Jewish National Fund' (1995: 235). A young communist Zionist in 1953, Wesker 'danced Israeli dances, the twist ... and [ate] the assorted cakes baked by my mother' at his twenty-first birthday party (343). At this stage, Wesker takes on the mantle of the 'Nice Jewish Boy' – celebrating his manhood with 'cakes baked by my mother' – the 'Nice Jewish Boy' who is also the 'Good Zionist'. Following disillusionment with Israel in the wake of the Six Day War, Wesker distances himself from the Jewish State. Occasionally, he falls into the discursive trap of 'Good (British) Jew' – 'Bad (Israeli)', for example, when he mentions an ex-girlfriend's Israeli son whom he imagines 'guards a prison camp'. Wesker asks for more details, but his former lover protects Wesker's innocence by simply stating: 'You wouldn't like what he is doing' (231).

Ultimately, Wesker eschews nationalism, depicting the 'Good Jew' as at home with all nationalities. We see this, for example, in Wesker's most performed play *The Kitchen*, which features French, German, Italian, Hungarian, British and other nationalities. In Wesker's novel *Honey*, 'Jew' becomes a signifier for all freethinkers; in effect, for all good people:

> 'We none of us round this table' [says Manfred], 'the three Jews that is, I can't speak for our lovely Gentile here, we none of us claim allegiance to either a religion or a nation but to a long line of freethinkers who've stood out [sic] against human injustice, cruelty and pathological fanaticism of any kind since the beginning of time. And such men and women have come from different religions, different cultures and different nation states.'
> 'And they are the glory of the human race,' said Tamara.
> 'Amen!' said Barney.
> (Wesker 2005: 289)

Here the very language is religious ('the glory', 'Amen!') while disclaiming 'either a religion or a nation'. Freethinkers are, apparently, *a self-chosen people without God* and a people who strive to create their own utopia, rather than waiting for the messiah to do it for them.

This is a key point. Wesker may deploy utopian and Judaic messianic tropes, but he writes as an atheist. As Joshua claims in *When God Wanted a Son*: 'But does the Jew listen? He can't! When you've invented God no other authority can be taken seriously' (Wesker 2009: 319). Joshua's point is that man comes before God, and not the other way round. This is fundamental to Wesker's humanism and his socialism. In some ways, Wesker resembles

Bertolt Brecht. His epic plays about the workplace, such as *The Kitchen* and *The Journalists*, are meant to make us think about a socialist transformation of society. It comes then as no great surprise that Wesker's *The Four Seasons* (1964) was premièred in Fidel Castro's revolutionary Cuba (Wesker 2008: 10).

Although Wesker is a utopian and didactic playwright, his utopias are always postponed. The traces of evil present in the plays – the Holocaust, cynicism and a mean-spirited worldliness – render utopia an aspiration rather than a realizable goal. As Andy says in *Their Very Own and Golden City*: 'Whether you stonewall, whether you legislate, whether you lobby, argue, deceive or apply your lovely reasonable sanity, the end is the same. A cheapskate dreariness, a dull caution that kills the spirit of all movements and betrays us all – from plumber to poet. Not even the gods forgive that' (Wesker 2010: 131). Similarly in *The Four Seasons*, the biblically named Adam descries people who are 'mean', 'bitter', '[s]our and hard' (Wesker 2008: 30, 43, 48), while he stays spiritually 'sweet' and sustains his messianic vision of 'the millennium … when Jerusalem is built' (27, 59).

Indeed, the evidence suggests that Wesker's vision of the world is fundamentally biblical. In *Fears of Fragmentation*, Wesker evokes Eden to allegorize the way politicians have impoverished people's spiritual lives: 'Do you know what happened to Adam and Eve when they were kicked out of Eden?' he asks, 'Do you know what the real torment was?' (Wesker 1970: 72, 85). Here Wesker reveals an essentially Judaeo-Christian vision of the Fall, its consequent torments and desired redemption. That he claims to be an atheist makes little difference to the Western religio-cultural teleology of utopia which Wesker espouses. This biblical genealogy is nowhere clearer than in 'The London Diary for Stockholm' (from *Six Sundays in January* (1971)). Here Wesker constructs a utopian tradition which is Jewish, Christian, secular and revolutionary: 'From Isaiah to hand a piece to Jesus, Jesus to Wat Tyler and he to Winstanley and he to William Morris and Marx to Lenin and Lenin to Castro and the students of Paris and the workers of Prague' (Dornan 1998: 55). Ultimately, it appears that Wesker's utopian *Weltanschauung* is both religious and secular, and we might best understand his theatre as Antonio conceives of Wesker's Shylock: 'religious, for all your freethinking' (Wesker 1990: 195).

## Notes

1   For a helpful discussion of this generic term, used since the 1950s to group together playwrights of the period, including Arnold Wesker, Harold Pinter, Peter Schaffer and Bernard Kops, see Taylor ([1962] 2014).

2   'Dodger' is possibly a reference to the Artful Dodger in Charles Dickens' *Oliver Twist* and thereby indirectly alludes to Dickens' Jewish creation Fagin. See Dickens ([1837-8] 2003).

## References

Dickens, C. ([1837-8] 2003), *Oliver Twist, or, The Parish Boy's Progress*, ed. P. Horne, London: Penguin.
Dornan, R. W. (1994), *Arnold Wesker Revisited*, New York: Twayne.
Dornan, R. W., ed. (1998), *Arnold Wesker: A Casebook*, New York: Garland.
Malkin, J. R. and E. Voigts (2018), 'Wrestling with Shylock: Contemporary British Jewish Theatre and Shakespeare's *The Merchant of Venice*', *European Judaism*, 51 (2): 175-85.
Osborne, J. (1978 [1956]), *Look Back in Anger*, London: Faber and Faber.
Ponnuswami, M. (1998), 'Histories of the New Left: Arnold Wesker and the Angrier Young Men', in R. W. Dornan (ed.), *Arnold Wesker: A Casebook*, 137-54, New York: Garland.
Roth, P. (1985), *Reading Myself and Others*, Harmondsworth: Penguin.
Taylor, J. R. ([1962] 2014), *Anger and After: A Guide to the New British Drama*, Oxford: Routledge.
'"The only thing necessary for the triumph of evil is for good men to do nothing." - Edmund Burke' (2016), *Open Culture*, 13 March. Available online: http://www.openculture.com/2016/03/edmund-burkeon-in-action.html (accessed 20 November 2018).
Wesker, A. (1970), *Fears of Fragmentation*, London: Jonathan Cape.
Wesker, A. (1971), *Six Sundays in January*, London: Jonathan Cape.
Wesker, A. (1974), *Love Letters on Blue Paper*, London: Jonathan Cape.
Wesker, A. (1990), *Shylock and Other Plays*, London: Penguin.
Wesker, A. (1995), *As Much as I Dare: An Autobiography (1932-1959)*, London: Arrow.
Wesker, A. (2001), *The Wesker Trilogy: Chicken Soup with Barley, Roots, I'm Talking about Jerusalem*, London: Methuen.
Wesker, A. (2005), *Honey: A Novel*, London: Scribner.
Wesker, A. (2008), *Wesker's Love Plays: The Four Seasons, Love Letters on Blue Paper, Lady Othello*, London: Oberon Modern Playwrights.
Wesker, A. (2009), *Wesker's Social Plays: The Kitchen, Voices in the Wind, Denial, The Rocking Horse Kid, When God Wanted a Son*, London: Oberon Modern Playwrights.
Wesker, A. (2010), *Wesker's Political Plays: Chips with Everything, Their Very Own and Golden City, The Journalists, Badenheim 1939, Phoenix Phoenix Burning Bright*, London: Oberon Modern Playwrights.

# 3

# Restaging the Jewish East End: Bernard Kops and Steven Berkoff

Jeremy Solomons

This chapter focuses on Bernard Kops[1] and Steven Berkoff,[2] playwrights who emerged from the Jewish East End of London. A significant tension in their work is between strong feelings for the place where they grew up and a wish to transcend that place. Like Harold Pinter[3] and Arnold Wesker,[4] Kops and Berkoff are the children of Jewish families, who in the late nineteenth and early twentieth centuries arrived from Europe and settled in London east of Aldgate particularly in Whitechapel and Stepney. Although Jews settled in other places in Britain, the East End came to be seen as the point of origin for British-Jewish culture. These four writers from the East End, grew up experiencing the close-knit Jewish community there, in a period of poverty, overt antisemitism and the Blitz. These intense experiences in their formative years inspired the careers of all these writers. They had leading roles in defining British-Jewish and British theatre from the late 1950s onwards. Pinter, Kops and Wesker came to prominence in the late 1950s, and because of their working-class backgrounds, theatre critics such as John Russell Taylor (1962) place them among the 'Angry Young Men'. Although only five years Wesker's junior, Berkoff is from a different generation. Berkoff's first plays, adaptations of Kafka, were staged between 1969 and 1971. *East*, his first original work, was staged at the Edinburgh Festival in 1975 and had the anger and frustration of the rising punk culture. This chapter focuses on Kops and Berkoff because they have made the lived experiences, urban landscape and language of the Jewish East End central to much of their work.[5]

## Location and Locution: Architecture and Language – Flights of Aspiration Rooted in the Urban Landscape

Kops and Berkoff build their East End plays around the physical geography of the area. They name streets, neighbourhoods and businesses. Lewis

Mumford writes of cities as 'theatre[s] of social action ... the city fosters art and is art; the city creates the theatre and is the theatre. It is in the city, the city as theatre, that man's more purposive activities are focused' (Makeham 2005: 150). The characters in Kops' and Berkoff's plays develop from the urban landscape and community, and even their dreams and aspirations to transcend their origins to leave the East End – physically, imaginatively and linguistically – are formed from that social and physical environment.

The naturalistic locations of the Jewish East End are central to many of Kops' stage and radio plays, his ten novels, hundreds of poems and two volumes of autobiography. His naturalism is evident in many scenes, especially in his London Plays (*The Hamlet of Stepney Green*, *The Dream of Peter Mann* and *Enter Solly Gold*) that were first staged in 1958, 1960 and 1970, respectively. The stage directions for *The Hamlet of Stepney Green* begin: 'The stage is in two sections ... the living room ... various pieces of furniture that one would expect in a Jewish lower-middle-class family ... the other half should be the garden ... flowers in rich profusion, but ... surrounded by a great area of bomb damage' (Kops 1999: 81). If a designer acts on these instructions, the aftermath of the Blitz is present on stage as a reminder of the horrors of the Second World War. The audience is meant to be aware of this history, even though there is no direct reference to the war in the play. Kops' next play, *The Dream of Peter Mann*, is set where 'several market stalls [stand] empty outside several closed shops' (Kops 2002: 13), and *Enter Solly Gold* begins outside 'a row of small houses near Aldgate in London's East End' (2002: 95). The precise designations of Jewish neighbourhoods to Stepney Green or Aldgate are for the producer. The audience will only be partially aware of it.

While Kops focuses on representing the East End on stage, Berkoff is not interested in sets, which he eschews in much of his work. *East* has the stage direction '*The stage is bare but for five chairs*.' Instead, Berkoff uses heightened, violent and sexually explicit language to set the location for the audience. In *East*, Mike introduces Les saying, 'Oh, he doth bestride Commercial Road like a colossus ... that's my manor ... he's my mucka, china or mate.' and Les replies, 'And he mine since those days at least twelve months ago when sailing out of the Black Raven pub where blessed Jack did rip' (15). Berkoff both names parts of the East End and uses words such as 'mucka' and 'china' which are local terms for a friend. The language is both accurately from the East End, although additions like 'doth' show Les' and Berkoff's ambitions beyond the quotidian.

Along with their characters, Kops and Berkoff aspire to leave the East End and to connect with British culture. One way Berkoff does this is through language in poetic speeches in which they combine patterns of East London speech with the heightened language of poetry and song and at times gesture towards Shakespeare. In *East* and *West* Berkoff 'constructs a cod Shakespeare … evoking and resignifying the kind of language associated with Shakespeare' (Cross 2004: 139). As Cross points out, Berkoff uses Shakespearean language to toy with the original meaning. For example, in an exchange between Les and Mike in *East* (34), Les says, 'I am no player who struts and frets his hour upon the stage and then is heard no more' (*Macbeth* 5.5.28–9). And Mike replies, 'I am that merry wanderer of the night' (*Midsummer Night's Dream* 1.2.43). The characters are playing. The writer is playing and showing how well he knows Shakespeare, and how easily he can insert the icon of British culture into the night-time banter of the young men of the East End. Later, Les is irreverent as he references *Hamlet* when he says of Sylv, 'I told her to get to a nunnery, in other words, piss off' (36) (Cross 2004: 139). Kops' *The Hamlet of Stepney Green* uses little of Shakespeare's language, but he takes part of the story and some characters from *Hamlet* and relocates them to the East End at the end of the 1950s. In doing so, he reflects the tradition of Jewish playwrights rewriting and claiming Shakespeare dating back to many Yiddish adaptations. Most notable is Jacob Gordin's *The Yiddish King Lear*, first performed in 1892, which first brought Shakespeare to Jewish immigrant communities and which like Kops' play is an adaptation set in Jewish community of Vilna, Lithuania. More recently, Arnold Wesker with *The Merchant* (which was renamed *Shylock*) and Julia Pascal with *The Yiddish Queen Lear* and *The Shylock Play* have adapted Shakespeare in order to comment on the plays and British antisemitism.

For Kops, aspiring beyond the everyday means to dream. He interrupts the action in his plays with dream scenes and songs and children's chants that interrupt the action. It is 'a mixture of fantasy and naturalism [with] a tone of poetic exuberance and apocalyptic rejection' (Cheyette 1998: xxviii). Cheyette's suggestion is echoed by the title of a critical study of Kops' work *Bernard Kops: Fantasist, London Jew, Apocalyptic Humorist* (Baker 2014). The area defines the characters and binds them in place as they dream. The dreams are of better worlds beyond the intensity of the crowded tenements in this urban landscape. The East End is not just poverty-stricken; it is the site of the apocalyptic history of Oswald Mosley's Brownshirts, the damage of the Blitz and, in the 1950s, the possibility of nuclear war.

In other plays not set in the East End, rather than Shakespeare, Kops aspires to connect with high modernism. The title of *On Margate Sands* (a novel and a play) is a quote from Part III of T. S. Eliot's *The Wasteland*.[6] It is 'about the emergence from mental breakdown' (Kustow 2000) drawing on Kops' experiences and advocating for people who are mentally ill. In *Ezra*, Kops builds a meditation on Ezra Pound's imprisonment in Pisa. At the end of the play, as the poet is on the 'verge of release and a possible catharsis' (Leigh 1999), Kops gives Pound, the notorious antisemitic[7] pioneer of modernist poetry, the line: 'Where have they gone? Where are my Jews? Why are their houses empty? The worst mistake I made is the stupid suburban prejudice of anti-Semitism' (Kops 1999: 196). These lines echo *Enter Solly Gold*, where Morry's family, who move to the suburb of Golders Green, give up the colour and spirit that they had in the East End. Kops and Berkoff connect their work to culturally admired icons in their journey to escape the East End. Kops bases *Solly Gold* on Moliere; Berkoff adapts Kafka (*The Trial*, *Metamorphosis* and *In the Penal Colony*), Aeschylus' *Agamemnon* and *Oedipus Rex* in his play *Greek*, which has more in common with Berkoff's *East* than with Sophocles.

## Alone and Together in the City

The particular experience of living in and hailing from the Jewish East End of London connects Kops and Berkoff, but they differ in how they regard the area. Berkoff's language is outspoken and often crude, and individualistic; Kops' language is gentler, lighter and more communal. Kops' characters are deeply connected to each other despite their differences. At the end of *The Hamlet of Stepney Green*, both David, who plays the Hamlet role, and his widowed mother, the play's Gertrude, are getting married. She is marrying Solly Segal, her deceased husband's friend, and David is marrying Hava, the Ophelia character, Solly's daughter. The families become even more closely connected. Kops believes in community. The world is a place where human beings must get along. And yet they must dream of a better world. The dreams developed in the East End strain the relationships with friends and family who wish or are unable to leave. In *The Hamlet of Stepney Green*, David Levy dreams of becoming a singer and is trying to escape what he sees as the limiting orbit of his parents and Hava.[8] But he does not leave. It is not until Hava agrees to leave with him and presumably start a family together that he finds the courage to go. In response, David's father, Sam, says, 'Make the most of your youth ... make the most of the world ... because the world is a wedding' (Kops 1999: 157). Family is central to other Kops plays as well. Hugo Bauer in *Call in the Night* (Kops 2000) longs for his lost family; Anne Frank in *Dreams of Anne Frank* (Kops 2000) fears losing hers.

Berkoff's playwriting is built on his own performance style. He is an individualist. He writes these mostly male characters who like Mike and Les in *East* compete for the limelight. Berkoff's characters look out for themselves. In *East*, in a speech that is for Mike and Les, 'to be split or spoken together, as suits the actors', they say, 'I'm sick of my house, I'm sick of my family – in fact they make me sick' (1978: 48). His performance style is focused on the individual performer. He made his own way in the theatre world. Instead of looking for parts in other companies' productions, after drama school, in 1968, he formed his own theatre company.[9] The character is always the centre of attention in any scene he is in. Mike in *East* is concerned with his own needs above all else. For Berkoff there is no such thing as society,[10] just individuals competing in the same space. He resists stories that need to be told to bring cohesion to community, while Kops seeks such stories at the family and local community level. Berkoff aims to disturb, and although the inspiration for his style and approach predates his work, the fact that his plays came to the fore as the punk culture was on the rise meant that the culture was ready for him, if never comfortable with what he has to say.

## Significant Works with Outline of Jewish Themes

Berkoff's and Kops' first plays explore their ideals in the most specific of East End contexts. Kops' first play, *The Hamlet of Stepney Green*, 'A Sad Comedy with Some Songs' (Kops 1999: 77), is set in a bombed-out, post–Second World War East End. Berkoff's first original work, *East*, was written in and set in the mid-1970s. In the published script of *East* on the title page, Berkoff calls it an '[e]legy for the East End and its energetic waste' (Berkoff 1978: 13). In *The Hamlet of Stepney*, all the main characters are Jews. In *East*, they are not, but Berkoff uses the same neighbourhood and still addresses Jewish themes. These Jewish themes are combined with ideas about family, and in both plays, a younger generation seeks to escape. David Levy in Kops' *The Hamlet of Stepney Green* is trying to escape his family to become a singer. However, he struggles to commit to what it would take to succeed. Despite his stated determination to leave, he cannot escape the pull of family and place and is unable to escape the orbit of his dying father. Mike, in *East*, seeks release from the restrictions of family on the streets with his friends Les and Sylv.

Berkoff said that these characters 'exorcise certain demons struggling within me to escape' (Cross 2004: 79), and they mythologize that escape. Mike and Les speak directly to the audience. Les introduces Mike, connecting him to the history of the East End, including the Black Raven pub in Whitechapel 'where blessed Jack did rip and tear in cold thick nights so long ago' (Berkoff 1978: 15–16). Mentioning Jack the Ripper revives a Victorian, antisemitic trope that the notorious serial killer was a Jew: Jacob the Ripper. Ethnic tension, especially antisemitism, sex and the threat of violence are central to East End Berkoff is presenting in *East*. 'What if sly old Sylv had led me on a touch by showing out to all the lads, provoking hard-ons and gang wars between opposing tribes from Hoxton to Tottenham from Poplar to Islngton. The clash of steel and crunch of boot on testicle has long disturbed the citizens of those battle-scarred manors' (16). It is as much a wish to sleep with Sylv as it is a wish to win the fight with the local gangs, but if you do succeed, '[t]hen you'd go to court, and it would be all over the Hackney Gazette' (*East* 1978: 21). Local notoriety would be combined with prison time. The violence leaves the characters in *East* in a constant state of anxiety. Later in *East*, Les' London-accented description of a bus ride is laced with nostalgia for the old and a keen awareness of the multicultural present day. Each location is not just a place, but a stage for what people once did there and what they do there now.

> I jumped on the 38 goin' towards Balls Pond Road ... it spins around the Centre Point Synagogue and skates down Holborn – up Mount Pleasant where the spade post office workers are skiving in the betting shop, past the Angel where Jo Lyons used to be, where one's mums supped famous cups of rosy amidst merry parlance, now it's boarded up, down Essex Road, past Collins Music Hall, now a rotten wood yard, past Alfredo's café, you know where one gets great toasted liver sandwiches, streaks passed the ABC, now a shitty Bingo Hall to the end of Essex road, now a casbah full of shishkebab.
>
> (Berkoff 1978: 37)

Berkoff addresses the Battle of Cable Street, which is the most dramatic performative event in the history of the Jewish East End. He shocks the audience into hearing the story anew by having Dad tell it. Dad is a racist, not a brave Jewish partisan standing up to Oswald Mosley and the British Union of Fascists: 'Ozzie had the right ideas ... That beautiful summer in '38 was it?' (Berkoff 1978: 22). It was 4 October 1936, but Dad does not care. Three thousand Blackshirts led by Mosley (German and Rees 2012: 199) approached the end of Cable Street which was 'barricaded by packing cases, an overturned lorry, a couple of carts [and more]'. As Dad describes the march towards Cable Street, Berkoff names street after street, all of which are real. Thus, he ties Dad and the march and the Jews to the precise neighbourhood. It doesn't matter that not every audience member will know all these places; the litany has the impact of truth:

> When we marched six abreast to Whitechapel ... We got to Aldgate ... you could smell it – and those long-nosed gits, those evil smelling

> kikes had barricades up – you couldn't even march through England's green and pleasant land where Jesus set his foot … but our lads let them have it … but Hebrew gold had corrupted our fair law, and we were outnumbered … by not getting down Whitechapel – Alie Street, Commercial Road and Cable Street, Leman Street we opened the flood gates for the rest – the Pandora's bleeding box opened and the rest of the horrors poured in.
>
> (Berkoff 1978: 22–3)

Berkoff's fascination with antisemites appears later in his career when he begins to write in earnest about Jews and Jewishness. In later plays, such as *How to Train an Anti-Semite*[11] (2012b) which is written in a cockney patois, he includes one possible reference to the East End: 'Look around ya … this country already been taken over … ain't it?! There's a mosque down the fuckin' street. The Greeks and Cypriots have taken over the whole high street' (267). For Berkoff, antisemitism is rarely simple and is bundled with other hatreds. In *Roast*[12] (2012b), Berkoff recreates a medieval antisemitic tale of a Jewish boy's life being saved because he has a communion wafer in his pocket. In *Pound of Flesh* (2012b), the Jew-hatred is directly focused on Israel. Berkoff turns this focus on negative attitudes towards Jews around to Jews' mistrust of outsiders in *Sit and Shiver* (2007).[13] It is early morning in the East End of London at the shivah for Debby's father, who it is revealed had a twenty-year affair and a son with his former shop assistant, Mrs Green, who is not Jewish. The scene is set during the seven days of mourning. The family are sitting on boxes; the mirrors covered; the strudel, blintzes and cheesecake are from Rinkoff's Deli, and a torrent of Yiddish to the extent that the published script has a glossary of approximately forty Yiddish words and phrases. The hatred comes from Debby's pain at hearing the news as she says, 'She's lying! My father never had nothing to do with a shiksa … Money she wants … The slut wants money' (Berkoff 2007: 56). Hatred is coming from a Jewish person now. Even if the anger is understandable, all the elements of a sentimentally staged mourning ritual set up this moment. Berkoff is at his strongest and most performative when he is not direct. His own sentimental feelings about the East End, about Jewish food and secular Jewish culture are there behind these harsh portraits. This is in striking contrast to Pinter, for whom the stage has no address, few, if any details of the present and no specific past.

In Kops' work, the past is never absent from the present. Sonia, Peter Mann's four times widowed mother in *The Dream of Peter Mann* (Kops 2002), imagines her friends back in Russia (it is Russia she remembers, not the Soviet Union) waving and smiling in Red Square saying, 'Where are you, Sonia? Remember the fun we had together? Come back to Russia?' (32). Sonia is not the only character who is pining for the steppes. Sam, the dying father in *The Hamlet of Stepney Green*, is also from Russia, but he has a perhaps more typical reaction to his origins: 'I was ... made in Russia, so I came to Tilbury' (1999: 89) and 'I came in at Odessa sixty-five years ago and today I'm going to die in Stepney Green' (1999: 85). Dying in the East End is what most of the characters in these plays expect to happen. The East End is the centre of their world. A few of the younger people, including David Levy and Peter Mann, in a theme common in Angry Young Men literature, both imagine a land beyond the neighbourhood. David and Peter draw a few other characters into their vision. *Enter Solly Gold* is different. Here the shoe magnate and patriarch, Morry, rather than the son, has moved to Golders Green and is the only one in his family who remembers the old life. He is brought back to an idealized view of the East End by Solly, a con man, whose lies remind Morry of the world he left to move to Golders Green. Morry is in the promised land that Peter and David aspire to and that Sam and Sonia would aspire to if they could imagine the move.

**Morry** So you're an East End boy – like myself. Well you made good, maybe there's a chance for me.

**Morry** The bedroom small, can't you see it? My father struggled and my mother worried and we played. I was rich then; caterpillars in boxes and conkers on strings ... and don't you remember the pillow fights and feathers everywhere? (Kops 2002: 126)

Despite the fact that Morry has moved to Golders Green and has more than enough money, all the successful shoe salesman can do is look back nostalgically to the place he came from, guided by Solly Gold's pandering lies. The characters in all three plays live with unrealistic yearnings for a better place.

It is not hard to imagine Morry as a young man, thinking just like David who says to his father: 'Why do you want to bequeath me the things you hated?' (Kops 2002: 93), and like Peter who tells a man he barely knows: 'I want money, sure, like the others, but I want something more ... I don't get on with the yobs round here. I think of the future ... I want to be stinking rich, open the most super-colossal Superstore you ever saw. If only I had the courage, to just go' (Kops 2002: 19). Neither of them quite does have the courage. Morry had the courage. Yet Morry is disappointed with his life in Golders Green.

## Position in Post-War British-Jewish Theatre

When Kops and Berkoff write about the East End, they are part of a tradition of ghetto writing that has often been marginalized. Brian Glanville in his 1960 article in *Encounter* about British-Jewish literature dismisses the overtly Jewish writing of Kops and Wolf Mankowitz[14] as '[g]lowing on the embers of a fire which went out with the death of Israel Zangwill' (1960: 62). Glanville also sees the East End writing as nostalgia for the past; however, he is ignoring the fact that both Kops and Berkoff are writing about their own time, as is Wesker in his *Trilogy*. Their work does look back, but it is about how Jews living in the present live with that past. This is a strong aspect of Jewish writing seen especially in Holocaust plays which are asking how the Jewish people live with the trauma of the Second World War and are most often set in the past. Kops' *A Call in the Night* (1993) is an exception, being a Holocaust play set mainly in the present about a Holocaust refugee and how he lives in the present. *Dreams of Anne Frank* (1997) is set in the 1940s, as are other British-Jewish Holocaust plays such as Peter Barnes' *Laughter* (1978), C. P. Taylor's *Good* (1981) and Diane Samuel's *Kindertransport* (1993).

Kops' and Berkoff's Jewish East End is not a good-to-be-forgotten past, but the experience of their particular urban landscape in the context of post-war Britain. Glanville has defined one strand of the British-Jewish literary tapestry. He acknowledges another strand by noting that Anglo-Jewish writers were not achieving the cultural currency of their American counterparts because – he uses Shaffer as a leading example – they 'are cutting themselves off from the best of their material [Anglo-Jewish life]' and they are often vilified by members of the Jewish community for being insufficiently Jewish.[15] Kops and Berkoff are actually writing about the Anglo-Jewish life that they know. They are rooting it in a place where British-Jewish culture formed, and Glanville and much of Jewish theatre is looking at life outside the ghetto.

## Reception

Rarely are Kops or Berkoff the recipients of full-throated praise from critics. Kops remains a minor figure in the theatre world. His plays, aside from *Dreams of Anne Frank*, are rarely produced. Still in the early 2000s, Oberon published three volumes of Kops' plays. He is admired for his ability to bring out the feelings of real human beings although he is not seen by critics as having the technical abilities to structure a play. In early reviews, he was praised for the full humanity of his characters. Donald Malcolm, in his review of *The Hamlet of Stepney Green*, writes, 'Few playwrights ever master the subtle dialectic of a living character. Mr. Kops is obviously a man to watch' (1958: 102–3). And the anonymous reviewer of the original production at the Oxford Playhouse writes that Kops 'tells his story with a zest that seems to flow from his own complete belief in the fable and in the characters with all their human possibilities' (*The Times* 1958). In 1962, as he honours Kops by including him in his seminal survey of the period, *Anger and After*, John Russell Taylor writes, '[T]he development [of *The Hamlet of Stepney Green*] is rather free and arbitrary, suggesting often inspired improvisation more than careful literary craftsmanship; the style is basically simple and unsophisticated – in many ways Kops remains even now something of a primitive – and the characters have a habit of speaking in asides to the audience and bursting from time to time into song' (171). *The New Yorker* review begins with the play's faults: the 'wobbly foundation' that connects this play to the original Shakespeare play and the way that Kops '[transposes] the soliloquies into a hideous mélange of slang and Yiddish'. It concludes, '*Hamlet of Stepney Green* is ... an entertaining work although the author has an occasional disregard to the niceties of plotting. And the character of Sam Levy, a gentle, latter-day Job, who persists in questioning the meaning of life is an extraordinarily mature creation on which Mr. Kops maintains a firm but tactful grip.' Berkoff also receives a mixed reception from critics. Charles Spencer writes of a revival of *East* in 1999. 'I have to admit that *East* is a drama of vitality and far-reaching influence ... it is easy to admire ... I find it impossible to like it.' Berkoff's position in the theatre world is one of antagonism. Michael Billington describes him as 'natural romantic haunted by a demonic genius whose spirit he can never quite exorcise' (Cross 2004: 79).

While Kops and Berkoff never achieve the level of acclaim Wesker and Pinter attained from critics or audiences, the East End plays discussed here bring an intense focus on how the history of the Jewish East End and the physical form of the neighbourhoods creates the contemporary communities that are the subject of the plays. Kops and Berkoff should be recognized as the definitive playwrights of the Jewish East End while they are central in building a British-Jewish theatre. These playwrights have continued in their own singular styles to explore the place and culture of the British-Jewish community's place of origin, even as they strive to connect with the wider British theatre and culture.

## Notes

1   Born in Stepney, 1926. Family origins: Holland.
2   Born in Stepney, 1937. Family origins: Romania/Russia.
3   Born in Hackney, 1930. Family origins: Poland/Odessa. See chapter by Mark Taylor-Batty.

4   Born in Stepney, 1932. Family origins: Hungary/Russia. See chapter by Peter Lawson.
5   Recently, late in their careers, they have begun using other genres to chronicle Jewish life in the East End: Berkoff's book of photographs: *East End Photographs* (2012), and *Bernard Kops' East End: By the Waters of Whitechapel* (2006), a collection of Kops' writings about the East End, are just two examples of Kops' and Berkoff's efforts to document the unique culture and history of their shared place of origin.
6   'On Margate Sands. / I can connect / Nothing with nothing. / The broken fingernails of dirty hands. / My people humble people who expect / Nothing' (Eliot 1963).
7   One of many antisemitic quotes from Pound made during his time in Italy. 'The sixty Kikes who started this war might be sent to St. Helena as a measure of world pro-phylaxis. And some hyper-kike, or non-Jewish kikes along with 'em.' From *'Ezra Pound Speaking': Radio Speeches of World War II*, ed. Leonard W. Doob (1978; p. 115; 30 April 1942) (qtd. in Pearlman 1981).
8   Hebrew name for Eve.
9   He formed the London Theatre Group in 1968.
10  'Who is society? There is no such thing!' Margaret Thatcher, 23 September 1987, *Woman's Own*.
11  First performance 2013.
12  First performance 2013.
13  First performance 2006.
14  Playwright, screenwriter and novelist born in Spitalfields in the East End to Russian parents, whose novel and film *A Kid for Two Farthings* and whose play *The Bespoke Overcoat* are significant works of Jewish East End drama.
15  Colin MacInnes' response to Glanville was published in *Encounter* and in his book *England, Half English*.

# References

Baker, W. and J. Roberts Shumaker (2014), *Bernard Kops: Fantasist, London Jew, Apocalyptic Humorist*, Madison, WI: Farleigh-Dickinson University Press.
Berkoff, S. (1978), *East*, London: John Calder.
Berkoff, S. (1985), *West*, London: Faber and Faber.
Berkoff, S. (2007), *Sit and Shiver*, London: Faber and Faber.
Berkoff, S. (2012a), *East End Photographs*, Stockport: Dewi Lewis.
Berkoff, S. (2012b), *One Act Plays*, London: Methuen.
Cheyette, B. (1998), *Contemporary Jewish Writing in Britain and Ireland*, London: Peter Halban.
Correspondent, S. (1958), 'Enter a New Playwright at Oxford Repertory', *The Times*, 20 May.

Cross, R. (2004), *Steven Berkoff and the Theatre of Self-Performance*, Manchester: Manchester University Press.
Eliot, T. S. (1963), *Collected Poems 1909–1962*, London: Faber and Faber.
German, L. and J. Rees (2012), *A People's History of London*, London: Verso.
Glanville, B. (1960), 'The Anglo-Jewish Writer', *Encounter*, 24 (2): 62–4.
Kops, B. (1963), *The World Is a Wedding*, New York: Coward-McCann.
Kops, B. (1999), *Plays One*, London: Oberon Books.
Kops, B. (2000), *Plays Two*, London: Oberon Books.
Kops, B. (2002), *Plays Three*, London: Oberon Books.
Kops, B. (2006), *Bernard Kops' East End: By the Waters of Whitechapel*, Nottingham: Five Leaves.
Kustow, M. (2000), 'Introduction', in B. Kops (ed.), *Plays Two*, 7–9, London: Oberon Books.
Leigh, M. (1999), 'Introduction', in B. Kops. (ed.), *Plays One*, 9–10, London: Oberon Books.
MacInnes, C. (1986), *England Half English*, London: Hogarth Press.
Makeham, P. (2005), 'Performing the City', *Theatre Research International*, 30 (2): 150–60.
Malcolm, D. (1958), 'Off Broadway: Import News', *The New Yorker*, 22 November: 102–3.
Pearlman, D. (1981), 'The Anti-Semitism of Ezra Pound', *Contemporary Literature*, 22 (1): 108.
Spencer, C. (1999), 'Unforgettable … Sadly', *The Daily Telegraph*, 17 September.
Taylor, J. R. (1962), *Anger and After*, London: Eyre Methuen.

# 4

# The Theatre of Harold Pinter: Staging Indefinable and Divided 'Jewishness'

Peter Lawson

This chapter considers to what extent, and in what ways, Harold Pinter (1930–2008) can be experienced as a Jewish playwright. In some respects, this may seem an impossible, even an unnecessary exercise. Impossible because 'Jewishness' is a notoriously contended, if not indefinable, term. And unnecessary because Harold Pinter is understood by most critics through the prism of a largely agreed, though various, critical terminology: as modernist, postmodernist, minimalist, absurdist, comedic and politically engaged. Moreover, since Pinter was awarded the Nobel Prize for Literature in 2005, he has been predictably approached as a universal voice *tout court* – in the spirit of the Swedish Academy. After his death on Christmas Eve 2008, the obituary in the *Guardian* newspaper described Pinter as a Nobel Prize winner and 'the most influential, provocative and poetic dramatist of his generation' (Wyllie and Rees 2017: 8). While there may seem no point at all in discussing Pinter's oeuvre from a Jewish perspective, I argue that Pinter is a Jewish playwright precisely because he brings 'Jewish' indefinability to his plays. Furthermore, it is in his relationship to the English language – as someone coming to it as might a foreigner or an immigrant – that there appears something refreshingly non-English in his plays, something which leads them out of a parochial and insular 'Englishness' towards a European and global *Weltanschauung*.

This chapter will also consider the Jewish memory, post-memory and trauma following the Holocaust as a primary point of implied reference throughout Pinter's oeuvre, from *The Birthday Party* (1958, Pinter 1996a) to *Ashes to Ashes* (Pinter 1996d). Born in 1930, Pinter's childhood and adolescence were overshadowed by fascism and the Second World War. It is, I would contend, no coincidence in this context that Pinter's plays depict both victims and torturers. Indeed, the relationship between the powerless and the powerful is central to Pinter's post-Holocaust dramaturgy. Somewhat controversially, I suggest that the negotiation of power in Pinter's plays speaks to 'Jewish' identity in its own dialectical conversation between subject positions of disempowered victim and empowered aggressor.

Let us begin with the notion of 'Jewish' indefinability. In a 1996 interview with Mireia Aragay and Ramon Simo, Pinter was asked about his Jewish identity. He replied: 'I've no religious beliefs whatsoever, but I'm still Jewish. I don't know what that means, really, nobody ever does' (Smith 2005: 104). The very absurdity of a term – 'Jewish' – without an agreed referent suggests 'the theatre of the absurd', a term coined by Martin Esslin in his 1961 critical study, which includes a chapter on Pinter. According to Esslin, plays such as Pinter's *The Room* (1957) show 'there is a world bearing upon them [Pinter's characters] which is frightening'; and he quotes Pinter as saying: 'There is a kind of horror about and I think that this horror and absurdity go together' (Esslin 2014: 192, 198). Taking this one step further, I want to relate Pinter's plays of 'horror and absurdity' to his notion of an absurdly indefinable 'Jewishness' which was faced with horror during the Holocaust.

Clearly, Pinter approaches the question of 'Jewish identity' seriously, and with what one might term existential responsibility. Although he has no idea what this 'absurd' term means, Pinter is aware of the baggage of horror that the sign 'Jew' carries. Pinter accepts this baggage in a manner redolent of Jean-Paul Sartre's 'authentic Jew', who 'makes himself a Jew, in the face of all and against all. He accepts all, even martyrdom' (Sartre 1948: 137). Indeed, responsibility in the face of the absurd and the horrific are shared by Sartre's existential philosophy and Pinter's plays. They both recognize the horrific and are ready to demonstrate 'even martyrdom' in confronting it.

Pinter began writing in the 1950s, when existentialism was pervasive in English theatrical circles and the wider intellectual culture (Stokes 2013: 30), and his 'Jewishness' can readily be understood within an existential paradigm. There is a stark contrast between understanding the epithet 'Jew' in existential terms and a fascist essentializing of 'Jewish' attributes. One might observe that the continuous negotiation of subject and power positions in Pinter's plays is similarly existential, since it reflects (in John Stokes' words) 'the existentialist's refusal to reduce a lifetime of decision-making to a predetermined pattern set in motion by origin or attribute alone' (40). Pinter's plays are the opposite of essentialist and therefore the opposite of fascist. Yet they do depict binary oppositions between the 'Jewish'-feminized victim and the fascist-masculinized torturer. I will return to this controversial point a little later.

If Pinter's plays are existentially and indefinably 'Jewish', concerned with victims and torturers as well as the negotiation of power and identity, they are also clearly plays which bring language to the foreground. This may well be because Pinter – according to critics, actors and directors – and not least Pinter himself – is a poet. As Richard Allen Cave typically remarks,

'*Ashes to Ashes* [is] theatre poetry of the highest order' (2013: 135). Indeed, Pinter is often grouped not just with such absurdist playwrights as Arthur Adamov, Eugène Ionesco, Samuel Beckett and Jean Genet, but also with poetic playwrights such as Samuel Beckett (again), T. S. Eliot, Edward Bond and, most obviously in England, William Shakespeare. Pinter's plays, in this heightened linguistic sense, are not *about* anything. They are linguistic games in which one-upmanship occurs purely in the region of the sign. As a result, identity and power are inextricably linked with performativity rather than possessing essentialized 'Jewish' or 'English' characteristics. Indeed, Pinter's plays are very much about play, deconstructing identity and power as linguistic games rather than demonstrable truths. Performance, comedy and heightened language together play at power. I would agree with Steve Waters that Pinter revels in 'language unmoored from its referential burden', which links him to 'Kafka, Joyce and Beckett rather than to an anodyne English comic tradition' (303). In this non-referential sense, Pinter's use of language is European and modernist rather than part of an 'English' realist stage tradition.

Interestingly, Pinter's linguistic games at times resemble a Jewish joke. Devorah Baum's twin publications of 2017, *Feeling Jewish* and *The Jewish Joke*, remind us how Pinter's plays share characteristics with such jokes. Like the Jewish joke, Pinter's early plays in particular, such as *The Caretaker* (1960), *The Homecoming* (1965) and *Old Times* (1971), 'sustain differences, contradictions and uncertainties, rather than seeking their obliteration' (Baum 2017a: 174). Baum cites Saul Bellow to the effect that 'laughter and trembling are so curiously intermingled that it is not easy to determine the relation of the two' (2017a: 179). One recalls here that the 1950s epithet attached to Pinter's plays by the critic Irving Wardle was precisely the contradictory term '*comedy of menace*' (Stokes 2013: 30).

Pinter's plays are 'Jew-*ish*', deploying Baum's sense of this epithet, in that they reveal apparently ordinary characters 'as strange, odd, ambivalent, out of place, and thus, in a certain sense, funny' (Baum 2017b: 24). The humour of Pinter's theatre enables emotional distancing from the horror which is implied just off-stage, in the brutal world beyond the performance. Baum reflects on the German-Jewish artist Charlotte Salomon's graphic novel *Leben? oder Theater? (Life? or Theatre?)* (1940–3) to argue that 'there may be no life without the possibility of a theatrical representation of that life in such a way as to enable the kind of emotional distancing and reintegration that makes even a terrible life somehow bearable' (2017b: 236). Following Baum, I suggest that Pinter's theatre similarly depicts the effects of trauma, making terror 'bearable' through 'emotional distancing and reintegration' in aestheticized language and performance.

Charlotte Salomon was murdered in Auschwitz. Pinter grew up safely in Hackney, East London. Yet the Holocaust is a resonating motif throughout his oeuvre. There was a powerful moment in Ian Rickson's sixtieth-anniversary production of *The Birthday Party*, which played in 2018 at the Harold Pinter Theatre in London's West End. Stephan Mangan, playing Goldberg, 'lights his cigarette with a lighter', precisely following Pinter's stage directions (Pinter 1996a: 66). If his name didn't make Goldberg 'Jewish' enough, there's a nod to the Levant as he offers Petey 'an Abdullah' cigarette (66). Rickson, as director, went further still, having Goldberg stare in a disturbed manner into the flame of the lighter after the cigarette was lit. Goldberg, we were subtly reminded, is haunted by the Holocaust.

Yet Goldberg behaves like a member of the Gestapo, which is to say that he arrives with McCann to torture Stanley Webber and to take him away to 'Monty' for 'special treatment' (Pinter 1996a: 79) – special treatment, *Sonderbehandlung*: the Nazi euphemism for extermination in the gas chambers. The name Webber evokes a German Jew, and certainly Stanley claims to have a job playing the piano in Berlin, although he adds significantly: 'We don't stay in Berlin' (16). This doubled 'Jewishness' of victim and torturer – Webber and Goldberg – calls to mind Baum's point that '[e]veryone is split by something unassimilable or strange: the sense of difference within that puts each of us in an *eternal double act with all others, including those others posing as ourselves*' [my italics] (2017a: 165). Baum notes too that 'there's always some sort of doubleness at play in Jewish identity, just as there is in joking itself' (2017a: 166). Bearing this in mind, we might consider Goldberg and Stanley as a traumatized Jewish double act, with Stanley the victim and Goldberg the aggressor of a Jewish joke and a Jewish melodrama. There may seem something static in this post-Holocaust double act, although with a drama as much as with a joke the audience plays a key role in unsettling the stasis by sympathizing with either the victim or the aggressor. As Francesca Coppa reminds us, 'we, the audience' (2013: 54) are fundamental to how a joke or a theatrical event works.

Victims and torturers feature more explicitly in Pinter's later plays, from *One for the Road* (1984) to *Ashes to Ashes* (1996). As Pinter points out, there is no negotiation of power in such overtly political plays as *Mountain Language* (1988), *The New World Order* (1991) and *Party Time* (also 1991). This is because the protagonists do not share a situation of existential freedom, in which power is shifting or ambiguous. 'These plays,' Pinter tells Mel Gussow in a 1993 interview, 'are to do not with ambiguities of power, but actual power. Now maybe this is not as appealing to some people as ambiguities of power, or shifting power' (Gussow 1994: 152). Pinter's later political plays are, in this sense of fixed, 'actual' and non-negotiable power, markedly un-'Pinteresque' (Wyllie and Rees 2017: 34). Yet they also resemble Pinter's early theatre of *The Birthday Party*, *The Caretaker* and *The Homecoming* in dealing with 'power and powerlessness' (Gussow 1994: 102). That this relates to the Holocaust becomes more overt in plays such as *Ashes to Ashes*, with its images of slave labourers and babies being torn from the arms of 'screaming mothers':

>    **Rebecca**   They were all wearing caps … the workpeople … soft caps … and they took them off when he came in, leading me, when he led me down the alleys between the rows of workpeople.
>
>    **Devlin**   They took their caps off? You mean they doffed them?
>
>    **Rebecca**   Yes.
>
>    **Devlin**   Why did they do that?
>
>    **Rebecca**   He told me afterwards it was because they had such great respect for him.
>
>    **Devlin**   Why?
>
>    **Rebecca**   Because he ran a really tight ship, he said. They had total faith in him. They respected his … purity, his … conviction [...] He was a guide. He used to go to the local railway station and walk down the platform and tear all the babies from the arms of their screaming mothers.
>
>    *Pause.* (Pinter 1996d: 23–7)

We witness in this dialogue the return of repressed trauma. Its relationship to the Holocaust is suggested in the play's title, *Ashes to Ashes*, which evokes the ashes of concentration camp crematoria. Indeed, the play concerns the re-enactment of traumatic experience. Intimations of Nazism and the Holocaust pervade the dialogue between Devlin and the 'Jewishly' named Rebecca: 'total faith', 'purity', 'guide' (in German, *Führer*), 'railway station' and 'screaming mothers'. Rather than being repressed and silenced in a Pinteresque '*Pause*', the trauma of the Holocaust becomes manifest and articulated in *Ashes to Ashes*. Moreover, the centrality of such trauma in Pinter's oeuvre becomes clearer if one considers some of his writing for the cinema;[1] for example, his screenplay for the film of Fred Uhlman's *Reunion* (1989) about a German Jew going back after the War to the Berlin he escaped as a boy, and Pinter's screenplay for Kazuo Ishiguro's *The Remains of the Day*, which also concerns Nazism. In the interview with Gussow, Pinter is explicit about the centrality of Nazism to his *Weltanschauung*: 'I read a lot about Nazi Germany,' he says. 'I think the whole period is probably the worst thing that ever happened' (Gussow 1994: 137).

Therefore, it is reasonable to suggest that Pinter's plays melodramatically hit back hard against the traumatic memory, or post-memory, of Nazism; much as Pinter, in one anecdote related to Michael Billington, recalls punching a Hitler enthusiast 'hard' in a bar brawl of the 1950s. 'Pinter had popped into a bar next to Sloane Square tube station for a quiet drink,' Billington writes. 'A well-dressed man at the bar suddenly said to his neighbour, "Hitler didn't go far enough. That's the big problem."' Pinter confronted the antisemite, who responded: 'I suppose you're a filthy Yid yourself.' The result was a fist fight, with the police eventually being called. Pinter explains to Billington that the reason he hit the antisemite so hard was 'because he wasn't just insulting me, he was insulting lots of other people. He was insulting people who were dead, people who had suffered ... [M]y fury with him came from some part of my being which I didn't consciously analyse or think about' (Billington 1996: 81). It is feasible to suggest that Pinter's plays manifest a similar, psychologically repressed 'fury', which the dramatist does not 'consciously analyse'. As readers or audience members, such psychoanalysis is left for us to conduct.

This returns us to the point that Pinter, as a 'Jewish' playwright, is split between the masculinized, empowered, worldly aggressor and the feminized, disempowered, theatrical victim. It is telling, for example, that the torturing man (Nicolas) and victimized boy (Nicky) in *One for the Road* share the same name. The issue of whether the torturer may be Jewish is also made explicit in this play:

> **Nicolas** You may have noticed I'm the chatty type. You probably think I'm part of a predictable, formal, long-established pattern; i.e. I chat away, friendly, insouciant. I open the batting, as it were, in a light-hearted, even carefree manner, while another waits in the wings, silent, introspective, coiled like a puma. No, no. It's not quite like that. I run the place. God speaks through me. I'm referring to the Old Testament God, by the way, although I'm a long way from being Jewish. (Pinter 1996c: 374)

Pinter's plays rely on the audience to take the side of the victim, but they also glorify power, machismo, worldliness and aggression. In short, they reflect a split 'Jewish' identity in the post-Holocaust world which allows for victimhood as much as aggression.

Before concluding, I want briefly to consider Pinter's relationship to the theatre and the world beyond the theatre. Although Pinter states in a reflective interview from 1993 that 'the theatre was my world. It was the only world I was happy in' (Gussow 1994: 142), I contend that his theatrical world is associated with the figure of a feminized, disempowered, theatrical victim as well as a suggestion of existential inauthenticity. Pinter relates an anecdote in which, like the 'Jewish' Rebecca with the 'Irish' Devlin in *Ashes to Ashes*, he is being strangled by a man. In Pinter's case, the strangler is Anew McMaster, the Irishman who gave Pinter his first acting job. The Irish actor is playing Othello to Pinter's Iago and strangles Pinter while saying the line: 'Villain, be sure thou prove my wife a whore.'[2] Pinter recounts: 'I can still feel his hand round my throat!' (110–11). Thus, Pinter's memory of his induction into the theatre is also a memory of his induction into the staging of 'Jewish' submissiveness and becoming a feminized, disempowered, theatrical victim, comparable to a 'whore'. It may be no coincidence that Pinter subsequently chose to play empowered aggressor roles in his own dramas: notably, Lenny in *The Homecoming*, Goldberg in *The Birthday Party*, Mick in *The Caretaker* and Nicolas in *One for the Road*. Pinter the actor appears to empathize with the aggressors rather than the victims in his plays, hinting again at a 'split' (Baum 2017b: 246) understanding of 'Jewishness'.

Moreover, existential authenticity requires engagement with the political world outside the theatre. As we have seen, critics tend to note that Pinter's theatre revels in modernist 'language unmoored from its referential burden' (Waters 2013: 303). It is the absence of clear referents in Pinter's plays which risks critical charges of 'mere posturing' (Aragay 2013: 293) and concomitant inauthenticity. I suggest that it is to avoid being dismissed as a disempowered, theatrical victim, as well as facing possible accusations of existential inauthenticity, which leads the later Pinter to stress his political engagement as 'a citizen' rather than as a mere 'entertainer' (Gussow 1994: 85). Pinter tells Mel Gussow in 1989: 'I'm also a citizen of the world in which I live. I take responsibility for that; I really insist upon taking responsibility' (1994: 85).

Existential responsibility, authenticated by Pinter's much publicized roles in PEN and Amnesty International (Wyllie and Rees 2017: 48, 55), places Pinter clearly as an authentic Jew in Sartre's formulation of this subject position. Perhaps related to being 'authentic', Pinter's role in the world makes him a 'Good Jew', as opposed to the villains he chooses to play in the theatre, from Iago to Goldberg to the devilishly named (old) Nicolas: an instance, perhaps, of managing the discursive split in 'Jewish' identity between the authentic 'Good Jew' and the inauthentic 'Bad Jew'.[3]

In summary, what I hope to have shown in this chapter is how reductive it would be to approach Pinter as either a British or a universal playwright.

To properly understand Pinter's oeuvre, we need to recognize that it also comprises 'Jewish' plays which – like the discourse of 'Jewishness' itself – dramatize a binary 'split' between feminized, disempowered, theatrical victims and masculinized, empowered, worldly aggressors. Moreover, it is important to note that Pinter's 'Jewish' dramaturgy and politics have significantly influenced contemporary British playwrights. Steve Waters is right to note that Pinter's plays following *One for the Road* 'find their counterpart in the work of Sarah Kane, Mark Ravenhill and even Caryl Churchill' (2013: 300). Furthermore, the Pinteresque 'confusions of masculine dialogue, of selves lost in language, pitted in unending competition' (301) reverberate in the twenty-first-century theatre of Joe Penhall, David Eldridge, Jez Butterworth and Patrick Marber.

## Notes

1   Unfortunately, it is beyond the remit of this chapter to consider Pinter's 'Jewish' screenplays, which include Kafka's *Der Prozess* (*The Trial*, Pinter 1993) and Proust's *A la recherche du temps perdu* (*The Proust Screenplay*, Pinter 2000). There is some interesting dialogue between 'Christian' aggressors and 'Jewish' victims in these screenplays, which echo the themes of power and powerlessness I have noted in the plays. For example, Josef K. experiences his powerlessness before the Priest in *The Trial*:

> **Josef K**   But I am not [guilty]. And anyway, how can any man be called guilty? We're all human beings, aren't we? One human being is just like another.
>
> **Priest**   That's true, but that's how all guilty men speak.
>
> **Josef K**   So you're prejudiced against me too?
>
> **Priest**   No, I'm not prejudiced against you.
>
> **Josef K**   Thank you. But people are prejudiced against me. My position is becoming more and more difficult.
>
> **Priest**   You don't seem to understand the essential facts. The verdict does not come all at once. The proceedings gradually merge into the verdict.
>
> *Pause.* (Pinter 1993: 59)

More than one critic has posited the debt that Pinter's theatre owes to Kafka's novel (Wyllie and Rees 2017: 43). Michael Y. Bennett goes further, making the astute point that Pinter's plays resemble the writings of Kafka in being 'ethical parables' (Wyllie and Rees 2017: 45).

2   This chapter has not considered Pinter's controversial sexual politics in any detail, and the problematic binary of feminized-disempowered-theatrical-victims versus masculinized-empowered-worldly-aggressors. Wyllie and Rees make another fascinating point about women as 'Jewish' mothers in Pinter's oeuvre: 'Women feature in a variety of important roles throughout the Pinter canon, but there are some particularly vital parallels between Ruth in *The Homecoming* and Rebecca in *Ashes to Ashes*. The first of these lies in the connotations of their names, both associated with Jewish motherhood' (2017: 92). More on Pinter's sexual politics can be found in a highly recommended essay by Drew Milne (2013: 233–48).

3   For a fuller discussion of this discursive split between the 'Good Jew' and the 'Bad Jew', see Chapter 2: 'The Theatre of Arnold Wesker: Didactic, Utopian, Biblical'.

## References

Aragay, M. (2013), 'Pinter, Politics and Postmodernism (2)', in P. Raby (ed.), *The Cambridge Companion to Harold Pinter*, 2nd edn, 283–96, Cambridge: Cambridge University Press.

Baum, D. (2017a), *The Jewish Joke*, London: Profile Books.

Baum, D. (2017b), *Feeling Jewish*, New Haven, CT: Yale University Press.

Billington, M. (1996), *The Life and Work of Harold Pinter*, London: Faber and Faber.

Cave, R. A. (2013), 'Body Language in Pinter's Plays', in P. Raby (ed.), *The Cambridge Companion to Harold Pinter*, 2nd edn, 123–45, Cambridge: Cambridge University Press.

Chiasson, B. (2017), *The Late Harold Pinter: Political Dramatist, Poet and Activist*, London: Palgrave Macmillan.

Coppa, F. (2013), 'The Sacred Joke: Comedy and Politics in Pinter's Early Plays', in P. Raby (ed.), *The Cambridge Companion to Harold Pinter*, 2nd edn, 43–55, Cambridge: Cambridge University Press.

Esslin, M. (2014), *The Theatre of the Absurd*, London: Bloomsbury.

Gussow, M. (1994), *Conversations with Pinter*, London: Nick Hern Books.

Ishiguro, K. (1989), *The Remains of the Day*, London: Faber and Faber.

Milne, D. (2013), 'Pinter's Sexual Politics', in P. Raby (ed.), *The Cambridge Companion to Harold Pinter*, 2nd edn, 233–48, Cambridge: Cambridge University Press.

Pinter, H. (1991), *The Homecoming*, in *Harold Pinter: Plays Three*, London: Faber and Faber.

Pinter, H. (1993), *The Trial: Screenplay*, London: Faber and Faber.
Pinter, H. (1996a), *The Birthday Party, The Room*, in *Harold Pinter: Plays One*, London: Faber and Faber.
Pinter, H. (1996b), *The Caretaker*, in *Harold Pinter: Plays Two*, London: Faber and Faber.
Pinter, H. (1996c), *Mountain Language, The New World Order, Old Times, One for the Road, Party Time*, in *Harold Pinter: Plays Four*, London: Faber and Faber.
Pinter, H. (1996d), *Ashes to Ashes*, London: Faber and Faber.
Pinter, H. (2000), *Reunion*, in *Collected Screenplays: Two*, London: Faber and Faber.
Salomon, C. (1998), *Life? Or Theatre?* Zwolle: Waanders Publishers.
Salomon, C. (2017), *Leben? oder Theater? Ein Singespiel*, Köln: Taschen.
Sartre, J.-P. (1948), *Anti-Semite and Jew*, trans. G. J. Becker, New York: Schocken.
Smith, I., ed. (2005), *Pinter in the Theatre*, London: Nick Hern Books.
Stokes, J. (2013), 'Pinter and the 1950s', in P. Raby (ed.), *The Cambridge Companion to Harold Pinter*, 2nd edn, 27–42, Cambridge: Cambridge University Press.
Uhlman, F. (1996), *Reunion*, London: Vintage Books.
Waters, S. (2013), 'Pinter Paradigm: Pinter's Influence on Contemporary Playwriting', in P. Raby (ed.), *The Cambridge Companion to Harold Pinter*, 2nd edn, 297–309, Cambridge: Cambridge University Press.
Wyllie, A. and C. Rees (2017), *The Plays of Harold Pinter*, London: Palgrave.

# 5

# A Jew Who Writes: The Shadow of the Holocaust in Harold Pinter's Work

Mark Taylor-Batty

Harold Pinter was a Jewish writer born in Hackney, East London, in October 1930.[1] He died in December 2008. His first work was staged in London in the late 1950s, and broadcast on BBC radio, placing him within the generation of British writers who are considered to have revolutionized stage writing in the wake of John Osborne's *Look Back in Anger* (1956). Pinter's early plays bore similarities with the 'Kitchen Sink' dramas of his cohort but eschewed social commentary in favour of menacing clashes of characters who seek to gain control of one another or of the spaces they occupy. These dramatic, menacing manoeuvres for control and status earned his emerging style the adjectival recognition 'Pinteresque'. This chapter will consider how, for Pinter, the troubled hyphenation in British-Jewish may have contributed to the unpacking of themes of belonging and calls 'home' in his early works, and how these might be read to have an association with Holocaust tropes through a concentration on the functions and consequences of authoritarian behaviour.

Pinter was brought up in the Jewish faith and as part of a tight community of Jewish families in East London. He enjoyed a happy childhood in Hackney, interrupted only by evacuation to Cornwall at the age of nine at the outset of the Second World War. This surely distressing experience aside,[2] his recollections of family life come across as ideal: '[T]he main feature of my family as I experienced it over some years, from childhood to late teens, was actually affection,' he recalled:

> I was born into a very large extended family, though I was an only child. On both sides there were lots of aunts and uncles, cousins, grandmothers, not many grandfathers by that time. We had a marvellous standard of living, given that my father worked for it … twelve hours a day. My mother was a *baleboosta*, a great cook; she looked after us wonderfully.
> 
> (Davis 1991: 9)

His relationship with Judaism, however, ended after having dutifully spent two nights a week learning Hebrew before his Bar Mitzvah at the Lea Bridge Road *shul* (synagogue) in 1943:[3]

> We were Jewish but I had a very odd relationship with being Jewish. I felt both Jewish and not Jewish, which in a way remains the case. After my bar mitzvah when I was 13, I hardly ever set foot in a synagogue again.
>
> (Moss 1999)

His reflection upon his identity in 1999 as 'both Jewish and not Jewish' as a duality or lifelong conflict is central to our understanding of how his heritage manifests itself in his art, in the form of contradictions or tensions it may have put in motion; an awareness of belonging coupled with a certain discomfort with its implications can be seen to haunt much of his writing. That this troubling of identity and rejection of religion coincided with the Second World War may only be incidental, but its significance for his Jewish community was to cast a shadow over much of his creative output.

If the young Pinter rejected the Jewish faith, he did not reject his Jewish identity. In 1991, he stated unequivocally: 'I've never had the slightest inclination to hide it. I've always been a Jew' (Davis 1991: 10). His adoption of the spelling Pinta for the publication of his earliest poems was, if anything, a celebration of his erroneously believed Sephardic origins.[4] When he chose the stage name of David Baron for his acting career, this choice was hardly one that sought to disguise his Jewishness: 'Harold Pinter is hardly a Jewish name. It just happens to be my name. David Baron, in fact, sounds much more like a Jewish name' (10). We know Pinter was meticulous in his choice of words when composing drama; it would not be credible that his choice of pseudonym was not equally as considered. The selection here seems deliberately balanced: both David and Baron have distinct etymologies in both British culture and in Jewish culture and, therefore, might represent a consciously balanced adoption of the hyphen that both joins and separates the compound British-Jewish.[5]

Growing up as part of a Jewish community in Britain during the pre-war years, Pinter was well aware of the home-grown Fascists who might have readily welcomed Hitler's armies onto our shores. The so-called Battle of Cable Street, between Oswald Mosley's British Union of Fascists and various anti-fascist groups, took place in London's East End in the week of his sixth birthday and set a precedent for such reactionary activities and counter-protests over the coming decades. As a child and teenager, he may have developed an awareness of the injustice and the vulnerability that was afforded by the police protection of the right of the Fascists to march and proclaim antisemitism, while a protesting Jew might be arrested for breach of the peace. Pinter's close friend Henry Woolf, in his recent biography, recalled the atmosphere that surrounded their gang:

> The six of us ran into ideology head on when the lovable lads of the British Union of Fascists were released from internment after the Second World War. They headed straight for their old stamping grounds in Hackney and picked up where they had left off: beating up Jews and defacing synagogues.
>
> (Woolf 2017: 53)

Hackney Gang member Mick Goldstein recalled an incident in March 1949 in which an eighteen-year-old Pinter and friends were targeted:

> We had decided to attend a meeting of the British National Party (or whatever they were called at the time) [...] We left the scene followed by a gang of thugs. [...] an enormous onion hit the wall of the bank Harold and I were just passing. I grabbed Harold by the arm to lead him quickly to catch up with the others but he shook me off and turned to face the thugs. I ran to the others and called out that Harold was in trouble. By the time we got back to him he was surrounded by about six of them. Some of them had bike chains, others carried broken milk bottles.
>
> (Billington 2007: 17–18)

The friends escaped a beating by jumping on a passing bus, which dropped them at Dalston police station, where they could report the incident. Their account, unbeknownst to them, was passed up to the Home Secretary of the time, James Chuter Ede, who had been charged to investigate the potential threat from the re-established fascist groups. It took fifty years – at the time of the declassification of documents from the 1940s – for Pinter to have confirmed what he suspected: that the Home Office was more concerned with the prospect of communism taking root in human rights movements than in the violent antisemitism of the far right (Bright 2002: 3). This seeming betrayal of his community by the British authorities no doubt played some part in disturbing that joint identity of being both British and Jewish.[6] But that moment of violence in 1949, in which Pinter himself fell to the tarmac, is the moment at which the British-Jewish hyphenation was most acutely troubled. That troubling was both deeply personal and communal. An understanding of Pinter's responses to those two facets is key to understanding his approach to the role of politics in acts of creative authorship.

Pinter's own recollection of the incident, briefly captured in his unpublished memoir *The Queen of all the Fairies*,⁷ is quite telling, in that he recalls how he dismissed the suggestion that he might join the 43 Group as a result of his bruising encounter.⁸ The teenage Pinter's rejection of the notion that he might join a politically engaged collective, and his dismissive reference to making speeches and waving banners, is of a piece with his later declared stance that he would not incorporate 'sermons, moral judgements, defined problems with built-in solutions' into his plays (Pinter 2009: 31). This has often been construed as a rejection of politics in his early dramas, but it is more clearly a reluctance to mobilize creative writing to make political statements. Similarly, with his rejection of the notion of participating in organized political movements, the young Pinter expressed a stubborn refusal to adhere to ready-made formats of responses; 'a body of active and positive thought is in fact a body lost in a prison of empty definition and cliché' (32).

In his chapter in this volume, Peter Lawson identifies a confrontation Pinter had in a Sloane Square pub a decade later. 'He was insulting people who were dead, people who had suffered,' he later explained:

**Harold Pinter** [M]y fury with him came from some part of my being which I didn't consciously analyse or think about.

**Barry Davis** A reaction against what you see as the oppressing personality who wants to deny other people's suffering?

**HP** Absolutely.

**BD** In the final analysis you feel a Jew when you feel beleaguered?

**HP** It is to identify with Jewish suffering.

Pinter answers the last question here by deflecting it and instead foregrounding his profound identification with the historic suffering of his community. The interview continued to pursue that angle:

**BD** That's when the emotional side comes out, but the connection, if it's not religious, is in the culture?

**HP** I think so, particularly in relation to the Holocaust. I find the poetry, the art that has come out of the Holocaust, is very strong and leaves a strong impression.

**BD**  You've read quite a lot?

**HP**  Paul Celan, Nelly Sachs, Primo Levi, Wiesel. The whole thing, and going back to the pogroms of the nineteenth century. (Davis 1991: 11)

Both intellectually and emotionally, Pinter clearly had a significant investment in cultural representation of the Holocaust. Back in the 1940s and 1950s, London's Jewish population must have acutely felt how close we had come in Britain to suffering a Nazi invasion, and all that it would have entailed for their community. A young Pinter, then, while refusing to belong visibly to any political movement beyond his unavoidable exposure as a conscientious objector, was nonetheless politically conscious and politically articulate. He chose to attend Fascist meetings with his friends to observe the rhetoric of those who would do him harm on racist terms. Despite his stance of not aligning himself with political movements, this one issue was the single concern that would mobilize him:

> In that war there was absolutely no question that I would have joined up. I would have accepted conscription. I would have fought against the Nazis, no question about that.
>
> (Davis 1991: 13)

And in relation to Nazi war criminals:

> I'm right on the side of the hangers in this case, if you see what I mean. As you know, I don't believe in capital punishment, but I would get these boys if they are murderers, and I think they should be judged.
>
> (16)

How, then, is this acute sense of awareness of recent, historic, existential threat, so large that it is inconceivable fully to absorb, one that participates in the troubling of the British-Jewish hyphenation and contributes to a distrust of authority and orthodoxy, manifested in his art without engaging in political posturing? There are well-documented traces of Jewish identity buried sparsely in Pinter's plays, and these are mostly to be found in some of the dramas written before 1965. *The Homecoming* (1964) is usually identified as signalling a Jewish family background and is indeed rooted in a real-life occurrence where a Jewish friend of Harold brought a non-Jewish wife back to meet his family, when none of them knew he had married (Billington 2007: 162–4). This is purely contextual, but the focus here is on the manner in which aspects of British-Jewish are being expressed and interrogated by Pinter, specifically in relation to the Holocaust.

Pinter's very first play, *The Room* (1957), captures something of that ambivalence over a hyphenated identity that its author claimed to experience. Ethnicity is quickly brought into the play when the character of Mr Kidd, the landlord, in conversation with his tenant, Rose Hudd, offers this recollection:

> I think my mum was a Jewess. Yes, I wouldn't be surprised to learn that she was a Jewess.[9]
>
> (Pinter 1991: 93)

In the script that was broadcast on television in 1960, there was also a line here that referred to Mr Kidd's belief that his sister was Jewish too, though this is excised from the published text. Mr Kidd's statement about his family is curious in this context. That he seems uncertain that his mother and sister were Jewish is bizarre in itself, unless we interpret it realistically to indicate he is suffering from memory loss, which fits with his other uncertainties about the dimensions of the house, the number of rooms it has and the origins of the furniture in the Hudds' room. But whatever the explanation, his failure to identify himself as Jewish, the natural conclusion from knowing his mother was, temporarily foregrounds that ethnicity as being both significant and anomalous. As with much in Pinter's early work, the nature of that significance is not pursued, outlined or spelled out, but once it has been uttered, an audience notes it. It is parked, and further indications of ethnicity mobilize it more precisely as the play progresses.

This issue of identity attaches itself to the issue of homecoming, or the retreat from a caring familial past, or a set of dominant cultural expectations, that is evoked in the appearance of Riley, a Black messenger who implores Rose to come home first on behalf of, and then seemingly as, her father. The use of name here is notable and deliberate: the fact that Riley has a traditionally Irish name seems to speak to the ugly reality of the 1950s rental market where both Black people and Irish workers experienced discrimination in applying for accommodation (*Guardian* 2015).[10] More of an index of that ideological position than a symbol, this contributes to the foregrounding of ethnicity that pushes a reading of the play closer to social realism than has applied to a play routinely characterized as 'Absurd', following Martin Esslin's lead.[11]

As for the naming of the main character, there is nothing more English than the rose. But Riley refers to Rose as 'Sal' when he calls her home. Sal, or Sally, is a diminutive of Sarah, a Hebrew name. It seems that the indicators of ethnicity are being deliberately mingled. Certainly, the unusual (for the time) physical presence of a Black actor in a lead role on stage in the late 1950s, when there were few Black actors and fewer roles for them, must have operated broadly outside of symbolic registers for its original audience. This is ethnicity writ large, in that context, stamping an undeniable visible ethnic identity in the place of one, Jewishness, that is not so readily visible, but which has been invoked in the drama: Mr Kidd's seeming separation from the Jewishness of his family chimes with the ethnic difference between Rose/Sal and her onstage 'father', Riley. Pinter is clearly deploying ethnicity as central to this first play of belonging. As the play was written at a time of growing racial tension as the Windrush generation of workers and families from the Caribbean established themselves in British cities, most notably manifested eventually in the 1958 Notting Hill riots, it seems misguided to ascribe a purely figurative reading to the stage actions.

When Rose's husband returns home to find his wife in the company of another man who is imploring her to return with him, he violently assaults him, exclaiming just one word as he does so: 'Lice!' (Pinter 1991: 110). This is an unambiguously racist attack, not least as the insult hurled is an accusation of parasitic character, something quite common to reactionary, anti-immigration rhetoric. The choice of the word 'Lice' here is uncomfortable: such a slur derives from institutional antisemitism. One needs to only remember Heinrich Himmler's April 1943 statement comparing the de-Judaification of Germany with delousing.[12] The violence that befalls Riley, a character that renders visible an ethnicity that has remained dormant, hidden in the dark basement – a violence that is accompanied by this insult which is core to the nastiest of antisemitic discourse – is a violence that splits the fault line between the British and the Jewish, between the Rose and the Sally. I argue it is the same violence that Pinter suffered on the Dalston Road in 1948, which perhaps viscerally exposed that fault line to him; 'a real particular rendering of trauma: a physical harm which operates at the level of acculturation, identity, to reorganise and marginalise existing formulations within subjectivity'.[13] In becoming a writer, Pinter was able to mobilize that personal and communal trauma not to ponder or resolve the problem, but to reveal it in all its unanswerable reality.

Pinter's next plays – *The Birthday Party*, *The Dumb Waiter* and *The Hothouse* (all 1958) – all sit in this same territory of the grip that some characters have over others in ways that impact on the victims' expression and experience of identity. *The Dumb Waiter* and *The Hothouse* consider aspects of authoritarian control and our interpellation into social systems, and the structures of authority that such interpellation facilitates and sustains. *The Birthday Party* engages in these ways too, but in this first full-length play Pinter introduces two characters who are constructed seemingly as representatives of social and religious orthodoxy, Goldberg and McCann. In a letter to the director Peter Wood, Pinter referred to this pair as '[d]ying, rotten, scabrous, the decaying spiders, the flower of our society. They know their way around. Our mentors. Our ancestry. Them. Fuck 'em' (Pinter 2009: 22–3). It becomes quickly evident that their arrival at Meg and Petey's seaside boarding house is part of a job that involves fulfilling the instructions of some higher authority to extract the sitting tenant Stanley and return with him.

Goldberg is the only overtly Jewish character in Pinter's writing for the stage. Interestingly, nonetheless, that character presents a number of instances of dislocated identity that are less overt than for example the folk tunes that his companion McCann sings, which unequivocally position McCann as not just Irish, but Republican and Catholic. Goldberg's numerous references to traditional London Jewish family and social realities root him in (and as a mouthpiece for) orthodoxy and tradition. He employs the word *Shabbuss* for Sabbath (Pinter 1991: 21), recalls being served gefilte fish by his mother (37), or rollmop and pickled cucumber by his wife (53), advises McCann about honouring his father and mother (71), refers to scroungers by the Yiddish term *schnorrers* (72), exclaims 'mazoltov' when raising a glass to toast Stanley (50), and finally promises that in his rehabilitation Stanley will be 'a mensch' (77).

In places, Goldberg's Jewish identity touches upon cliché in his manifestation of the vocal rhythms and idiosyncrasies of certain archetypes: 'Culture? Don't talk to me about culture'; 'True? Of course it's true' (Pinter 1991: 22); 'Lulu, schmulu' (74). Goldberg's statement to Stanley 'May we only meet at simchas' (50) is in fact what is said as form of greeting, or farewell, at Jewish funerals. This either indicates that he recognizes Stanley as Jewish, and passive-aggressively threatens him with the reference to a funeral, or that he self-indulgently enjoys the joke for himself: that this event is Stanley's figurative funeral. When McCann tells Stanley that 'you betrayed our land' (which chimes with his Irish Catholic interrogations over Drogheda, Oliver Plunket and the Albigensenist heresy), Goldberg follows up with 'You betray our breed' (46), suggesting something genetic or communal that he has in common with his victim. These indications and the fact that Stanley's surname 'Webber' is a not uncommon Jewish surname permit us to conclude that Pinter perhaps thought of Stanley as Jewish too, but as distinctly distanced from the orthodoxy and social obligation that Goldberg annunciates in his interrogations of Stanley, which Arnold Wesker contemporaneously observed 'could have taken place in the Jewish Board of Guardians' (Wesker 1960: 29). Goldberg, then, enacts a similar call back home to that which Riley performs to Rose/Sal in *The Room* and his Jewishness is therefore connected to the theme of belonging, but to imply that his victim is Jewish too does something more than indicate the restrictive imposition of orthodoxy, demanding obedience. The shadow of the Holocaust is cast in the composition of this play by the central act of an outsider being found, identified, processed and dragged away. But if Pinter was channelling these dark cultural tropes, then his making the chief agent of oppression Jewish is a deliberate provocation.

There are nonetheless enough indicators within the play to partially trouble this rooting of Goldberg in orthodoxy. While his references to childhood seaside holidays in Brighton, Canvey Island and Rottingdean accurately capture the vacation habits of many a London Jewish family in the mid-century, they manage to simultaneously represent very distinct destinations for different wealth brackets, which might originally have caused a knowing 1950s audience to query the authenticity of these recollections. Associated with this disorientation, locating his Uncle Barney in Basingstoke is a seemingly deliberate act of placing a wealthy Jew in a distinctly non-Jewish area of the 1950s – not incredulous of course, but, again, enough to raise curiosity: Pinter was doing something knowingly askew with this character's reminiscences.

Another notable reference Goldberg makes is to the Ethical Hall in Bayswater where he claims to have given a well-received lecture (Pinter 1991: 51). This is the only point at which the character locates his acknowledged esteem and authority in the real world beyond the environments of the play. The Ethical Hall in Bayswater was built as a Methodist chapel in 1868 but was acquired by the British Humanist Society in 1909.[14] The building was bought by the Catholic Church in 1953. It is plausible that Pinter himself appreciated lectures there[15] and that he was likely to have known of the controversy of the change of ownership in 1953.[16] One might wonder why a character given as so embedded in and indebted to tradition, Jewish or otherwise, might be so displaced as to give a lecture in a forum of progressive liberal humanism. It is clear that by inserting this location into his play, the Pinter of the late 1950s could site Judaism, Catholicism and Humanism in one package and deposit it casually and covertly at the centre of his play. As if to emphasize this displacement of tradition and orthodoxy when speaking of his triumphal speech at the Hall, Goldberg points out that '[t]hey were all there that night' and that 'Charlotte Street was empty' (Pinter 1991: 51), referring no doubt to the popular Fitzrovia haunts of London intellectuals, famously including the Fitzroy Tavern on Charlotte Street, popular among members of the London Jewish community.[17]

If Goldberg speaks with the voice of orthodoxy, he is not necessarily always serving that orthodoxy or is manifesting a hubristic overconfidence from his position of authority and power. His lack of self-assurance late in the play, manifested by his inability to complete the sentence 'I believe that the world ... ' (Pinter 1991: 72), is a symptom of that hubris. McCann's earlier expressed hope that their 'job' of admonishing Stanley and reintegrating him into whatever system he has escaped would be 'accomplished with no excessive aggravation' (24) is clearly unfulfilled. Goldberg's insecurity here is paralleled in *The Dumb Waiter*, in which two hitmen seem to be tested by their paymasters, and independent thought and critical attitude are seen as the reasonable cause for one of the men to be eliminated. If we are to extract any commentary from Pinter in these plays, it is that the system you serve and feed can consume you too. Fellow East End Jewish writer Arnold Wesker dismissed this approach as constructing 'fables' and questioned Pinter's seemingly deliberate obscurity and failure to address his heritage head-on:

> Pinter is a Jewish writer and this a play out of his experience in the Jewish community ... but the character of Stan is not strong enough to demand our sympathies. ... The world is complicated and we demand of art a clarification. ... It should all have taken place in a Jewish setting.
> (Wesker 1960: 23, 29)

When a journalist followed up on this issue and asked Pinter why he had made Goldberg a Jewish character, Pinter replied that he 'only knew that one of the men who called for Stanley was a Jew and the other an Irishman' and that he had 'no desire to write a whole play about Jews or a Jewish situation' (Pinter 1960: 27). Contrary to what Wesker and other 'angry young men' (and women) were demanding, his plays were not concerned with representing the plight of victims and appealing for corrective measures but instead were composed to demonstrate the construction of victimhood by authoritative systems. Those persuaded by Wesker might read Pinter's work as unfocused in its anti-authoritarianism, failing to declare a real-world enemy and the means by which we should be rallied against them. But what Pinter achieved with those first plays is to compose a theatrical experience that causes audience discomfort precisely because there is an ethical gap which calls for them to make judgement. Without real-world context, that emphasis on ethical judgement is both emphasized and extended. Our hands are not washed of it through cathartic applause at the performance's end.

A 1958 play by a Jewish author that shows a man being sought out, singled out, interrogated, tortured and abducted is of course not necessarily a Holocaust play, but the evocation of those historic behaviours across Europe participates in asking the question of how they come about, in plain sight, in domestic environments and welcoming neighbourhoods. We know beyond moral doubt that the circumstances that permitted the Holocaust to take place are to be condemned, but to ask how such circumstances could come about in civilized society is to ask how it might be that we too could see them being established and, like Petey at the end of *The Birthday Party*, fail to resist, or even facilitate their growth. Politically, one might argue that to activate such ethical enquiry is of more value than to present to the form of unquestionable, ready-made moral conviction that Wesker and other adherents of the 'vital' theatre might have preferred.[18]

As Pinter rose to fame in the 1960s, and as his stage writing shifted to focus on the emotional risks and betrayals of domestic relationships, his work for cinema would return again and again to the Nazis and neo-Nazism: *The Quiller Memorandum* (1966) is a spy film set in post-war West Germany, centred around the scrutiny and capture of a neo-Nazi cell in Berlin. In 1989, he took an option on and wrote the screenplay for Kazuo Ishiguro's *The Remains of the Day* (1993), for which he had an opportunity to write scenes concerning not just the Nazis' pro-appeasement propaganda, but to consider the symptoms of complicity and political apathy that are the fertile soil for fascist exploitation.[19] He would later say that one of his most satisfying film projects was his work on adapting Fred Uhlman's novella *Reunion* (1978), concerning the blossoming friendship over the summer of 1932 between two schoolboys, one a German Jew and the other a member of an aristocratic German, pro-Nazi family, set against the background of increased hostile environment being constructed for the German Jewish population. We know he read *The Diaries of Etty Hillesum* (1986) and the biography of Albert Speer around the same period, and it was believed he was thinking of taking out an option on the first for a screenplay (Gale 2003: 376). What *Reunion* and *Etty Hillesum* have in common, and what was no doubt compelling for Pinter, is the detail of everyday life as Nazism slowly takes grip and annexes people's domestic lives and friendships, and how complicity and failure to resist form part of the growing strength of reactionary thought.

Pinter's work as a director of other people's work also afforded him opportunities to consider these matters: his productions of Robert Shaw's *The Man in the Glass Booth* (1968) and Ronald Harwood's *Taking Sides* (1995) gave him an opportunity to stage the trial scenes of two German war criminals, one fictional and one biographical. Both plays clearly stamp the perpetrators of the Holocaust as condemned beyond redemption, and both plays temper this clear fact by considering the conflict between a personal appraisal of individual guilt and the implications of that guilt being manipulated as part of the self-validating processes of political ideology, specifically the ideology of victors. This may have been the attraction to Pinter of such work: both plays address the issue of complicity in atrocity and of the moral disingenuousness of the Allied governments, matters that are central to an understanding of Pinter's political dramas and political activism.

Early in 1996, Pinter interrupted a conversation he was having with his costume designer Tom Rand over their work on the production of Reginald Rose's *Twelve Angry Men*.[20] He politely but hurriedly ended their discussion in order to respond to a sudden compulsion to write. It was an all too infrequent instance of the muse striking and thoughts needing to be committed to paper before they lost form. The two men's conversation had strayed into discussion of Rand's parents leaving Vienna in 1939 after the *Anschluss*,[21] and this perhaps stimulated creative impulses concerning the historical events Pinter had been researching in recent years, firstly for his screenplay of *Reunion*, and just the year before for Harwood's *Taking Sides*. The play he began to write was *Ashes to Ashes* (1996).

When writing on this play elsewhere, I have adopted the perspective that the drama addresses and offers a solution to the ethical conundrum first articulated by Elie Wiesel, that to represent the Holocaust in art is to falsify memory, while recognizing the duty to sustain the cultural memory of that atrocity (Taylor-Batty 2009: 106). The text of *Ashes to Ashes* states that the play takes place 'now' (i.e. 1996 at the earliest) and gives the ages of its two characters as 'in their forties': before the drama begins, the text makes plain that neither of its characters had experienced the events of the Second World War. And yet Devlin and Rebecca, seemingly husband and wife, are caught in a tense discussion over her previous relationship with another man, and the more the conversation continues, the more details Rebecca gives that evoke instances of the Nazi treatment of Jews: a factory where there were no toilet facilities, people being herded into the sea to drown, babies being snatched from their mothers' arms on a railway platform. Devlin is frustrated by these extreme incongruities:

> **Devlin**   A little while ago you made … shall we say … you made a somewhat oblique reference to your bloke … your lover? … and babies and mothers, et cetera. And platforms. I inferred from this that you were talking about some kind of atrocity. Now let me ask you this. What authority do you think you yourself possess which would give you the right to discuss such an atrocity?
>
> **Rebecca**   I have no such authority. Nothing has ever happened to me. Nothing ever happened to any of my friends. I have never suffered. Nor have my friends. (Pinter 2011: 413)

Pinter here, again, spells out the distance in experience between Rebecca's 'memories' and her actual exposure to the events she recounts. This might also be read as the author acknowledging that he has no authority from personal experience to discuss these matters that urgently must always retain a high profile, must always be discussed and be remembered. In 'What Remains? *Ashes to Ashes*, Popular Culture, Memory and Atrocity', I argue that within Rebecca's memories, Pinter mobilizes examples of arguably contentious representations of the Holocaust, such as *Sophie's Choice* (Alan Pakula, 1982) or *Schindler's List* (Steven Spielberg, 1993), in order to suggest that cultural memory is absorbed, internalized and personalized by various routes, including populist art (Taylor-Batty 2009: 107). A dysfunctional link between personal trauma and cultural memory of trauma is being activated, and as a consequence a vital ethical question about the act of perpetuating cultural memory of trauma in non-documentary modes, including the play that is projecting these matters itself.

Caught between true personal suffering – perhaps of childlessness – and the populist narratives of Holocaust terror (such as *Sophie's Choice* and *Schindler's List*) that she may be investing in through adopted memories, Rebecca attaches her emotional suffering to these via the narrative of her sadomasochistic relations with the man who tore children from the arms of their mothers. This has the effect of rendering her complicit with the atrocities she recalls, binding heightened eroticism with authoritarianism. And yet, by possibly triggering our recognition of the narrativized Holocaust tropes that Rebecca recalls, Pinter is troubling our too-easy consumption of them. *Ashes to Ashes* thereby achieves two things; it realizes the Holocaust as a shared narrative grounded in indisputable, awful but inaccessible reality and at the same time problematizes any reproduction of aspects of that narrative, or the trauma that arises from it, in any mediated form. Articulation is necessary but impossible.

As the play comes to a close, Pinter shifts the theatrical discourse from a broadly realistic domestic dialogue between man and wife to a brief epilogue that is more interior, suffocating, exiled from the real world: the lights dim on the scenery to illuminate Rebecca alone as she regresses into the memory of the station platform, and an echo repeats the last words of each of her lines recollecting having a baby snatched from her. The tension between the 'truth' of the event, realized in tense audience empathy for manifest suffering, and the denial of her ever having experienced this in the final moments, when she confesses 'I don't have a baby … I don't know of any baby' (Pinter 2011: 432), opens that ethical gap in us. The loss is devastating, because while conjuring the abject horror of atrocity, we are left appreciating that we cannot know it and that our own access to the history is predominantly through mediated narratives, which can never be truly authentic. The ethical gap opens up, and we must digest it and take it with us from the auditorium to process. This is Pinter's art and his political act.

## Notes

1 Research for this chapter was funded by the Arts and Humanities Research Council (grant number AH/P005039/1) as part of the research project 'Pinter Histories and Legacies': http://pinterlegacies.com/.
2 Pinter recalled his predominant experience of evacuation as 'bewildered'. After a year he pleaded successfully to return home (Pinter 2009: 6). He spent further periods away from London in Reading and West Yorkshire.
3 We learn from Antonia Frasier's book *Our Israeli Diary, 1978* that the young Pinter's decision to leave the faith took place when he was fifteen: 'How astounded his parents were by his gesture of revolt against formal religion two years later' (9).
4 Pinter was later to learn that he was in fact of Ashkenazic descent (Billington 2007: 2).
5 David needs no explanation as a Jewish name; it has also been a common Christian British first name since the first centuries ACE. The etymology of the surname Baron equally has alternative roots in both British traditions, originating in Norman culture after 1066, and in Jewish history, understood either to originate in Bar-on (i.e. son of strength) or Bar-Aron (i.e. son of Aaron). As Aaron was the brother of Moses, and his intermediary in communicating with the Pharaoh, perhaps this was an attractive and suitable choice of name then for the role of actor, the intermediary between an author and an audience. It is also unlikely that Pinter was not aware of the work or reputation of David Baron (1855–1926), a London author and Christian Jewish missionary. If so, perhaps something about that split identity attracted him to the pseudonym.
6 In his biography, Henry Woolf recalls how increased incidents of antisemitic violence in the East End were countered by drafting in extra police from the recently disbanded Palestine Police Force, whom he points out had origins in the Black and Tans. He sardonically considered how their reputation for 'a hearty dislike of Jews' made them 'ideal intermediaries in a largely Jewish area like Hackney' (53–4).
7 This biographical early prose work is available to read in the manuscripts room at the British Library, with catalogue number Add MS 88880/4/17/1.
8 The 43 Group was a collective established by British-Jewish ex-servicemen in 1946 in order to actively counter the unchecked growth of British fascism after the war.
9 The word 'Jewess' is now dated in usage and can connote antisemitic intent when not used by and within Jewish company (Oppenheimer 2016).
10 The intention is not to suggest that one cannot be Black and Irish, but that in 1957 there were very few people who might have identified thus.
11 Esslin refers to Riley as a 'near-parody of a death symbol' (Esslin 1991: 237).
12 'Anti-semitism is exactly the same as delousing. Getting rid of lice is not a question of ideology.' (Office of the United States Chief of Counsel for Prosecution of Axis Criminality 1946: 574).

13  Extract from an email discussing this issue from Basil Chiasson to the author, 21 August 2018.
14  George Bernard Shaw frequented the meetings at the Ethical Church and his image is captured in a stained-glass window in the building. Arthur Conan Doyle is known to have given lectures at the venue.
15  The bus routes that Pinter's characters describe in the short sketch *The Black and White* (1959, Pinter 1991), when compared to bus timetables from the 1950s, represent a trajectory from the Bayswater area to Hackney.
16  The purchase of the Ethical Church in 1953 was so controversial to the humanist movement that Virginia Coit (the daughter of Stanton Coit who had purchased the chapel in 1909) originally cancelled the sale when she discovered who was buying. The Catholic Church later sent a neutrally dressed representative to a subsequent auction and secured their purchase on that second attempt.
17  Perhaps it is incidental, but nonetheless pertinent to this thematic strand, that the street address of the London Central Synagogue, Hallam Street, was 'Charlotte Street' from its construction until 1905.
18  Theatre criticism championing the new social realist writers of the 1950s mobilized the word 'vital' to describe engaged dramatists. In 1956, the theatre magazine *Encore* changed its subtitle to 'The Voice of Vital Theatre'. Notable articles include Lindsay Anderson's 'Vital Theatre?' (1957) and Penelope Gilliatt's 'Vital Theatre: A Discussion', (1959).
19  Pinter had his name removed from the final credits and screenplay after his work was edited, adjusted and added to by Ruth Prawer Jhabvala, Merchant/Ivory's in-house screenwriter.
20  The production opened in March 1996 at the Bristol Old Vic.
21  The Anschluss was the name given to the German annexation of Austria in March 1938.

# References

Anderson, L. (1957), 'Vital Theatre?' *Encore*, 4 (2): 10–14.
Billington, M. (2007), *Harold Pinter*, London: Faber and Faber.
Bright, M. (2002), 'The Day a Teenage Pinter Defied East End Fascists', *The Observer*, 6 January: 3.
Chiasson, B. (2017), *The Late Harold Pinter*, London: Palgrave Macmillan.
Davis, B. (1991), 'The 22 from Hackney to Chelsea: A Conversation with Harold Pinter', *The Jewish Quarterly*, 38 (4): 9–17.
Esslin, M. (1991), *The Theatre of the Absurd*, 3rd edn, London: Penguin.
Fraser, A. (2017), *Our Israeli Diary, 1978*, London: Oneworld.
Gale, S. H. (2003), *Sharp Cut: Harold Pinter's Screenplays and the Artistic Process*, Lexington: University of Kentucky Press.
Gilliat, P. (1959), 'Vital Theatre: A Discussion', *Encore*, 6 (2): 21–7.

Gordon, R. (2012), *Harold Pinter*, Ann Arbor, MI: University of Michigan Press.
Grimes, C. (2005), *Harold Pinter's Politics*, Madison: Fairleigh Dickinson University Press.
Hall, A. (1965), *The Berlin Memorandum*, London: Collins.
Harwood, R. (1997), *Taking Sides*, London: Dramatists Play Service.
Hillesum, E. (1996), *An Interrupted Life: The Diaries and Letters of Etty Hillesum 1941–43*, London: Picador.
Ishiguro, K. (1989), *The Remains of the Day*, London: Faber and Faber.
Moss, S. (1999), 'Under the Volcano', *The Guardian*, 4 August. Available online: https://www.theguardian.com/stage/1999/sep/04/theatre (accessed 30 August 2018).
Office of the United States Chief of Counsel for Prosecution of Axis Criminality (1946), *Nazi Conspiracy and Aggression*, vol. IV., Washington, DC: US Government Printing Office.
Oppenheimer, M. (2016), 'Is It Cool to Say "Jewess"', *Tablet*, 8 June. Available online: https://www.tabletmag.com/scroll/204697/is-it-cool-to-say-jewess (accessed 14 December 2018).
Osborne, J. (1978 [1956]), *Look Back in Anger*, London: Faber and Faber.
Pinter, H. (1960), 'I Am a Jew Who Writes', *The Jewish Chronicle*, 11 March: 27.
Pinter, H. (1991), *The Birthday Party, The Dumb Waiter, The Room, The Hothouse*, in *Harold Pinter: Plays 1*, London: Faber and Faber.
Pinter, H. (1997), *The Homecoming*, in *Harold Pinter: Plays 3*, London: Faber and Faber.
Pinter, H. (2000a), *The Quiller Memorandum*, in *Collected Screenplays 1*, London: Faber and Faber.
Pinter, H. (2000b), *Reunion*, in *Collected Screenplays 2*, London: Faber and Faber.
Pinter, H. (2009), *Various Voices: Sixty Years of Prose, Poetry, Politics, 1948–2008*, London: Faber and Faber.
Pinter, H. (2011), *Ashes to Ashes*, in *Harold Pinter: Plays 4*, 3rd edn, London: Faber and Faber.
*The Quiller Memorandum* (1966), [Film] Dir. Michael Anderson, USA: Twentieth Century Fox Home Entertainment.
*The Remains of the Day* (1993), [Film] Dir. James Ivory, US and UK: Merchant/Ivory Productions.
Rose, R. (1965), *Twelve Angry Men*, London: Samuel French.
*Schindler's List* (1993), [Film] Dir. Steven Spielberg, USA: Universal Pictures.
Sereny, G. (1995), *Albert Speer: His Battle with Truth*, New York: Albert A. Knopf.
Shaw, R. (1968), *The Man in the Glass Booth*, New York: Grove.
'Sign of the Times of Racism in England That Was All Too Familiar' (2015), *The Guardian*, 22 October. Available online: https://www.theguardian.com/world/2015/oct/22/sign-of-the-times-of-racism-in-england-that-was-all-too-familiar (accessed 30 August 2018).
*Sophie's Choice* (1982), [Film] Dir. Alan Pakula, USA: Universal Pictures.

Taylor-Batty, M. (2009), 'What Remains? *Ashes to Ashes*, Popular Culture, Memory and Atrocity', in C. Owens (ed.), *Pinter et Cetera*, 99–116, Newcastle: Cambridge Scholars Publishing.
Uhlman, F. (1978), *Reunion*, London: Fontana.
Wesker, A. (1960), 'A Plea for a Play', *The Jewish Chronicle*, 12 February: 23 and 29.
Woolf, H. (2017), *Barcelona Is in Trouble*, Warwick: Greville Press.

Part Two

# Force Fields and Fault Lines: The Holocaust, Antisemitism and the Israel-Palestine Conflict

6

# British Holocaust Memory and Polish Holocaust Commemoration: Eva Hoffman's Play, *The Ceremony*

Phyllis Lassner

Questions of representing the Holocaust as cultural artefacts remain challenging. Whether concerns emphasize ethical or aesthetic limits, scholars continue to debate the necessity for historical accuracy, the vicissitudes of individual and cultural memory, and the appropriate roles of imagination and humour. Questions of national identity and its relationship to the Shoah are particularly vexing because of the vast reach of Nazi destruction that implicated so many bystanders across Europe. However, despite Germany's airborne invasions in the Battle of Britain, the Blitz, and the V1 and V2 bombings, Britain's place in these discussions has only recently been investigated.[1] The reasons relate in part to the historical record. With the exception of the Channel Islands, Germany did not conquer and occupy Britain and therefore did not construct ghettoes and concentration camps on British soil. Nonetheless, as Caroline Sharples and Olaf Jensen observe, 'the path towards establishing a Holocaust consciousness in Britain has been protracted and politicised, and the manner in which the nation remembers this genocide remains imperfect' (Sharples and Jensen 2013: 1). For example, although the mass slaughter of the Jews was featured regularly on British TV 'from 1955 onwards', its purpose was primarily 'the British experience and the heroics of non-British helpers' (Jensen 2013: 116). As many scholars have observed, it was only in 1978, when the American TV miniseries *Holocaust* was broadcast in Britain, that the word itself, and the process and tortures that comprised its horrors, became widely known and discussed by general audiences.[2]

Before and through the 1990s, scholars argued that there is a 'lack of a specifically *British* critical discourse on dramatic representation and the Holocaust' (White 1999: 1). However, during the same decade, a body of British creative work, including plays, novels and memoirs, was published and performed, evincing a rich variety of genres and narrative approaches that grappled with the difficulties of representing the Shoah's excruciating experiences, responses and memories. Among these productions, a prominent subject has been the Kindertransport, Britain's celebrated rescue of approximately 7,800 Jewish children between the ages of three and sixteen from Central Europe, beginning immediately after *Kristallnacht* on 9 November 1938 and lasting until war was declared on 3 September 1939. Without that effort, those children would have been murdered along with the other 1.5 million. Yet this heroic British rescue was not publicly commemorated until its fiftieth-anniversary reunion in 1989 when survivors shared their stories and realized that theirs represented a significant event in the unfolding of the Holocaust and in modern British history. As her 1996 play *Kindertransport* demonstrates, British playwright Diane Samuels was inspired by the British rescue effort and the transmission of its traumatizing effects on successive generations. In the same period and later, the experiences of Holocaust refugees in Britain were imagined by other British women playwrights, including Sue Frumin's *The Housetrample* (1989) and Charlotte Eilenberg's *The Lucky Ones* (2002). Julia Pascal's Holocaust Trilogy (2000) includes the play *Theresa*, based on the denunciation and deportation of an Austrian-Jewish woman seeking refuge in Guernsey.[3] Antony Sher's *Primo* (2004), based on Primo Levi's memoir *Survival in Auschwitz*, introduces the death camp experience into British theatre.

British theatre of the Holocaust integrates modern European history into Britain's memory of the Second World War in contrast to British films that during the war were designed to uphold morale and even in the aftermath focused primarily on Britain's military and domestic heroism. A key element in that cultural integration has been the shifting political landscape of European Holocaust memory that European-born writers have brought with them when they emigrate to Britain. Eva Hoffman, whose 1989 memoir *Lost in Translation* established her as a major post-Holocaust writer, represents this transnational trend in contemporary British writing of the Holocaust and its aftermath. Her journey of identity, of belonging and in exile, from her birthplace in Cracow, Poland, to immigration to Canada, and the United States, led ultimately to London because it represents 'a kind of halfway return to Europe' (Hoffman 2013: 56). With this liminal destination, Hoffman acknowledges her complex cultural place in contemporary British theatre. Like other playwrights in Britain today, such as Bola Agbaje, of Nigerian descent, and Tanika Gupta, of Bengali ancestry, she is an outsider/insider, bringing her transnational identity and experience to broaden the meanings of multicultural Britain. While she acknowledges that 'the upheaval of exile is undoubtedly dramatic, and often traumatic', it is also 'dynamic' and in her case, the terrain on which her historical consciousness continues to develop and find a place in British cultural production. Her extensive writing about exile reveals it to be a condition of her identity and sense of belonging to the European past that has shaped her creative and reflective writing. As a point of departure from being the child of Holocaust survivors, exile has yielded a multivalent perspective on the shifting meanings of cross-cultural and intergenerational historical memories, in particular, Holocaust memory and the history of Polish-Jewish relations:

> I feel myself to be shaped by the rupture of that uprooting as deeply as I do by my parents, say, or my historical background. There were lessons that followed from it which, in their wider implications, have affected much that I think and write. Basically, these have to do with the extent to which language and culture construct us; the degree to which they are not only supra-personal entities, but are encoded in our selves and psychic cells.
>
> (Hoffman 2013: 56)

Even as she has made London her home and has been recognized as a significant contributor to contemporary British literature and culture, Hoffman's experience and interpretation of exile remain determining factors in her writing. Shaping the historical ethics that characterize her writing is one constant: she was born of the Holocaust past, whose horrors her parents barely escaped. Resonant with that past, her memories of life in 1950s Poland have and continue to inspire her work, defined by 'dark political rumblings, memories of wartime suffering and daily struggle for existence ... yet when it came time to leave I felt I was being pushed out of the happy, safe enclosures of Eden' (Hoffman 1989: 5).

Hoffman expresses her ambivalent memories of Poland in an amalgam of discursive registers: historical and ethical investigation and a lamentation for a lost idyll. Her continuing investigation of Poland's wartime past and shifting political present remains infused with the 'memories of wartime' that shape her parents' lives and characters, shade her portraits of Poland, and motivate her efforts to integrate that past into British historical memory. Despite the growing distance of time, as new emanations of 'dark political rumblings' trouble her, her personal ties to Poland remain steadfast. Poland remains a vital part of her identity and memory, not just as a backdrop or context for her development as a writer, but as a questing core of her critical imagination.

Hoffman's 1997 history, *Shtetl: The Life and Death of a Small Town and the World of Polish Jews*, explores the thousand-year entangled relationship between Poles and Jews as it was enacted in the shtetl of Bransk, in northeastern Poland.[4] A documented history, the book also confronts the relations between the two communities as they were bound in taut recognition of their indelibly separate social and cultural traditions. If this recognition was always edgy, both mutually suspicious yet forbearing, pogroms against the Jews demonstrated the fragility of the shtetl's ambivalent stability. It took the German occupation and construction of death camps on Polish soil to shatter that thousand-year relationship. Hoffman writes:

> As an example of Polish-Jewish relations during World War II, the shtetl offered the most extreme scenario. The villages and small towns were where Jews and Poles were at their most exposed and vulnerable, and where ongoing political conflicts were at their sharpest. This was where Jewish inhabitants experienced acts of the most unmediated cruelty from their neighbors – and also of most immediate generosity. In the dark years of the Holocaust, the shtetl became a study in ordinary morality tested, and sometimes warped, by inhuman circumstances.
> (Hoffman 1997: 13)

The dramatic effect of Hoffman's account is borne by her efforts to portray both Jews and Poles with an ethics of sympathetic tension. On the one hand, she offers a social history of both communities sustaining their cultures in the face of external threats. At the same time however, illuminating the troubling absence of Polish mourning for the nation's lost Jews becomes a critical counterpoint. As she says in *Shtetl*'s introduction, 'Because the extent of the loss was so great – so total – the act of remembering the vanished world has become fraught with painful and still acute emotions' (Hoffman 1997: 1). This pain has become even more intense since the fall of communism and the trajectory of Poland's parliamentary democracy shifting rightwards. An excruciating event that lacerated the nation's sense of its independence and ethical progress was the 2001 publication of Jan Gross's book *Neighbors* which exposed the July 1941 massacre of the Jews of Jedwabne by the town's Polish residents. Gross revealed that while German-occupying forces thoroughly approved the massacre, the perpetrators were Polish villagers. As that history continues to reverberate in Polish efforts both to confront and defend against the charges of complicity, in 2006 Hoffman argued that the breakdown in Polish-Jewish relations 'was a mutual failure on the part of the Jews and the Poles. Yes, the majority people did have the power. But the Jews were, in my view, too separatist. ... This was understandable, but nevertheless a mistake – and I'm afraid it redounded on their fate during the Holocaust' (Levin 2006: 7).[5]

When Hoffman's play *The Ceremony* was performed at London's JW3 (Jewish Cultural Centre) on 21 May 2017, the historical supports on which she based her balanced analysis of Polish-Jewish relations were already under siege. In a March 2018 article, Hoffman acknowledged that the Polish government's 'hard-right turn' is consistent with its unwillingness to accept any Polish responsibility, participation or complicity in the Holocaust (Hoffman 2018b: 4). She argues that the government's 'defiance of democratic principles' is 'once again ... unsettling the Polish polity and the passions that historical disputes continue to arouse' (4). The title of her article, 'Hearing Poland's Ghosts', refers to her critical survey of the nation's new museums that document and commemorate the history of Poland's Jews. The word 'Ghosts' in the title is especially resonant. While the investigation of Polish-Jewish history and its commemoration remains vibrant, the nation is almost empty of actual Jews. Jews occupy a spectral presence in Polish memory, and with few material and human traces. But perhaps like the ghost of Hamlet's father, they remain a determining force in the nation's identity and destiny. In its interpretive guise, Hoffman's title also insists on unsilencing the voices of the slaughtered Jews who have shaped Poland's historical narrative and identity in the past and continue to do so in their absence.

That these efforts remain controversial is the subject of *The Ceremony* which dramatizes the 2011 Polish event commemorating the massacre of Jedwabne's Jews and its haunting questions about responsibility and intervention in any genocide. Like the *Polin Museum* reviewed by Hoffman, *The Ceremony* confronts history through the display of commemoration where, according to Bryce Lease, 'history in the museum is experienced within the discursive space of loss and mourning' (2017: 386). At the same time that Hoffman's play enacts loss and mourning, it also questions the ethical and psychological viability of commemoration in Poland. Significantly, given the play's British audience, it was calling for enlivening British Holocaust memory beyond the stillness of the nation's Holocaust exhibition at the Imperial War Museum.

A rehearsed reading of *The Ceremony*, directed by Braham Murray, was followed by a discussion among some of the actors and the director and moderated by Nick Temko.[6] The panellists then responded to questions from the audience.[7] The play's title signifies Hoffman's imagined recreation and interpretation of the 10 July 2001 commemoration in Poland. Although the play is based on Hoffman's attendance at the event, the script does not identify the setting. Rather than avoiding the slaughter's horrors, however, the unarticulated name Jedwabne echoes widely. The unspoken not only evokes an all-encompassing Holocaust, but also recalls the genocidal slaughter of neighbours by neighbours anywhere in the world at any time. For example, during the ceremony, a visiting envoy receives a phone call from an unidentified speaker who, the stage directions tell us, could be from 'Africa, or the Middle East, or India, or Central Asia or the Balkans' (2017: 11). Calling twice more and with escalating terror, he pleads for rescue from an unspecified massacre by yet another group of neighbours. Although the audience hears his voice and sees his cell phone image projected onto a screen, these devices dramatize his presence as both virtual and overdetermined. The magnified image representing the reality of his humanity and its threatened state confronts and involves the audience with its urgency, but also creates the possibility of defensive alienation. Like responses to other genocides, an audience member asked, 'What would we have done then and now, with child refugees?' The question recalls Britain's courageous Kindtertransport but also evokes today's political, ethical and emotional discomfort with accepting and integrating migrants. As though responding to this question with a challenge, later in the play the nameless young man confronts those at the ceremony: 'I am Tiresias ... and I'm always with you. I've been man and woman. I've killed and I've been killed' (2017: 40). Dramatically condensing and expanding the story of Jedwabne, he embodies a fusion of victim, perpetrator and prosecutor, confronting the spectators, participants and ghosts of the victims as well as the British audience with the ethical if controversial challenge that anyone of them could become any other.

In Hoffman's interpretation, the breadth of Jedwabne's terror has extended beyond historical time and memory to contemporary confrontation, as more mass murders are recited and then projected onto a screen, prodding the British audience's memory and ethics: 'Yugoslavia, Rwanda, Kashmir ... Srebrenica, Syria' (2017: 9). Indeed, the nameless victim intruder comments to the ceremony's spectators and participants, 'with biting humor, "We live in a small world, don't we"' (38). As Joanna Zylinska posits, such a gesture universalizes 'issues of proximity and neighborliness in the transnational political landscape of the early twenty-first century', inviting us to ponder the intensifying 'xenophobia of contemporary Western democracies' and whether and how alternatives might be possible (2007: 279). In the discussion following the play, the director cautioned the audience about the 'danger of lapsing into generalities and that *The Ceremony* remains about individual memory and motivation, requiring deep, true emotion'.

At the same time that the play evokes geographical breadth and a historical continuum of neighbourly violence, it explores the specific question or quest for a politically and morally responsible commemoration of Poland's slaughtered Jews. For as Zylinska reminds us, '"Event Jedwabne" needs to be seen as part of the Polish narrative of the Holocaust ... and we need to acknowledge ... its unspeakable and horrifying singularity' (2007: 280). Reverberating throughout Hoffman's play is a triangular question: how to offer official and public recognition of the complicated history of Poland's Jews, including not only their dehumanized treatment but that would also preserve the Poles' sense of their own humanity. In short, how might it be possible to include a Jewish presence in Polish historical and cultural memory of the Second World War when, as Joanna Tokarska-Bakir observes, 'for the majority of Poles', historical 'memory is a place without Jews' (in Ziarek 2007: 302). The deep ambivalence implied in this empty memory is echoed in Polish Christian diarists studied by Rachel Brenner:

> Despite their firm commitment to humanism, the Warsaw diarists [Maria Dąbrowska, Jarosław Iwaszkiewicz, Zofia Nałkowska, Aurelia Wyleźnsńska, and Stanisław Rembek] did not display a uniform response to the Jewish genocide, whose evolution – the establishment of the Ghetto, the deportations in 1942, and the Uprising and liquidation of the Ghetto in 1943 – they all saw, heard and smelled. Their reactions ranged from deliberate evasion of the victims' plight, to paralyzing dismay at the unfolding horror, to active participation in altruistic rescue operations. ... the diarists' contemporaneous responses to the Jewish genocide deepen our understanding of the ethical, mental, and emotional challenges that face any witness of terror.
>
> (Brenner 2014: 4)

In her reflections on Holocaust memory in her book *After Such Knowledge*, Hoffman declares that 'recognition is the salutary balm most needed by those who have been targets of brutality and injustice. It is also perhaps the only redress we can offer to the victims of great wrongs' (2004: 57).

Hoffman's play insists on instantiating the Jews' destroyed presence in both Polish and British Holocaust memory by dramatizing it as disembodied human remnants, as spectral performances of their own memories. Reminiscent of pre-war and wartime events, these performances confront the ceremony's participants and audiences with their suppressed, ignorant or erased Holocaust knowledge. In Freddie Rokem's terms, 'The cathartic processes activated by the theatre performing history are more like a "ritual" of resurrection, a revival of past suffering, where the victim is given the power to speak about the past again' (2000: 205). In *The Ceremony*, the ghostly victims appear as belated witnesses to the crimes that destroyed them, fulfilling the Latin designation of *superstes*, which, according to Giorgio Agamben's discussion of Auschwitz prisoners, 'designates a person who has lived through something, who has experienced an event from beginning to end and can therefore bear witness to it' (1999: 17). In *The Ceremony*, the witnesses add their performed memories as an aftermath to the end.[8]

Hoffman's source for the depiction of Holocaust memory and its lasting effects emerges from her evocation of her Polish childhood experience, as in *After Such Knowledge*, where she describes her family home as haunted by the unresolved fears embedded in her parents' inescapable and inconsolable Holocaust memories. The challenges of translating the ineffable images of trauma into a language of shared intergenerational meanings are visible in Hoffman's tentative, oblique language:

> In our small apartment, ... memories – no, not memories but emanations – of wartime experiences kept erupting in flashes of imaginary; in abrupt, fragmented phrases; in repetitious, broken refrains. They kept manifesting themselves with a frightening immediacy in that most private and potent of family languages – the language of the body.
> (Hoffman 2004: 9)[9]

A second-generation survivor, Hoffman represents the transmission of Holocaust memory by filling the gaps of disrupted, fragmented and discontinuous narratives with ghostly 'emanations' that call attention to how her play, a work of memory, imagination and testimony, is constructed. In the above passage, as in *The Ceremony*, Hoffman represents the challenges of revitalizing and preserving those memories and achieving narrative coherence through images of the fantastic which in turn acknowledge the transitory, tremulous nature of traumatic memory. That she chose this non-realist fictional form coincides with her reflections on how narrative responds to the cataclysms of history:

> It certainly seems to me that the changing topography of the world profoundly alters our consciousness of the world. The task, for a certain kind of writer, is precisely to catch these deeper shifts – to imagine the present, so to speak, in all its flux and unfamiliar strangeness. How to grasp it, articulate it, narrate it? What forms are sufficient to the distinctly non-linear circumstances which increasingly define us? ... What styles, or stories, or genres will be invented to describe a world which is no longer divided between peripheries and centres, but in which movement is multidirectional and no centre privileged; in which the individual self is shaped less by history or culture than by other factors entirely; in which the very idea of the 'cultivated', stable self may be losing its significance and hold? In short, the kind of literature we need to represent our

fast-changing present and rapidly approaching future, and to interpret
these for ourselves and others, remains to be seen.

(Hoffman 2013: 60)

Theoretically, the non-realist form of *The Ceremony* raises questions about
the historicity and ethics of imaginative Holocaust stories in general and in
British theatre specifically.[10]

The setting of the play is an official occasion in the town centre in
which fearful villagers witness their leaders proclaiming recognition of
the slaughtered Jews as a national tragedy. In the discussion following the
performance, Hoffman noted that the officials' speech in 'high discourse'
resonates with 'classical Greek drama' that is a 'potent template of other
events, like the Holocaust and how it unfolds' (David 2017: 2). Although
there is no conventional plot, the dramatic arc is given shape by 'distinct
registers of voice: fragments of documentary speeches ... by the Polish
President and other dignitaries; fierce "debates" among contemporary
guests; haunting encounters with Shades of lost ancestors; and crucially, the
disturbing and rarely heard voice of the Perpetrator' (Hoffman 2018a). The
stage set, interpolations of music, and the ghostly appearance and voices
of the murdered Jews create the provocative atmosphere. Hoffman has
described the staging 'as taking place in a circle or a space of light ... which
would evoke not so much the dead, as a space of memory' (2018a). Within
this space the Jewish ghosts interrupt the ceremony with their insistent
refusal to stay buried and quiet, that is, to remain a suppressed memory. The
psychological viability of this representation for audiences is questioned by
Vivian Petraka:

> And what happens when the actor's body is signifying not an individual
> death, which presumably all of us can conceive of, but a mass death,
> which basically none of us can conceive of? It may be that representing
> genocide theatrically means the absence/presence of the body and the
> ruining of representation.
>
> (Petraka 1999: 98)

The dramaturgy of *The Ceremony* presents the 'absence/presence' of the
victims as both individuals and a collective. In movement and speech, their
enshrouded, depersonalized bodies suggest resistance to decomposition
and dissolution, in effect prodding the British audience's attention to how to
represent a destroyed community as a traumatic historical memory that they
don't share but about which they should care. At issue here is an enactment
that suggests the spasms of both violent death and its disjunctive impact on

memory. One aspect of this issue is addressed by the performances of actors, whose significance, according to Rokem, makes

> it possible for the spectators, the 'bystanders' in the theatre, to become secondary witnesses, to understand and, in particular, 'to form an opinion' about the forces which have shaped the accidents of history. ... it is the actor's role as a witness which determines the kind of relationship a certain production develops with the historical past. One of the aims of performances about history is to make it possible for the spectators to see the past in a new or different way.
>
> (Rokem 2000: 9)

In *The Ceremony* the actors performing the victims challenge audiences to recognize the reality of traumatic memory in a non-realist performance that fuses the presence of their living humanity with their imaginative roles as ghosts. Simultaneously, because the ghosts' individual names and voices distinguish one from the other, the play resists a homogenized sense of the lost as an undifferentiated mass. Instead, the liminal embodiment of the ghosts – there and not there – resurrects the Polish community as comprised of internal differentiation among individual perspectives that form a multicultural testimony to terror. The ceremony as Hoffman represents is not scripted to recognize the victims' individual selves and stories. Instead it is depicted as designed by the officials to be a ritual offering that in effect occludes the victims' voices. The clash between the ghosts' insistent presence and their erasure is expressed by including fragments of the 'Shema' repeated intermittently by a chorus in masks and a 'piercing piece of music' by a Polish composer (Hoffman 2018a). This ensemble of sight and sound suggests an 'uncanny' return of suppressed Polish Holocaust memory, representing what Hoffman refers to in her book *Shtetl* as 'a layer of the past so close to the surface and yet so perplexing' (1997: 25). During the discussion following the play's reading, she stressed that 'even memory is complicated in its transfer of intense, contradictory emotions. [Therefore] dialogue between Poles and Jews is difficult because both parties see themselves as victims'.

The script's description of the set confirms the presence of the uncanny and the fear it invokes: 'The play opens on a darkened stage. We hear muffled country sounds – crickets, rustling leaves, the barking of a dog – and a low clangor of metal being struck' (2017: 1). The cacophonous chorus of natural sounds chafing against the mechanical creates the play's sinister atmosphere, intensified by sounds of the murdered Jews' rustling that blend with 'the piercing squeals of a pig being slaughtered', and the fragmented, interrupted dialogue of the characters (21). In dramatic effect, it is as though the violence of the Jewish massacre rejects translation into realistic conventions of historical and dramatic narratives which, for reasons of verisimilitude and verification, would omit the non-empirical sensory experiences embedded in memory. Realism could not adequately address a pivotal question shaping Hoffman's entire oeuvre: 'What meanings does the Holocaust hold for us today – and how are we going to pass on those meanings to subsequent generations?' (Hoffman 2004: ix). Susan Russell synthesizes the problem inherent in resolving Hoffman's question: 'In a sense, a "successful" representation of the Holocaust may occur only when the representation fails, when it points to its own limits, and occludes permanent answers, whether the representation purports to be "history" or historical fiction' (2001: 128). For Freddie Rokem, theatre proposes a viable response: 'What may be seen as specific to the theatre in dealing directly with the historical past is its ability to create an awareness of the complex interaction between the destructiveness and the failures of history, on the one hand, and the efforts to create a viable and meaningful work of art, trying to confront these painful failures, on the other' (2000: 3).

Instead of a traditional three-act structure and linear narrative, *The Ceremony* assumes a non-realist, expressionist form that from the perspective of the victims challenges the viability of Polish commemoration and the Polish president's apology.[11] In response, the ghosts assert their subjectivity even as they embody the destruction of their agency. Their simultaneous presence and absence disrupts the ceremony, critiquing and undermining the effort to create a ritual that will unify the participants and spectators as a community acknowledging and memorializing its Jewish history. The dead reject closure as a false premise and promise – a psychological lie that must fail as a defensive strategy for those still haunted by their hatred of the Jews. At this moment of stalled recognition, the dramatic and interpretive effect of the play's persistent dissonance between the Poles and the Jews questions the past and future meanings of neighbour anywhere. As a disjunctive ensemble, the collective audial and visual metaphors and the dramatis personae enact the question of whether the Jews can be integrated into Poland's history and memory as neighbours, considering that their difference is steadfast and therefore an alien and suspicious presence.

In *The Ceremony*, the spectral bodies and anguished, fragmented but insistent pleas of the slaughtered interrupt the public commemoration to demand recognizance, that is, a binding commitment to reinsert a Jewish presence in Polish Holocaust memory. The play does not, however, present this petition as producing and integrating an enlightened acknowledgement of the Jews as participating and contributing to Polish culture and society. Instead, the Jews' pleas are dramatized as being stonewalled by the villagers' menacing memories of their neighbours' incorrigible strangeness, as illustrated by this stage direction: 'The SHADES' rumble, made up of a rustle of Hebrew sounds – *tss, male, rachmonim*' (2017: 15). As expressed early in the play, the Jews and their culture remain in the shadows yet their voices haunt Polish cultural consciousness:

> **Man No. 1**   Remember, how they moaned in those shuls of theirs ... Like they were possessed. Why couldn't they pray like normal people ...? (2017: 3).

Described by Hoffman as 'shades', in their spectral presence and appeals, the Jewish victims reanimate the dormant but indelible memory of the living selves the villagers continue to fear as uncanny Others and therefore threatening. Hoffman's interpretation of Freud's definition of uncanny is pertinent here, as

> the sensation of something that is both very alien and deeply familiar, something that only the unconscious knows. If so, then the second generation has grown up with the uncanny. And sometimes, ... wrestling with shadows can be more frightening, or more confusing, than struggling with solid realities.
>
> (Hoffman 2004: 66)

Hoffman here is referring to children of survivors, who even in their historical distance from terror suffer from their inheritance of 'fear and darkness' inspired by their parents' indelible but shadowy losses (2017: 20). For the Jewish second generation present at the ceremony, the entreaty to remember is baffling at first and yet a challenge they realize they cannot resist. Hoffman's take on this uncanny, unsettling responsibility also applies to second-generation Poles.

In the play the phantom victims assume the form of embodied reconstituted memories still struggling to establish a subjectivity and ethical impact of their own making. As the ghost of a grandfather tells his granddaughter attending the ceremony, 'If you forget us *we* are nothing' (2017: 13). The imperative here implies that historical knowledge by itself will always carry insufficient meaning and impact. Indeed, as Bryce Lease declares about Holocaust museums, 'This history unadulterated by memory can be concatenate with a betrayal of the dead' (392). One meaning of such betrayal was noted by the woman actor participating in the post-performance discussion. She confessed that she had lost her family in the Holocaust but had not wanted to talk about it until recently in response to Holocaust denial and to those who wrongfully claimed victimhood. In *The Ceremony*, as reimagined by the Polish second generation, the dead cannot escape another form of betrayal: the prevailing 'latent prejudices' and suspicions, such as 'trusting the Russkies' or hiding their wealth 'under the mattress' (Hoffman 2018a; 2017: 4). The temporal and geographical breadth of such antisemitic stereotypes was noted by a Polish-Jewish audience member at the play's reading whose personal experience led her to conclude that 'antisemitism was everywhere the Jews lived but that each national place tells a different story'. In the play, overriding memories of Jewish generosity and sentimental nostalgia for their 'funny' way of talking, suspicions remain a form of defence and motivation for killing (2017: 4). The solution to the insistent presence of the Jewish ghosts and the villagers' inadequately defensive memories of their Jewish neighbours is to '[d]amn their souls', banishing the Jews' bodies and spirits from Poland and Polish history.

The centrality of the Jews' ghostly presence and pleas as testimonial evidence establishes Hoffman's play as an expressionist drama exploring the ethical and cultural role of historical memory in any nation's identity. At stake are the questions of whether contested cultural meanings of human identity can be resolved or mutually integrated as a new historical reality and in what representational form or dramatic style can that proposal persuade audiences. In Vivian Petraka's terms, *The Ceremony* challenges 'realism's normalizing concepts of what it means to be "human" to a particular "category" of humans' (1999: 45). In turn, a pivotal challenge for Hoffman was how to articulate the Poles' demonization of the Jews and, at the same time, express understanding of the Poles' continuous if irrational fear of the Jews. Complicating this presentation would be an enactment of the humanly possible destroyed Jewish presence. Hoffman's solution is to have one of the Jewish ghosts provide an ambivalent explanation – a stereotypical yet sympathetic response to the Poles' fearful antipathy towards the Jews: 'Full of superstition, all of them ... You see, this village was all they ever knew' (2017: 17). The play encapsulates the Poles' fears of these unfathomable strangers in a curse uttered by one of the Polish spectators: 'Damn their eyes' (5). Resonant with the timelessness and transcultural language of folklore and fairy tales, this is an expressionistically logical riposte to the superstitious belief in the evil eye, a demonic feature attributed to the uncanny, spellbinding power of the Jew but also a belief that stereotypes the Polish peasant as irredeemably superstitious. That Hoffman should choose this non-realist mode of expression is consistent with Tzvetan Todorov's discussion of the fantastic in Holocaust drama where 'the very heart of the fantastic [emerges] when in a world which is indeed our world, the one we know, a world without devils, sylphides, or vampires, there occurs an event which cannot be explained by the laws of this same familiar world' (1975: 25).

The play's dramatization of the past occurs through flashbacks that enact the ghosts' recollections of interactions between themselves and non-Jewish Poles. Regarding this dramatic method that crosses 'the threshold between the "normal" and the "fantastic"', Rokem observes that '[i]t is only through such a flashback technique that the place of memory itself is brought back, the place where it happened' (2000: 46). Despite the wider resonances of ongoing genocides and massacres and the performance site as British, the place in *The Ceremony* is that of Polish-Jewish encounters, in the remembered past and in the present. In concert, these encounters respond to persistent questions about the historically tremulous relations between Jews and Poles. In one example, a character named Hanna, daughter of one of the murdered, is described in the stage directions as a liminal, destabilized figure. She is 'a Jewish woman of uncertain nationality', but who admits she was born not far from the ceremonial site and 'who has stood a little apart from the others, with a look of wonderment, or perplexity, on her face. In all the group scenes, we should remain aware of her as a kind of central consciousness' (2017: 10). Encountering her mother's ghost at the commemoration, Hanna expresses her uncertain relation to the uncanny past: 'what happened here … the people … What they were like. You knew them so well' (16).

Without transitional markings, but indicating the presence of the past in the present, the scene switches to an ordinary pre-war day at Hanna's mother's shop, where a peasant woman customer, accompanied by her husband, comments favourably on the fabric on display. The drift into neighbourly conversation between the two women suddenly turns ominous when the peasant husband begins interrupting. Defending his authority, he denigrates his wife and targets the Jews with increasingly angry condemnations:

**Man** (in an undertone):   Eh, what do you know woman … Our priest has warned us, they're not like us … They don't believe the same things …

**Man** (louder this time, as if he didn't care who hears):   You don't understand, woman … (On the way out of the shop) They're not like us, who knows what she writes in that big book of hers … (2017: 18)

Returning to the present, Hanna comments:

> Such small things ...
> **Mother** (to **Hanna**):
> This is how it begins ... (18)

Re-enacting the past here is an attempt to fill the emotional and epistemological void implied by Hanna's question and the shadowy presence of her mother. The distance between the mother's murder and the daughter's survival is too great to accommodate a direct address in which speaker and listener are capable of the same cognitive understanding. Nonetheless, embedded in both methods is the same assumption: that a survivor-witness or, in this case, the ghostly witness has '"too much" knowledge or experience' for any straightforward, realistic narrative form to be able to convey (Rokem 2000: 34). Both representations of victim witnesses and their listeners, including the audience, are attempts 'to make it possible for "naïve" listeners to understand, and at the same time also to show implicitly that they probably never really will. The realities of the Shoah are too ominous to be rationally understood' (Rokem 2000: 34). *The Ceremony* depicts Hanna's exchange with her mother's ghost and her mother's memory of interacting with non-Jewish Poles as confronting the audience with the question of how to assess Holocaust memory as a reality. Instead of the involuntary, invasive and lacerating nature of traumatic memory, the enactment of the mother's memory contributes to her construction of a vigorous and self-affirming self-image.[12]

Together, the juxtaposition of Hanna's mother's elliptical answer and the brief tableau of a past Polish-Jewish encounter can only suggest an explanation. How it might end is proposed by the play's conclusion. *The Ceremony* ends with a voice-over, described as 'a gentle voice, not heard before' (2017: 54):

> Let us therefore pray for those who died here on that awful day sixty years ago. For those who have died elsewhere, on their awful days. Let us pray that the letters of consolation are reunited with their souls. Let us pray that letters of consolation and compassion enter our souls and flower there into full and beautiful texts.
>
> (54)

As in Hoffman's other writing, this peroration remains hopeful. Despite the continuation of mass atrocities around the globe and indifferent, inadequate or misguided and destructive responses, she remains committed to the idea of reunion and integration of the stranger or Other into our own sense of selves as a new social politics of enlightenment. For example, she has posited that

> the need for both individual and collective recognition is deep. ... In our multi-cultural societies, as long as we expect new generations of immigrants, we need to make room for forums in which ... particular pasts and cultural sensibilities can be lived and recognised ... We also need to meet on the 'objective' ground of shared interests and responsibilities – perhaps even responsibilities to and for each other.
>
> (Hoffman 2008: 212)

For British theatregoers, as with Julia Pascal's *Holocaust Trilogy*, *The Ceremony* imprints the plea to accept the role of secondary witnesses as a way of mourning the lost.

## Notes

1. See the volume *Britain and the Holocaust* (Sharples and Jensen 2013), and Stone (2006).
2. Tim Cole discusses the miniseries *Holocaust* and its British reception in '"Marvellous Raisins in a Badly-Cooked Cake": British Reactions to the Screening of *Holocaust*' (2013).
3. For further discussion of these plays, see my *Anglo-Jewish Women Writing the Holocaust* (Lassner 2007).
4. As expressed in novels, memoirs and the media, memories of wartime Polish Jewish relations remain vexed. Under Nazi threats of retaliation, Poles recall the near impossibility of helping their Jewish neighbours, but many also viewed Jews as colluding with the Soviet occupation of 1939–41. Polish Jews recall the antisemitism promulgated by the Catholic Church and political factions as well as the indifference and treachery of ordinary Poles. The post-war communist regime exploited continuing antisemitism to claim that American and Israeli forces were undermining the security of the nation, leading to the 1968 antisemitic campaign that drove Polish Jews to leave. For cultural representations of these memories, see Baron (2005) and Michlic (2006). For historical analysis see Lucas (2005), Heller (1977), Gutman and Krakowski (1986), Cooper (2001) and Zimmerman (2002).
5. Rachel Brenner's study of five notable Polish writers shows reactions ranging from 'deliberate evasions of the victims' plight, to paralyzing dismay at the unfolding horror, to active participation in altruistic rescue operations' (Brenner 2014: 4).

6   I am very grateful to Eva Hoffman for sending me a copy of the script. The musical director was Michael Zev Gordon, the casting director, Ginny Schiller, and the stage manager, Sarah Longson. The actors, some of whom played more than one role, included Niall Buggy, Joe Murray, Charlotte Harwood, Oliver Gomm, Jay Benedict, David Horovitch, Amy Marston, Paul Herzberg, Ben Caplan, Helen Ryan, David Fielder, David Fleeshman, Trevor Cooper and Ruth Posner.
7   The JW3 production team generously shared the recording of the play and discussion.
8   The scholars who have debated the challenges of representing Holocaust atrocity and memory include Saul Friedlander, Dominick La Capra and Berel Lang. Recent perspectives comprise the collection of essays *After Testimony* (Lothe, Suleiman and Phelan 2012).
9   Ernst Van Alphen assesses the difficulties of representing and analysing the possibility of transmitting Holocaust trauma from the first generation to the second, a relationship that 'utterly fails to establish continuity between generations' and 'that causes the intense desire for it on the side of the children' (2006: 478).
10  Different perspectives on the ethics of Holocaust representation appear in Gigliotti, Golomb and Gould while Glenda Abramson analyses British theatre. I discuss other British Holocaust playwrights in *Anglo-Jewish Women Writing the Holocaust* (Lassner 2007).
11  See Walker (2005) for a discussion of Expressionist theater. Lawrence Baron's analysis of assessing Holocaust films applies to Hoffman's experimental method: 'whether they figuratively or literally evoke a sense of the collective and individual choices and historical circumstances that enabled Hitler to persecute or liquidate millions of civilians he designated as asocial, deviant, ideological, racial, or religious enemies' (2005: viii–ix).
12  Hoffman's representation interprets Holocaust memory differently than Rippl et al. (2013) who argue that the traumatic past is too disorienting to be witnessed and understood at the time and narrated coherently.

## References

Abramson, G. (2001/02), 'Anglicising the Holocaust', *Journal of Theatre and Drama*, 7 (8): 105–23.

Agamben, G. (1999), *Remnants of Auschwitz: The Witness and the Archive*, trans. D. Heller-Roazen, New York: Zone Books.

Baron, L. (2005), *Projecting the Holocaust Into the Present: The Changing Focus of Contemporary Holocaust Cinema*, Lanham, MD: Rowman and Littlefield.

Brenner, R. (2014), *The Ethics of Witnessing: The Holocaust in Polish Writers' Diaries from Warsaw, 1939–1945*, Evanston: Northwestern University.

Cole, T. (2013), '"Marvellous Raisins in a Badly-Cooked Cake": British Reactions to the Screening of *Holocaust*', in C. Sharples and O. Jensen (eds), *Britain and the Holocaust: Remembering and Representing War and Genocide*, 115–28, Basingstoke: Palgrave.

Cooper, L. (2001), *In the Shadow of the Polish Eagle: The Poles, the Holocaust, and Beyond*, New York: Palgrave.

David, K. (2017), 'Eva Hoffman's First Play', *The Jewish Chronicle*, 18 May. Available online: www.thejc.com/culture/theatre/eva-hoffman-1.438805 (accessed 6 October 2018).

Gigliotti, S., J. Golomb and C. S. Gould, eds (2014), *Ethics, Art, and Representations of the Holocaust*, Lanham, MD: Lexington Books.

Glowacka, D. and J. Zylinska, eds (2007), *Imaginary Neighbors: Mediating Polish-Jewish Relations after the Holocaust*, Lincoln: University of Nebraska.

Gross, J. T. (2001), *Neighbors: The Destruction of the Jewish Community in Jedwabne*, Princeton, NJ: Princeton University.

Gutman, I. and S. Krakowski (1986), *Unequal Victims: Poles and Jews during World War Two*, New York: Holocaust Library.

Heller, C. S. (1977), *On the Edge of Destruction: The Jews of Poland between the Two World Wars*, New York: Columbia University.

Hoffman, E. (1989), *Lost in Translation*, New York: Dutton.

Hoffman, E. (1997), *Shtetl: The Life and Death of a Small Town and the World of Polish Jews*, New York: Houghton Mifflin.

Hoffman, E. (2004), *After Such Knowledge*, New York: Public Affairs.

Hoffman, E. (2008), 'Talking across Cultural Differences', *Aspasia*, 2 (1): 201–13.

Hoffman, E. (2013), 'Out of Exile', *European Judaism*, 46 (2): 55–60.

Hoffman, E. (2017), *The Ceremony*. Unpublished playscript.

Hoffman, E. (2018a), email correspondence, 20 June.

Hoffman, E. (2018b), 'Hearing Poland's Ghosts', *New York Review of Books*, 22 March: 4, 6, 8.

Jensen, O. (2013), 'The Holocaust in British Television and Film: A Look over the Fence', in C. Sharples and O. Jensen (eds), *Britain and the Holocaust: Remembering and Representing War and Genocide*, 115–25, Basingstoke: Palgrave.

Lang, B. (2000), *Holocaust Representation: Art within the Limits of History and Ethics*, Baltimore, MD: Johns Hopkins University.

Lassner, P. (2007), *Anglo-Jewish Women Writing the Holocaust*, Basingstoke: Palgrave.

Lease, B. (2017), 'Shared Histories and Commemorative Extensions: Warsaw's POLIN Museum', *Theatre Journal*, 69 (3): 383–401.

Levin, J. (2006), 'Eva Hoffman: Interview', *Jewish Renaissance*, 5 (2): 6–7.

Lothe, J., S. R. Suleiman and J. Phelan, eds (2012), *After Testimony: The Ethics and Aesthetics of Holocaust Narrative for the Future*, Columbus: Ohio State University.

Lucas, R. C. (2005), *The Forgotten Holocaust: The Poles under German Occupation 1939-1944*, New York: Hippocrene Books.

Michlic, J. B. (2006), *Poland's Threatening Other: The Image of the Jew from 1880 to the Present*, Lincoln: University of Nebraska.

Petraka, V. M. (1999), *Spectacular Suffering: Theatre, Fascism, and the Holocaust*, Bloomington, IN: Indiana University.

Rippl, G., P. Schweighauser, T. Kirss, M. Sutrop and T. Steffen, eds (2013), *Haunted Narratives: Life Writing in an Age of Trauma*, Toronto: University of Toronto.

Rokem, F. (2000), *Performing History*, Iowa City: University of Iowa.

Russell, S. (2001), 'Holocaust History as Postmodern Performance', *Essays in Theatre*, 19 (2): 127-39.

Schumacher, C. (1998), *Staging the Holocaust*, Cambridge: Cambridge University.

Sharples, C. and O. Jensen, eds (2013), 'Introduction', in C. Sharples and O. Jensen (eds), *Britain and the Holocaust: Remembering and Representing War and Genocide*, 1-12, Basingstoke: Palgrave.

Stone, D. (2006), 'Britannia Waives the Rules: British Imperialism and Holocaust Memory', in D. Stone (ed.), *History, Memory and Mass Atrocity: Essays on the Holocaust and Genocide*, 174-90, London: Valentine Mitchell.

Todorov, T. (1975), *The Fantastic: A Structural Approach to a Literary Genre*, Ithaca, NY: Cornell University.

Van Alphen, E. (2006), 'Second-Generation Testimony, Transmission of Trauma, and Postmemory', *Poetics Today*, 27 (2): 473-88.

Walker, J. (2005), *Expressionism and Modernism in the American Theatre*, Cambridge: Cambridge University.

White, N. J. (1999), 'In the Absence of Memory?: Jewish Fate and Dramatic Representation; Production and Critical Reception of Holocaust Drama on the London Stage 1945-1989', PhD diss., City University London.

Ziarek, E. P. (2007), 'Melancholic Nationalism and the Pathologies of Commemorating the Holocaust in Poland', in D. Glowacka and J. Zylinska (eds), *Imaginary Neighbors: Mediating Polish-Jewish Relations after the Holocaust*, 301-26, Lincoln: University of Nebraska.

Zimmerman, J. D., ed. (2002), *Contested Memories: Poles and Jews during the Holocaust and Its Aftermath*, New Brunswick, NJ: Rutgers University.

Zylinska, J. (2007), '"Who Is My Neighbor?": Ethics under Duress', in D. Glowacka and J. Zylinska (eds), *Imaginary Neighbors: Mediating Polish-Jewish Relations after the Holocaust*, 275-300, Lincoln: University of Nebraska.

# 7

# Dramatic Responses to the Resurgence of Antisemitism: On Trial – the Blood Libel, Arnold Wesker and Steven Berkoff

Axel Stähler

It is a fine line that separates a play about antisemitism from promoting the prejudices it seeks to denounce or, as the British-Jewish dramatist Stephen Laughton found to his cost, from provoking a surge of abuse. While receiving much critical acclaim in the national and international press, Laughton's *One Jewish Boy* (2018),[1] which is described by the *Jewish Chronicle* as 'a play about rising antisemitism' (Sugarman 2018), occasioned a flurry of hate mail. As one reviewer succinctly put it: 'Life imitates art as play about antisemitism faces wave of abuse' (Sherwood 2018).

To some extent, *One Jewish Boy* is based on an incident of antisemitic abuse suffered by its author which erupted from the projection of anti-Israeli sentiments onto diaspora Jews (Frazer 2018). In the play – which is also a probing exploration of how race and gender, class, culture and anxiety impact on the relationship between a 'nice educated' Jewish boy from North London (Laughton 2018: 66) and a young woman of mixed heritage with her own experience of racism – a similar incident scares and scars the protagonist to such a degree that he can no longer escape the pernicious impact and inexorable persistence of 'inherited trauma' (28). Jesse insists: 'It defines me. There's scar tissue in my DNA' (89). The uncomfortable associations of heredity in the context of racism aside, Jesse's 'poisonous' (87) preoccupation with antisemitism escalates and eventually irreversibly fractures his relationship with his wife and child.

Laughton (b. 1981), whose own heritage is Greek-Cypriot and Jewish, and who embraced his Jewish identity not before adulthood, said that the play 'has been written from a place of tangible fear' in post-millennial Britain. He elaborated: 'Things that were on the fringes of the far right and the far left started creeping in to the mainstream. In the last few years it seems like people feel they have permission to be antisemitic' (Sherwood 2018). Indeed, even a cursory look at almost any number of the *Jewish Chronicle* of the past decade will convey a mounting sense of dread that antisemitism is on the rise in Britain. A particular concern of Laughton's play is the refutation of the conflation of Jews and Israel, because, as the author insists, 'If we're ever going to actually tackle modern anti-Semitism, we have to pull that apart' (Laughton 2018: 104). Yet *One Jewish Boy* also traces the provenance of antisemitism. Its persistence is attributed by Jesse to its 'four pillars': 'Loyalty. Oppression. Control and' – perhaps the most potent and enduring among them – 'the blood libel' (69).

The allegation that Jews murder Christian children in a mockery of the passion of Christ in order to obtain blood for ritualistic purposes, known as blood libel, originates in medieval England. Various references in *One Jewish Boy* to the blood libel attest to its persistence and continued cultural relevance, even though in recent decades the fallout of Israeli policies appears to have generated a substitute of sufficient weight to eclipse the blood libel as a topic of dramatic engagement with antisemitism. Yet to Arnold Wesker (1932–2016) and Steven Berkoff (1937–), representatives of an earlier generation of British-Jewish playwrights, historical instances of the blood libel appear to have offered a pertinent means of responding to the resurgence of antisemitism specifically in Britain.

Near contemporaries, who shared their roots in the working-class milieu of the impoverished Jewish East End, both Wesker and Berkoff gravitated towards the theatre. While they could hardly have been more different, Wesker and Berkoff curiously each wrote a play repudiating the fabricated antisemitic ritual murder accusation. After the Holocaust, dramatic engagement with this persistent calumny has been rare,[2] and Wesker's *Blood Libel* (1994)[3] and Berkoff's *Ritual in Blood* (2000)[4] are uncharacteristic of either playwright's work. Yet the thematic convergence, revisionist approach and enduring topicality of the two plays ensure their significance as contributions to contemporary British-Jewish theatre even though their actual stage life – barring any unforeseen revivals – was very brief.

## Arnold Wesker and Steven Berkoff in Context

Arnold Wesker was a central figure in the New Wave of British theatre in the 1950s and 1960s alongside playwrights like John Osborne, Shelagh Delaney and Harold Pinter (whose origins were also in Jewish East London) (Lacey 1995). Wesker's early plays, such as *Chicken Soup with Barley* (1959), *Roots* (1959) and *I'm Talking about Jerusalem* (1960), commonly referred to as the *Wesker Trilogy*, drew in a social realist mode on his Jewish working-class background and the experience of farm labourers in Norfolk. His plays gained immediate prominence and were followed by the similarly successful

*The Kitchen* (1960) and *Chips with Everything* (1962), which were inspired by the dramatist's own experiences as a kitchen help in a large restaurant and as an RAF recruit, respectively.

In 1961, Wesker's active social and cultural engagement led him to establish Centre 42 in London, where he served as the artistic director until his experiment to provide workers with access to high art and culture ultimately failed in 1970. Frequently of a didactic nature and focusing on family life and disappointed idealism, such as in *Their Very Own and Golden City* (1966), Wesker's later plays are increasingly diverse in content as well as in. These later plays include comedies such as *The Old Ones* (1972) and *The Wedding Feast* (1974); the farce *One More Ride on the Merry-Go-Round* (1990); and historical plays, such as *Caritas* (1981), a play about 'the pursuit of the ideal through dogmas which lead to the destruction of things human' (Wesker 2012b: 253), and *Longitude* (2002), which chronicles the tribulations of the eighteenth-century clockmaker who discovered the solution to determining the longitude of a ship's position at sea.

Jewish concerns were initially coincidental to Wesker's plays and subliminal rather than explicit. Yet his critical rewriting of Shakespeare's *Merchant of Venice* (c. 1596) in *The Merchant* (1977), later renamed *Shylock*, marked the beginning of Wesker's direct dramatic engagement with Jewishness. From 1983 to 1985, Wesker worked on the script for a TV adaptation of Arthur Koestler's *Thieves in the Night* (1946). Though his screenplay was never produced (Stähler 2017), it arguably attuned Wesker to the impact of the Middle East conflict on the perception of Jewishness in Britain and to the persistence of antisemitism. With *Badenheim 1939* (1994) completed in 1987 and possibly inspired by his abortive reworking of Koestler's novel, Wesker offered a stage adaptation of Aharon Appelfeld's eponymous allegorical satire on the beginnings of the Holocaust (1978). *When God Wanted a Son* (1990) is, in Wesker's words, a play 'about anti-Semitism and the indigestibility of Jews' (Heathman 1989: 19). It ventures into comedy with its main character, Connie, an aspiring stand-up comic who finds herself entrapped between her Jewish father and English mother.

Though initially very successful, Wesker found himself increasingly marginalized on the British stage. Many of his later plays premiered abroad and the embittered dramatist, who gained a reputation of being not easy to work with, eventually sought seclusion in the Black Mountains in Wales (O'Mahoney 2002). Like Wesker, Steven Berkoff (born Leslie Steven Berks) has a reputation of being difficult (Cross 2004: 99). Yet there is a very different quality to their obstinacy. Where Wesker was loath to make artistic compromises and felt alienated, Berkoff seems to thrive on confrontation. For many years the *enfant terrible* of British theatre, Berkoff has been described as a 'phenomenon' in his own right (13). Trained as an actor at the Webber Douglas Academy of Dramatic Art and the École Internationale de Théâtre Jacques Lecoq with a strong focus on physical theatre and mime, Berkoff emerged as a playwright with adaptations of Kafka's *In the Penal Colony* (1969), *Metamorphosis* (1969) and *The Trial* (1971), all of which were performed by the London Theatre Group, formed by Berkoff in 1968.

Acclaimed by Aleks Sierz as a pioneer of 'in-yer-face' theatre (2001: 25–6), Berkoff infused his following plays with a pervasive sense of violence and conflict: *East* (1975), as indicated by its subtitle, is an *Elegy for the East End and Its Energetic Waste* and was described by its author as a 'scream or a shout of pain' (Sierz 2001: 25). *East* was followed by *Greek* (1980), a reworking of Sophocles' *Oedipus Rex*; *Decadence* (1981), which explores class tensions; and *West* (1983), a play about identity and violence in the West End of London. The verse satire *Sink the Belgrano!* (1986) condemns the Falklands War (1982). Berkoff's most recent as yet unpublished play, *Harvey* (written 2018), targets the alleged sexual misconduct of Hollywood producer Harvey Weinstein (Sommers 2018).

Berkoff wrote also a number of 'Jewish' plays which confirm his penchant for provocation. With *Messiah* (2000), he offered a controversial reinterpretation of the crucifixion that examines 'what we believe and why we believe it' (Gardner 2000). In *Biblical Tales* (2010), Berkoff was said to have 'plunder[ed] biblical narratives to promote his own view of the world' (Billington 2010). Berkoff commented that the play's four scenes launched an investigation of 'ancient Jewish values' prompted by 'the appalling flack that Israel received' (Berkoff 2010) in response to its recent military intervention in Gaza (Operation Cast Lead, 2008–9). Attacking what has been described as 'new' antisemitism, Berkoff denounced those who claim, 'We hate Israel, we hate Zionism, we don't hate Jews' because, as he confrontationally maintained: 'Zionism is the very essence of what a Jew is. Zionism is the act of seeking sanctuary after years and years of unspeakable outrages against Jews.' (Round 2009).

## The Persistence of Antisemitism and the Blood Libel

Gaza is also the trigger in Berkoff's 'How to Train an Anti-Semite', the first of five 'shorts' produced under the title *Religion and Anarchy* (1992). It takes the audience from the mindless antisemitism of two benefit cheats to a Jewish couple's delight in kosher delicacies ('Guilt'), to an antisemitic bedside story of medieval provenance ('Roast'), to the selection on the ramp of a concentration camp ('Line-Up'), and finally – unnervingly and problematically – into the gas chamber ('Gas'). Yet engaging with antisemitism informed already Berkoff's first dramatic effort, which remained unpublished and unperformed for more than three decades. Like Wesker's *Blood Libel*, it challenged the blood accusation. Completed in 1965, the play about the alleged ritual murder of little Hugh of Lincoln by the Jews in 1255 was eventually published in 2000. Berkoff may have felt that it was his indictment of the history of antisemitism in Britain that frustrated his initial efforts to see his play staged or published. He certainly sensed latent antisemitism in the British theatrical establishment. Referring to the *Marranos*, the 'secret Jews' of early modern Spain, Berkoff insisted with regard to his own Jewishness: 'Well, I've never been secret' (Round 2009).

In fact, as Robert Cross observes, Berkoff 'makes no mention in his writings or interviews of having practised Judaism in any form during his childhood and youth' (2004: 26). The writer's early dramatic engagement with Jewishness in *Ritual in Blood* and his adaptations of Kafka are explained by Cross through the prism of psychology. Cross suggests, perhaps simplistically, that Berkoff applied the narrative of 'the victimisation and persecution of the Jews' to himself 'at a time when he considered (or projected) himself as an artist systematically marginalised by the British theatre Establishment' (26–7). At a later date, the actor and playwright emphasized in an interview with Angela Lambert that his Jewishness – 'such as it is' – is cultural and acknowledged the Jewish influence in particular on the interiority of his theatrical approach: 'seeing the dreams and haunting fears underneath the reality' (Lambert 1989: 16).

Wesker, though not observant, also never denied his Jewishness. Like Berkoff, Wesker was very much aware of his Jewish heritage, which he considered part of his cultural identity and literary production (Bigsby 1976). Wesker too was concerned about what he perceived to be pervasive antisemitism in English theatre. Historically, antisemitism in Britain between the beginning of the twentieth century and the Second World War has been described as endemic but 'quiet' (Julius 2010: 303) and 'civil' (Trubowitz 2012: 1–2). After the Second World War, British antisemitism surfaced mainly during three episodes: 'the final years of the Mandate [for Palestine], the trajectory of the fascist and far-right parties in the 1950s and 1960s, and the controversy over the War Crimes Act 1991' (Julius 2010: 330). In recent years, the perception of antisemitism in Britain – and in Europe – has changed (Kahn-Harris and Gidley 2010: 148).

'New' antisemitism – mostly 'disguised behind a new non-racial language of anti-Zionism' (ibid., 136) – may be different in kind from its previous manifestations. Even so, as experienced also by Jesse in Laughton's *One Jewish Boy*, it is only another permutation of a variegated phenomenon that – as political and religious anti-Judaism or pseudo-scientific and racial antisemitism – has blighted Jewish life even prior to the destruction of the Second Temple in 70 CE (Schäfer 1997: 1–8). A predicament of immeasurable impact, antisemitism has spawned a plethora of calumnies against the Jewish *other*. Of these, the blood libel is probably the most perfidious, pernicious and persistent.

The first recorded instance of the blood libel occurred in Norwich in 1144, when the mutilated body of a young boy was found, and the city's Jews were blamed for his death. Eventually William was sainted; his corpse was translated successively from the churchyard to the chapter house, to the high altar and finally to a side chapel of the cathedral (Rose 2015: 99). The calumny and the persecution of the Jews it provoked quickly spread across England and Europe, exacerbated by the fanaticism engendered through the debacle of the unsuccessful Second Crusade (1147–1149) (Rose 2015: 3–11). Instances of the blood libel surfaced throughout the Middle Ages and into the twentieth century. There was an unprecedented number of blood accusations in the period between 1870 and the beginning of the Second World War, 'more, in fact, than all the previous recorded instances put together' (Band 2001: 113). Whereas there seems to have been no explicit occurrence of the accusation in Britain during this period, belief in the charge continued to have an 'amorphous existence' (Holmes 1991: 122). Yet while the emergence of the blood libel and the occasionally insensitive journalistic response to it was confronted vigorously by the *Jewish Chronicle*, Jewish literary production in Britain offered no notable engagement with the calumny during this period.

Wesker and Berkoff reimagine in their plays medieval instances of the blood accusation in England which mark the early period of its snowballing dissemination. Though none of the alleged victims of ritual murder remain in the Roman Catholic calendar of saints (Rose 2015: 1), the historical instances of the blood libel offered Wesker and Berkoff a poignant metonymy for the continuing persecution of Jews. Its recorded origins in Britain allowed Wesker and Berkoff to confront British audiences with a seminal myth of antisemitic provenance that was uncomfortably close to home.

Short of attempting to engage with the Holocaust, *Ritual in Blood* and *Blood Libel* nevertheless add to the historical specificity of either case the sense of their universal relevance in relation to the later occurrence. By revisiting the presumed origins of the calumny in the English Middle Ages, they evoke an intensely disturbing manifestation of antisemitism that comprises Christian anti-Judaism and pseudo-scientific antisemitism. By emphasizing the spatial proximity of the historical blood libel cases to their audience, both playwrights arguably sought to dispel any resistance to the implicit moral imperative suggested by the events through their temporal distancing: they jolt the audience and create an immediate rapport which in a more roundabout way sustains ethical interpellation and supports a revisionist objective.

Though very different in detail, *Ritual in Blood* and *Blood Libel* consequently share a number of essential similarities. They present the blood libel as the result of selfish intrigues of individuals or small interest groups who by means of demagogy and the exploitation of superstition as well as economic anxieties incite an eruption of collective hysteria directed at the Jewish other. These plays also engage with the specific juridical discourse that has developed around the commemoration of ritual murder accusations and whose trajectory they seek to subvert through their interpellation.

## Trying the Blood Libel on Stage

Wesker was commissioned in 1989 to write a play on the legend of William of Norwich for the opening of the Norwich Playhouse. Earlier draft versions of the play were provisionally entitled *Martyrs for Sale* and *Saints for Profit* (Wesker 1991a, b). Though completed in 1991 and published in 1994, *Blood Libel* was not performed until February 1996 as the third production of the new theatre which had finally opened in December 1995.

Berkoff chose to engage with another instance of the blood accusation, which proliferated in medieval England before the expulsion of the Jews in 1290: in Gloucester (1168), Bury St Edmunds (1181), Bristol (1183) and Lincoln (1255). Written twenty years after the Holocaust, Berkoff's play is about the alleged martyrdom of Hugh of Lincoln in 1255, which is probably best known through Geoffrey Chaucer's late fourteenth-century allusion to the events in 'The Prioress's Tale' (1392). As mentioned above, the play was Berkoff's first dramatic effort and was completed in 1965 with the title *Hep, Hep, Hep*, later to be changed to *Blood Accusation*. As Berkoff notes in his autobiography, neither any stage nor any television production firm 'would touch' (1996: 277) the play. It remained unpublished until it was included in the third volume of Berkoff's collected plays (2000) under its new and final title, *Ritual in Blood*. Once published, *Ritual in Blood* soon premiered at the Nottingham Playhouse in May 2001.[5] Berkoff was inspired to write his play by a plaque in Lincoln Cathedral that was installed in 1955 at the site of the former shrine of Little St Hugh, replacing an earlier inscription. The new plaque acknowledged the historical fabrication of the blood libel and asked for forgiveness (Hick 1993: 64) – but only of the Lord and not of the Jewish victims of the detestable calumny.[6]

When intermittently unemployed as a young actor, Berkoff took to researching the blood libel in the British Library. Looking back to his efforts, the dramatist noted that '[t]he most illuminating aspect of the many hours in the museum was the sheer amount of material I found on antisemitism' (1996: 278). At the same time, Berkoff acknowledged that '"Jewy" themes are difficult to set down without falling into the trap of making all the Jews holy, good, decent and all the gentiles villains and cold-blooded tyrants'. And he conceded: 'I fell right into it and I had to find another way.' Yet he nevertheless felt that he had 'assuaged a great deal of guilt' (278).

Wesker too was concerned about representing Jews on stage; he maintained that it is 'very difficult to portray them properly, they become stage Jews' (Lyndon 1996: 58). With his initially perplexing decision not to include any Jewish characters in *Blood Libel* – with the exception of the convert Theobald – Wesker deftly evaded the issue. Wesker's *Blood Libel* engages directly and critically with Thomas of Monmouth's *Life and Miracles of St. William of Norwich*. Though composed over the course of more than two decades and years after the fact (1150–73; Rose 2015: 17, 110), this is the main contemporary source for the murder of William and his subsequent sanctification. Wesker's play intervenes on different levels in the juridical discourse on the blood accusation introduced by Thomas, which has been described as 'a fundamental precedent for discussions about the ritual murder accusation that has persisted down to the present' (Johnson 2012: 32). It is, in effect, integrated into the play's very conceptualization and structure. The dramatist's production note suggests that *Blood Libel* should be staged so that the actors 'are witnesses and jury both' (Wesker 2012a: 109) – with the exception of the rape scene. This was enacted for the benefit of the audience, while the actors on stage remained oblivious to it and its various reiterations (113).

In his notes, later partially included in the programme booklet, Wesker considered three different approaches to his controversial source: '*to select from Thomas's record and assume it is the truth/or to ignore everything in the record of Thomas of Monmouth and invent an entirely new scenario/or to select from Thomas's record and comment on its veracity*' (Programme 1996; Wesker 1991c). Wesker opted for the third approach, and *Blood Libel* is very clear in suggesting the fabricated nature of the proffered testimony and miracles.

Wesker unravels the strategies used by Thomas of Monmouth to turn the murdered child into a martyr by confronting superstition with reason. The conflict is succinctly articulated by bringing Thomas onto the stage in *Blood Libel* and suggesting that the play reflects the process of the creation of the monk's account of the death and sanctification of the murdered boy. Prior

Elias, the voice of reason in the play, maintains: 'A martyr is not a martyr unless he die for his religion.' He insists: 'The boy William was murdered I strongly suspect by a mad and cruel stranger for cruel obscene desires of the flesh' (Wesker 2012a: 136). The historical Thomas' response to such doubts, as noted by Johnson, was to emphasize instead of the martyr's intention, that of his alleged persecutors (2012: 41). In Wesker's play, Elias' interlocutor, the prior of a rivalling house who is keen to acquire the profitable relic for his own use, shrewdly delivers the punch line: 'But prove it was the Jews, you prove a martyr' (Wesker 2012a: 136). Because, as Thomas maintained and as Wesker has Elias assert: 'Not suffering but why he suffered is what lays claim to martyrdom' (136; Johnson 2012: 38). This point is crucial because it allows Thomas to contend that it is the imitation of Christ's passion and its mockery through the ritual murder which constitute William's claim to sainthood (ibid., 39–40).

With the repeated stark juxtaposition of the brutal rape of William at the hands of the stranger with 'revelation' (Wesker 2012a: 148), the 'evidence' of dreams and visions (129), Wesker invalidates the very premise on which the case for sanctification – and for the blood accusation – rests. Berkoff employed this same strategy of revealing the evidence as fabrication. In the case of little Hugh, no single hagiographic source exists but a diffuse tradition which ranges from annals to histories and folklore (Sicher 2017: 25–32). Berkoff confronts this tradition by suggesting that little Hugh was the victim of his own mischievous behaviour: in evocation of the Fall, the boy plunges to his death into the Jew's well as he is about to steal his apples. Wesker and Berkoff's interventions in the established narratives are decisive; not only do they subvert the attribution of the martyrdom to the children, but they also acquit the Jews of the murder charge and, more importantly, of ritual murder.

Like *Blood Libel*, *Ritual in Blood* also participates in the juridical discourse established by Thomas. Most obviously, Berkoff's play too includes a trial scene. Structurally, the elaboration of the historical context and the alternative explanation of what happened to the unfortunate child are followed by the escalation, which culminates in the accusation of ritual murder and the trial. This reveals the Jews, beyond the religious intolerance to which they were subjected, to fall victim to economic considerations and intrigues and the trial, too, is shown to legalize the exploitation and destruction of the Jews. It is in fact only on the substratum of the political machinations that the religious dimension of the accusation is elaborated. It is refuted with the notion of 'projective inversion' that suggests a sense of displaced guilt in relation to the symbolic cannibalism of the Eucharist (Berkoff 2000: 88; Dundes 1991: 354).

In conspicuous contrast to *Blood Libel*, the trial in *Ritual in Blood* is nevertheless suggested to offer the Jews an opportunity to articulate their own voice and resist victimization. The notion of Jewish resistance to antisemitic excesses suggested here and throughout the play on different levels sets Berkoff's play apart from Wesker's, in which the Jews neither have nor contemplate any agency. But ultimately, in *Ritual in Blood* Jewish resistance remains verbal and ineffectual. Resistance is frustrated not only by external factors but also by internal division, which the author portrays by appropriating from Holocaust discourse (Berkoff 2000: 19-20).

In Wesker's *Blood Libel*, the audience, initially guided by Elias, is compelled to form their own judgement. They are, in effect, as are the actors, witnesses and jury. The dramatic intention of Berkoff's trial scenes is less subtle. In *Ritual of Blood*, accusation and defence are played out for the audience. Berkoff instead conveys a sense of the intransigence of the antisemitic mentality and the seeming inevitability of a catastrophic conclusion. Yet he nevertheless conveys a moral imperative, no less than Wesker's appeal to reason.

## Reception

Neither *Blood Libel* nor *Ritual in Blood* was successful on the stage. Wesker's expectations to take his ritual murder play to London and Broadway were disappointed (Wesker 1996) and it only ever ran for a fortnight in Norwich, in the spring of 1996.[7] Berkoff's play was performed only during one season in Nottingham in the early summer of 2001. This makes the significance of either play on a national scale in relation to British-Jewish drama questionable. However, considering their affirmative stance and potentially conflictual nature, there may be a deeper reason for the failure of both plays on the British stage and for their continued relevance. Uncharacteristically for both Wesker and Berkoff, both plays – if in very different ways – directly confront British antisemitism. They challenge complacency and demand rethinking the Jewish/British encounter. Sadly, although both productions were reviewed in the national papers, this process appears to be largely limited to the dissemination of *Blood Libel* and *Ritual in Blood* in print.

The Nottingham production of *Ritual in Blood*, directed by Timothy Walker, received mixed reviews. The play's topicality was observed by Alfred Hickling in the *Guardian*, who noted that its themes of 'superstition, bigotry and revenge' never change: 'The year is 1255, but the costumes are modern' (2001). The critic described *Ritual in Blood* as 'a multidimensional drama of great intellect and style' and asserted the dramatist's unbridled ambition and vastness of scope, noting that Berkoff 'turns dry chronicle into well-lubricated drama in a way that courts comparison with Shakespeare'. This favourable assessment was not shared by Ian Shuttleworth, who considered the play 'at times clumsily patterned' and deemed the courtroom sequence, in particular, a failure that accomplished 'the rare, unfortunate achievement of going most noticeably awry during what is usually one of theatre's most solid bets' (2001). This was perceived very differently by the reviewer of the *Telegraph*. Dominic Cavendish felt that 'only in the trial scene does Berkoff and Walker's theatrical treatment ignite the subject-matter' (2001). The rest of the play he described as 'frequently fascinating', though 'no shrine to dramatic complexity'. Like Hickling, yet less enthusiastically, Cavendish compared the trial scene in *Ritual in Blood* to Shakespeare's *Merchant of Venice*: 'It's a compelling scene – but you can't help recalling the grimmest hour of one Shylock, and a far, far better play.'

It has also been observed that *Ritual in Blood*, naturalistic in acting style and dialogue (Cross 2004: 211), is to some extent atypical of Berkoff's writing. Considering its textual genesis, this should be no surprise. Hickling nevertheless emphasized that the author abandoned 'his familiarly mannered verse style – the language is brutally simple, the execution simply brutal' (2001) in his play on ritual murder, while Shuttleworth opined: 'What's peculiar about *Ritual in Blood* is that the attitudes aren't clothed in the writer's notoriously impassioned, verbally opulent style. The dialogue is drably naturalistic without being true to the dialect of the time' (2001). Arguably, Berkoff's linguistic and stylistic choices reflect his desire to bridge the historical distance of a dramatic episode whose explosive geographical proximity might otherwise be defused. Wesker, arguably for the same reason, favoured a simple and modern style that was simultaneously terse and poetic. With the considered use of a Norfolk accent, he emphasized the geographical proximity of the historical incident.

With one notable exception, *Blood Libel* was positively received. In the *Sunday Times*, John Peter pronounced caustically: 'Arnold Wesker's new play is beyond any doubt the worst new work by an internationally established playwright I have seen in the past two decades' (1996). Peter denounced what he perceived to be the play's 'plodding tameness' and reiterated the same adjective also in his assessment of Irina Brown's production. The critic pounced on what he considered the 'tedious preliminaries' of 'chanting, sermons' and 'a clumsily mimed account of William's birth and a prophecy about his uniqueness'. Yet Peter seems not only to have missed the point but also to have misunderstood the programmatic doubling of actors. In Norwich, the actor who played the Stranger also played Theobald. Peter's exasperation with what he considered the 'final, bizzare [sic] revelation that

William's murderer is a converted Jew who nurses a deep hatred for his former co-religionists' reveals his complete confusion.[8] Even so, the notion of Theobald's guilt was in fact already entertained by M. R. James, one of the editors of Thomas' *Life and Miracles* (Thomas of Monmouth 1896: lxxix). The doubling of the actor playing Theobald and the Stranger in the Norwich production of *Blood Libel* (Toby Davies; Programme 1996), closely observed by Wesker who attended rehearsals, may respond to this suggestion.

In the *Guardian* and the *Times*, Michael Billington (1996) and Jeremy Kingston (1996) respectively emphasized what they perceived to be a lack of historical context. Billington, more specifically, pointed out that *Blood Libel* 'never puts the Jewish community on stage, so we have no idea of their learning, financial structures or religious rituals, nor indeed of how they reacted to their widespread victimisation'. These aspects were covered by Berkoff in order to flesh out his representation of the historical conflict and its context. Yet they were of no concern to Wesker, whose aim was rather to universalize the impact of the historical precedent.

Intriguingly, Berkoff's *Ritual in Blood* was not reviewed in the *Jewish Chronicle* – nor was Laughton's *One Jewish Boy*. But David Nathan's review of Wesker's *Blood Libel* was full of praise. The critic asserted that the play 'imaginatively, shrewdly, powerfully deals with the legend of Jews as killers of Christian children' (1996). Nathan emphasized the representation of 'the potent combination of superstition, fanaticism and greed' among the clergy, which in conjunction with the ignorance of the masses inexorably led to 'the damnation of the Jews'.

Writing for the local *Eastern Daily Press*, Charles Roberts felt that the play would benefit from some judicious cuts and observed that Brown's production self-indulgently put too much emphasis on mystery (1996). Roberts interpreted the play as 'a drama whose roots reach back to morality and mystery plays where all was absolute and dogma with no room for shades and doubts' and believed that it represented 'mindless enmities whipped up to frenzy by ranting, fundamentalist clerics'. He enthused: 'Text and direction combine to hypnotic effect as hysteria begins to build.'

## Conclusions

In *Blood Libel*, Thomas' concluding exultation in his litany of miracles is horribly subverted with the final agonized scream of the rape victim in the darkness and the frantic cry: 'The Jews! The Jews!' (Wesker 2012a: 159). *Ritual in Blood* ends with the suppression of the truth: little Hugh's traumatized brother who witnessed but kept silent about the child's accidental death is silenced by his confessor decades after the event and, tormented by dreams, hangs himself. The plays' cynical conclusions may reflect the resignation of their authors. After all, irrational accusations and calumnies tend to persist. The attempt to reason with manifestations of antisemitism, as sustained in the juridical discourse into which Wesker and Berkoff's plays intervene, may ultimately be futile. While some of the parameters of antisemitism may have shifted in recent decades, the blood libel, as emphasized also by Laughton, remains one of its main pillars. Trying the blood libel on the stage is a valiant endeavour.

## Notes

1   *One Jewish Boy* was first performed at the Old Red Lion Theatre, London, in 2018.
2   The trial of Mendel Beilis in 1913 triggered an 'epidemic' of *tsaytbilder*, plays on current affairs that briefly swept Yiddish theatres in North America and Britain (Berkowitz 2001). Just after the Second World War, Heinz Herald and Geza Herczeg's *The Burning Bush* (1947) about the ritual murder accusation of Tiszaeszlár (1882–3), translated by Noel Langley, was successfully staged at the small New Lindsey club theatre in London (1948) and later also variously in America (1949–50); in the UK, a TV adaptation, now lost, was broadcast by BBC Two England in 1967. Yet a play by the American Jewish academic Paul M. Levitt appears to have been the first dramatic engagement with the medieval blood libel to find an audience in Britain and in all probability far exceeded the reach of either *Blood Libel* or *Ritual in Blood*. Only partially published (Levitt 1975), *The Norwich Incident* was aired in August 1980 as a radio play on BBC Radio 4. Wesker presumably read Levitt's script in the early 1970s when he first met its author, who was to become a close friend (Levitt 2014: 99), but it did not directly influence his own effort; nor is it likely that either Wesker or Berkoff was familiar with the Yiddish *tsaytbilder* of 1913–14 whose texts did not appear in print.
3   *Blood Libel* was first performed at the Norwich Playhouse in 1996.
4   *Ritual in Blood* was first performed at the Nottingham Playhouse in 2001.
5   The textual genesis of Berkoff's play cannot be fully ascertained but the author's preface suggests that the text remained unaltered (Berkoff 2000: 4). Intriguingly, *Ritual in Blood* is not mentioned in Berkoff's most recent 'attempt to describe his multifarious dramatic works', *A World Elsewhere* (2020).
6   In 2008 a new plaque was installed which was devised jointly by the Jewish and Christian communities of Lincoln. Following a detailed historical explanation, it links the historical accusation with contemporary racism

and invites visitors to pray: 'The libel against the Jews is a shameful example of religious and racial hatred which, continuing down through the ages, violently divides many people in the present day. Let us unite, here in a prayer for an end to bigotry, prejudice and persecution./Peace be with you: Shalom.'

7   It should, however, be noted that *Blood Libel* was recently recommended for student productions (Binnie 2017).
8   Wesker, perhaps because he foresaw the problem, originally suggested different groupings (2012a: 108).

## References

Band, A. J. (2001), 'Refractions of the Blood Libel in Modern Literature', in M. A. Signer (ed.), *Memory and History in Christianity and Judaism*, 113–33, Notre Dame: University of Notre Dame Press.
Berkoff, S. (1996), *Free Association: An Autobiography*, London: Faber and Faber.
Berkoff, S. (2000), *Ritual in Blood*, in *Plays*, 3: 1–92, London: Faber and Faber.
Berkoff, S. (2010), 'Press Release for *Biblical Tales*'. Available online: http://www.stevenberkoff.com/resources_biblical_tales.html (accessed 14 December 2018).
Berkoff, S. (2020), *A World Elsewhere*, Abingdon: Routledge.
Berkowitz, J. (2001), 'The "Mendel Beilis Epidemic" on the Yiddish Stage', *Jewish Social Studies*, 8 (1): 199–225.
Bigsby, C. W. E. (1976), 'In Conversation with Christopher Bigsby', *British Council Literature Study Aids*, 4 March.
Billington, M. (1996), 'Lies of the Saint', *The Guardian*, 5 February: T40.
Billington, M. (2010), 'Biblical Tales', *The Guardian*, 11 August. Available online: https://www.theguardian.com/stage/2010/aug/11/biblical-tales-review (accessed 14 December 2018).
Binnie, E. A. G. (2017), 'The Norwich Blood Libel Mounted Once Again: A Pedagogy for Tolerance in Arnold Wesker's *Blood Libel* (1991)', in M. A. Krummel and T. Pugh (eds), *Jews in Medieval England: Teaching Representations of the Other*, 171–90, Cham: Palgrave Macmillan.
Burke, H. (1995), Fax to Arnold Wesker, 1 December, Harry Ransom Humanities Research Center, University of Texas at Austin, Wesker Box 19/5.
Cavendish, D. (2001), 'Pale Shadow of Shylock's Finest Hour', *Telegraph*, 8 June. Available online: https://www.telegraph.co.uk/culture/4723974/Pale-shadow-of-Shylocks-finest-hour.html (accessed 11 January 2019).
Cross, R. (2004), *Steven Berkoff and the Theatre of Self-Performance*, Manchester: Manchester University Press.
Dundes, A. (1991), 'The Ritual Murder or Blood Libel Legend: A Study of Anti-Semitic Victimization through Projective Inversion', in A. Dundes (ed.), *The Blood Libel Legend: A Casebook in Anti-Semitic Folklore*, 336–66, Madison: University of Wisconsin Press.

Frazer, J. (2018), 'How a Fringe Anti-Racism Play Has Upset London's Streets and Exploded Twitter', *Times of Israel*, 21 December. Available online: https://www.timesofisrael.com/how-a-fringe-anti-racism-play-has-upset-londons-streets-and-exploded-twitter/ (accessed 14 February 2020).

Gardner, L. (2000), 'God's Spin Doctors', *The Guardian*, 10 August. Available online: https://www.theguardian.com/culture/2000/aug/10/artsfeatures.edinburghfestival2000 (accessed 14 December 2018).

Heathman (pseud.) (1989), 'Wesker Musical', *Ham and High*, 19 February: 19.

Hick, J. (1993), 'Interpretation and Reinterpretation in Religion', in S. Coakley and D. A. Pailin (eds), *The Making and Remaking of Christian Doctrine: Essays in Honour of Maurice Wiles*, 59–72, Oxford: Clarendon Press.

Hickling, A. (2001), 'Ritual in Blood', *The Guardian*, 8 June. Available online: https://www.theguardian.com/stage/2001/jun/08/theatre.artsfeatures1 (accessed 11 January 2019).

Holmes, C. (1991), 'The Ritual Murder Accusation in Britain', in A. Dundes (ed.), *The Blood Libel Legend: A Casebook in Anti-Semitic Folklore*, 99–134, Madison: University of Wisconsin Press.

Johnson, H. R. (2012), *Blood Libel: The Ritual Murder Accusation at the Limit of Jewish History*, Ann Arbor: University of Michigan Press.

Julius, A. (2010), *Trials of the Diaspora: A History of Anti-Semitism in England*, Oxford: Oxford University Press.

Kahn-Harris, K. and B. Gidley (2010), *Turbulent Times: The British Jewish Community Today*, London and New York: Continuum.

Kingston, J. (1996), 'Catch in His Martyr's Voice', *Times*, 5 February: 15.

Lacey, S. (1995), *British Realist Theatre: The New Wave in Its Context 1956–1965*, London: Routledge.

Lambert, A. (1989), 'Dramatic Passions of a Beverley Hills Cop', *Independent*, 13 November: 16.

Laughton, S. (2018), *One Jewish Boy*, London: Nick Herne.

Leeman, S. (1996), 'English City Corrects Record on Medieval Death Blamed on Jews', *Independent*, 11 March.

Levitt, P. M. (1975), 'Act the Second: The Norwich Incident', *The Ohio Review*, 17 (1): 25–40.

Levitt, P. M. (1980), *The Norwich Incident*, *The Monday Play* [radio programme], BBC Radio 4 FM, 4 August and *Afternoon Theatre* [radio programme], BBC 4 FM. Available online: http://genome.ch.bbc.co.uk/schedules/radio4/fm/1980-08-04 and http://genome.ch.bbc.co.uk/schedules/radio4/fm/1980-08-10 (accessed 12 April 2018).

Levitt, P. M. (2014), 'Well-Nigh Wesker', in R. W. Dornan (ed.), *Arnold Wesker: A Casebook*, 97–108, London and New York: Routledge.

Lyndon, S. (1996), 'Blood Libel. A Norwich Scenario', *Jewish Quarterly*, 43 (1): 57–9.

Nathan, D. (1996), 'Libel Action', *Jewish Chronicle*, 9 February: 36.

O'Mahoney, J. (2002), 'Piques and Troughs', *The Guardian*, 25 May. Available online: https://www.theguardian.com/books/2002/may/25/arts.artsfeatures (accessed 12 February 2020).
Peter, J. (1996), 'Blood Libel', *Sunday Times*, 11 February: 8.
Programme (1996), *Arnold Wesker's Blood Libel*, Norwich Playhouse.
Roberts, C. V. (1996), 'Wallowing in Medieval Mysteries', *Eastern Daily Press*, 2 February: 13.
Rose, E. M. (2015), *The Murder of William of Norwich: The Origins of the Blood Libel in Medieval Europe*, Oxford: Oxford University Press.
Round, S. (2009), 'Interview: Steven Berkoff', *Jewish Chronicle*, 22 January. Available online: https://www.thejc.com/lifestyle/interviews/interview-steven-berkoff-1.7222 (accessed 13 December 2018).
Schäfer, P. (1997), *Judeophobia: Attitudes toward the Jews in the Ancient World*, Cambridge, MA: Harvard University Press.
Sherwood, H. (2018), 'Life Imitates Art as Play about Antisemitism Faces Wave of Abuse', *Observer*, 9 December. Available online: https://www.theguardian.com/news/2018/dec/09/one-jewish-boy-abuse-campaign-play-london-antisemitism (accessed 14 February 2020).
Shuttleworth, I. (2001), 'Ritual in Blood'. Available online: http://www.cix.co.uk/~shutters/reviews/01051.htm (accessed 11 January 2019).
Sicher, E. (2017), *The Jew's Daughter: A Cultural History of a Conversion Narrative*, Lanham, MD: Lexington Books.
Sierz, A. (2001), *In-Yer-Face Theatre: British Drama Today*, London: Faber and Faber.
Sommers, J. (2018), 'Playwright Steven Berkoff: I Want to Play Harvey Weinstein in My One-Act Play about Him', *Jewish Chronicle*, 21 November. Available online: https://www.thejc.com/news/the-diary/playwright-steven-berkoff-i-want-to-play-harvey-weinstein-in-my-one-act-play-about-him-1.472847 (accessed 14 December 2018).
Stähler, A. (2017), '"Historical Argument" or "Cowboys and Indian"? Arnold Wesker's TV Screenplay of Arthur Koestler's *Thieves in the Night*', *Jewish Film & New Media*, 5 (2): 199–226.
Sugarman, D. (2018), 'Jewish Writer's Play about Antisemitism in the UK Attacked by Antisemites', *Jewish Chronicle*, 20 September. Available online: (accessed 14 February 2020).
Thomas of Monmouth (1896), *The Life and Miracles of St. William of Norwich, Written by Thomas of Monmouth*, ed. and trans. A. Jessopp and M. R. James, Cambridge: Cambridge University Press.
Trubowitz, L. (2012), *Civil Antisemitism, Modernism, and British Culture, 1902–1939*, New York: Palgrave Macmillan.
Wesker, A. (1991a), Fax to Henry Burke, 22 March, Harry Ransom Humanities Research Center, University of Texas at Austin, Wesker Box 19/3.
Wesker, A. (1991b), Note, 30 July, Harry Ransom Humanities Research Center, University of Texas at Austin, Wesker Box 18/7.

Wesker, A. (1991c), 'Notes on – *William of Norwich*', 23 October, Harry Ransom Humanities Research Center, University of Texas at Austin, Wesker Box 18/5.

Wesker, A. (1994), 'Blood Libel,' in *Wild Spring and Other Plays*, 281–353, London: Penguin.

Wesker, A. (1996), Fax to Jack Temchin, 9 January, Harry Ransom Humanities Research Center, University of Texas at Austin, Wesker Box 19/4.

Wesker, A. (2012a), 'Blood Libel,' in *Wesker's Historical Plays*, 103–59, London: Oberon.

Wesker, A. (2012b), 'Caritas,' in *Wesker's Historical Plays*, 249–306, London: Oberon.

# 8

# Representing the Israel-Palestine Conflict in Contemporary British-Jewish Theatre

Mike Witcombe

In December 2018, Stephen Laughton's play *One Jewish Boy* began its debut run at the Old Red Lion Theatre in Islington, London. Laughton, whose previous work had explored Jewish topics, was shocked by the reaction to the play on social media; the title alone provoked anger, with Harriet Sherwood writing in the *Guardian* that 'Palestinian flags were posted online in response to mentions of the play', as an attempt to turn conversations around Jewish identity to the subject of crimes committed by the Israeli state – a common antisemitic trope (Sherwood 2018). As the *Guardian* article noted, it was ironic that the play was the subject of antisemitic abuse, given that antisemitism is one of the key themes in the play itself. A pivotal theme in *One Jewish Boy* is the conflation of diaspora Jewish identity with contemporary Israel. As Jesse, the protagonist of Laughton's play, argues: 'I am a diaspora Jew. I have very little ... in fact nothing to do with Israeli foreign policy.' However, his partner Alex, who is not Jewish, answers back: 'Well it's not quite foreign' (Laughton 2018). Jesse eventually comes to regard Israel as somewhat of a safe haven for Jews compared to the abuse (and violence) he receives in London. This precipitates the couple's eventual break-up.

Laughton's play debuted in an increasingly volatile political atmosphere in Britain, and one of Jesse's points of contention in the play is that the Labour Party, led by Jeremy Corbyn, was enabling the kind of guilt-by-association towards British Jews that Alex cites (and that the play itself generated among online commentators). Given the international reach of social media, it remains unclear how many of these commentators were based in Britain – nonetheless, the combination of online antisemitic abuse about Israeli sympathies and the ambivalence towards Israel within the play itself is telling.[1]

For the majority of people involved, debates around British-Jewish loyalties have become increasingly entrenched and intense, with little sense of action or resolution. In another sense, the tone of the debate is familiar to many British Jews, and Laughton's depiction of ambivalence within the British-Jewish community emerges from perspectives that have been quantitatively verified. In 2015, a group led by Stephen Miller concluded that British Jews identify strongly with Israel but have a wide range of opinions about both its military activities and what its future ambitions should be.

Miller stated that debates around Israel raised issues about the 'future cohesiveness of the Jewish community' in Britain (Miller, Harris and Shindler 2015: 10). His report noted that the majority of British Jews felt pride in Israel's achievements but also felt its current government was damaging its international standing. Miller also noted that British Jews often failed to measure how popular their own ideas on Israel were within the community. A later study by Toby Greene and Yossi Shain expanded on this by arguing that recent years had seen an 'Israelization of British Jewry', citing developments in culture, political affiliation, religion, communal politics and the increasing prominence of the Haredi community (Greene and Shain 2016: 848). From being a subject about which a certain commonality of communal feeling could be assumed, Israel is now a central topic of debate.

The ambivalence of Laughton's play, combined with the centrality of discussions around British-Jewish Zionism in the media and the divisiveness of the topic within the British-Jewish community itself, highlights the importance of theatrical interpretations of the debate by British-Jewish playwrights. Talking about a revival of her play *Crossing Jerusalem* in the *Jewish Chronicle*, Julia Pascal argued that British plays about Israel that explore Israeli perspectives were uncommon when she first wrote the play – that there were no British plays offering an Israeli (or even a Jewish) perspective at the time, and most of the plays that did discuss the conflict were anti-Zionist polemics (Nathan 2015). One of the counter-influences Pascal references is Caryl Churchill's play *Seven Jewish Children*, arguably the most well-known British play on the subject. A twenty-minute 'playlet' structured around adults explaining the conflict to an unseen child, the play remains controversial for its supposed pro-Palestinian bias (Churchill 2009).

There were at least four plays written in direct response to Churchill's work, which attempt to give alternative perspectives. One of these is Stephen Laughton's *Three* (Laughton 2018), which Laughton introduces by noting that 'we diaspora Jews are no more responsible for what happens in Israel than any other person on the entire planet' – echoing his character Jesse in *One Jewish Boy*, who states that he has 'nothing to do with Israeli foreign policy'. The mixed reception of Churchill's play by reviewers shows how easily discussion of the Israel-Palestine conflict within theatre can enact familiar ideological divisions.[2] While there is more to Churchill's play than many of its polemical critics are willing to acknowledge (Laughton himself calls the play 'beautifully written and confronting'), its chief purpose is to serve as a political intervention (Laughton 2018). What Laughton attempts to engage with in both *One Jewish Boy* and *Three* is how this debate takes on a different valence when writers come from within the Jewish community itself.

*One Jewish Boy* emerges from a distinct tradition within British-Jewish theatre, part of a growing list of works within British-Jewish theatre that have taken on the subject of the Israel-Palestine conflict. This chapter asks whether the twenty-first century has given us a canon when it comes to British-Jewish plays about this conflict and will ask what unites and separates the plays themselves. Pascal's claim that plays about the conflict can have a simplistic political worldview is not new, and the impulse she felt to challenge this has been shared by others. If anything unifies British plays about the conflict, it is a collective desire to be involved in ongoing debates and discussions. The plays this chapter will discuss often have a sense of urgency to them and are attuned to how debates over the conflict manifest within the British-Jewish community. By engaging in internationally resonant political debates, these plays also comment on the community that they emerged from.

This chapter will thus explore representations of the Israel-Palestine conflict in plays by four British-Jewish playwrights – Ryan Craig, Mike Leigh, Julia Pascal and Shelley Silas. These plays could be said to represent a significant wave of new plays on the subject within British-Jewish theatre in the early years of the twenty-first century; moreover, the debates these plays have initiated may have exerted an influence on more recent plays, such as *One Jewish Boy*.[3] Taken together, these plays are a diverse, challenging group of texts. None of these plays attempts to cover the views of the British-Jewish community in their entirety; however, they all convey a sense of fraught debate around Israel, reflecting the way the topic is discussed in British-Jewish culture at large. They are also keenly contemporary in their dialogue, often referencing recent or near-current events. Beyond their political complexities, they all demonstrate that there is theatrical – and perhaps ethical – value in critically analysing debates on the conflict within the British-Jewish community.

Rather than attempt a comprehensive overview of this theme within British-Jewish theatre, this chapter will offer readings of British-Jewish plays that focus on the Israel-Palestine conflict as a primary theme, oriented around differences in setting. This elides a number of earlier works by British or British-located Jewish playwrights which have explored similar territory, some of which have already received significant critical attention. For example, the American-born playwright Charles Marowitz wrote several plays after Shakespeare during the 1970s, when he was residing in London. One of these, *Variations on the Merchant of Venice* (Marowitz 1978), depicts

Shylock as a Jewish nationalist in Mandatory Palestine during the period leading up to the establishment of the state of Israel. In Marowitz's text, Shylock's eventual turn to violence is defended by the character as the obverse of the oppression directed against Jews by the British authorities. Marowitz's portrayal of Shylock's self-defence thus lies at the nexus of both historical and thematic continuities that can be detected in later theatrical works; it reflects an ambivalence towards Israel that has to be understood in reference to both American and British attitudes in the era of production and the fact that, as Jeanette R. Malkin and Eckart Voigts note, 'Marowitz was in general less invested in his Jewish identity than in the renewal of the theatre' (2018: 179).

Contemporary plays arguably differ from this approach in that the internecine conflicts implicit in plays such as *Variations on the Merchant of Venice* have been rendered explicit; the debates shape the plot rather than vice versa. The plays discussed in this chapter dramatize the process of debate in compatible but divergent ways. Work by Craig and Leigh will be the focus of the first part of this chapter, which will explore the representation of the Israel-Palestine conflict as a debate within a domestic and familial British environment. This will enable a contrasting reading of plays by British writers set in Israel or Palestine itself, focusing on Julia Pascal's *Crossing Jerusalem* and Shelly Silas' *Eating Ice Cream on Gaza Beach*.

What unites these two approaches is the sense of ongoing debate without a possibility of reconciliation. This sense of hopelessness encompasses both the ideological combatants within the Israel-Palestine debate as well as those within British-Jewish community itself. There are a range of different opinions within the plays, sometimes within individual characters, always within any group of Jewish characters. As such, the plays serve as layered microcosms, symbolizing the impossibility of consensus. The plays are thus concerned with the results of the operation of rhetoric rather than functioning as rhetorical or ideological devices themselves. They enact the process that rhetorical theorist Dilip Parmeshwar Gaonkar describes as where 'opinion … comes into its own as the inescapable scene and substance of human deliberation, judgement, and action' (2004: 11). The plays are less concerned with the objective truth of the conflict than with the ramifications of the debate itself – of the inevitability and impossibility of agreement or even of persuasion. Trapped in a domain of pure and inescapable opinion, rhetorical impossibility leads to aesthetic and affective complexities. This interpretation is rooted in Ruth Gilbert's claim that 'contemporary British Jewish writers highlight the desire to identify the particularity of their difference, whilst acknowledging that such difference is neither fixed nor final, but always open to change, resignification and reinterpretation' (2014: 19). British-Jewish playwrights focusing on the Israel-Palestine conflict similarly understand the unique significance of their position but maintain a liminality in their representations of it that defies stable ideological categorization.

This ambivalence and uncertainty has specific historical origins. For example, the association between antisemitism and Zionism in England is not a new phenomenon; its history has been discussed in some detail by Geoffrey Alderman and Anthony Julius, among others.[4] Moreover, the plays discussed in this chapter should also be seen in light of broader trends in British-Jewish literature. For example, Axel Stähler noted in a 2013 article that 'much of recent British Jewish literature challenges traditional and frequently ossified markers of Jewishness' and that novels such as Howard Jacobson's *The Finkler Question* (2010) represent the increasing prominence of the Israel-Palestine conflict within this trend (112). While comparative analysis of theatre and novels about the conflict is beyond the scope of this chapter, the simultaneous sense of a forthright discussion of Jewish topics and a willingness to challenge markers of Jewishness, are also key aspects of the plays discussed and may represent a similarly important development to that identified by Stähler.

## Home Fires: Ryan Craig and Mike Leigh

Mike Leigh's *Two Thousand Years* and Ryan Craig's *What We Did to Weinstein* were first produced in 2005, their production runs coinciding.[5] The plays have a lot in common aside from this apparent coincidence, although their authors came from different backgrounds and had different approaches to similar subjects. Leigh had a significant career prior to the production of *Two Thousand Years*, with an established reputation as a playwright and film director, and the success of the play may have owed a great deal to his celebrity and to his reputation.[6] The play was also performed at the National Theatre, giving the play the imprimatur of one of the country's leading venues and one of the very few to directly receive significant funding from the British government. Ryan Craig was a lesser-known playwright at this time, although he too would eventually stage a Jewish domestic drama revolving around issues about Israel in 2011, when the National Theatre debuted his play *The Holy Rosenbergs*.

*What We Did to Weinstein*, as with much of Craig's work, has inter-family conflict as its central theme. A dying writer, Max, is visited by his estranged son, Josh. The two have become estranged since Josh left London to join the Israeli Defence Forces. The play starts with Josh visiting his father's deathbed, before we see him as a younger man trying to convince his girlfriend, Sara, to join him in Israel. We also see him as an IDF soldier, being interrogated after an incident with a Palestinian prisoner. In between this, we see Sara arguing with her father, as well as an argument between two young British Muslims, one of whom wants to become a terrorist. In addition to this, there is the revelation of the family secret that gives the play its title.

The play had a mixed reception, reflected in the range of reviews written about it. Writing for the *Guardian*, Lyn Gardner advised that

> [i]f you want one view of the crisis of faith in a contemporary London-based Jewish family you can go and see Mike Leigh's *Two Thousand Years* at the National. For another snapshot, you could [see] Ryan Craig's story about Josh, who moves from north London to Israel ... You could, but you shouldn't.
>
> (Gardner 2005)

Gardner's polemic prompted the play's director to respond in the form of a letter shortly afterwards. He argued that Gardner's attack prevented people from seeing the play, limiting the potential for dialogue on the play's central topic: 'where then is the debate – the rich mess of thoughts, discussion and feeling?' Leigh's play may have been more commercially successful, but Gardner's depiction of both plays as dependent on a 'crisis of faith' diminishes the factors influencing these crises themselves, as well as the complexities of debate identified in the director's response.

The varied responses that Craig's play received may be related to this focus on dialogue and debate. For example, generational conflict is discussed through the alignment of separate strands of plot narrative, enabling Craig to expand the debates around identity in the younger generation beyond his own specific experience of Jewish identity – arguably, one of the central topics in his work. Discussing Jewishness in an interview with the *Evening Standard*, Craig argued that 'sometimes, your limitations can be your strengths'; through focusing on this supposed limitation, Craig has come to see himself as a chronicler of Jewish identity issues. In the case of *Weinstein*, this can be seen in Craig's using scenes of Muslim sibling conflict predominantly as a means to shed light on the play's central debate over British-Jewish attitudes towards Israel. Though it projects its concerns beyond the British-Jewish community, Craig's play still has the British-Jewish community as its core analytical model for other identities it examines.

Josh, the play's protagonist, is the focus for most of these debates. Both his father and his ex-girlfriend Sarah find his newfound love for Israel baffling. In the case of his father, this leads to some of the play's most memorable comic lines, such as: 'Israel's a madhouse. It's no place for a nice Jewish boy' (Craig 2012: 100). In this manner, Craig highlights both the inevitability of thought processes about Israel within the community at the same time as he comically incites the differences between them. The play's most important line about the arguments created by Josh comes where Josh and Sara argue over the Israel-Palestine conflict, when Josh petulantly cries, 'This is the subject! There is no other subject. Not for us.' It is ambiguous who 'us' refers to. In one sense, this refers to the two characters' opposing views on Israel. In another sense, it refers to the British-Jewish community as a whole. We see the community split generationally along different lines, with some older members opposing Zionism and some supporting it. If the play seems almost incoherent in its sprawling meshwork of debates, that might be in part because British-Jewish attitudes on the topic are so messy themselves. Craig's work arguably reflects the constant process of 'change, resignification and reinterpretation' that Ruth Gilbert discusses as being core components of contemporary British-Jewish writing.

As Gardner's review noted, Craig's ambitious play might have suffered from the simultaneous success of Mike Leigh's *Two Thousand Years*, a more contained play on similar themes. As with *Weinstein*, *Two Thousand Years* is a domestic drama, set in the home of a North London Jewish family. The focus in this instance is on a younger son who seems to have 'converted' from a secular to a religious Jewish identity. This provokes one of a series of family feuds, concluding with the arrival of an exaggeratedly selfish Aunt. In between, we meet the family's cheerful daughter, Tammy, who introduces the family to her sardonic Israeli boyfriend, Tzachi. In interviews about the play, Leigh, much like Craig, emphasized the Jewish character of his oeuvre as a whole. Although he described *Two Thousand Years* as his 'Jewish play', Leigh also argued that 'all of my work has a certain Jewishness because it is always tragi-comic'. Leigh's definition of Jewishness may be tongue in cheek, but his description of *Two Thousand Years* as a 'Jewish play' invites consideration of what this term might encompass. Characters argue about Tony Blair and then-contemporary British politics, locating the play firmly in its time of writing. Like Craig's work, *Two Thousand Years* grapples with contemporary debates in the Jewish community. If Leigh's attempt is more successful, it may be because he aimed more deliberately at the Jewish community, rather than trying to give a panoramic overview that situated British-Jewish debates within broader cultural trends.

Discussions of Israel within the play need to be interpreted alongside other cultural trends, as Leigh develops a sense of changes in attitudes within the British-Jewish community. In particular, Leigh depicts Josh's newfound interest in the religious elements of Jewish identity as perplexing to his family. When Rachel, his mother, walks in on him praying, Leigh playfully invites associations with furtive adolescent masturbation:

**Rachel**     What are you doing?

**Josh**     I was praying.

**Rachel**     What?!

**Josh**     How was your holiday? (Leigh 2006: 20)

Josh thus negates Rachel's shock, and the masturbatory associations of the scene, by responding directly and then attempting to turn a scene of domestic drama into a casual conversation. Perhaps tellingly, he also responds to her second question (or interrogation) with a question, following the Talmudic trope of answering a question with another question. Josh's father, Danny, reacts by cooking himself bacon and eggs in a petulantly emblematic assertion of British cultural norms over Jewish religious norms that recalls the antisemitic trope of Jewish otherness.

Josh's grandfather Dave is a former *kibbutznik* and is more receptive to Josh's religious turn than his parents, whose antipathy can be interpreted as symptomatic of second-generation assimilation into British-Jewish identity. Tzachi, Tammy's Israeli boyfriend, is taciturn – at once careful about etiquette ('I cannot kiss you in your father's house') (Leigh 2006: 58) – and corrective ('You're not dealing in reality, you are being idealistic') (70). On the topic of Israel and Palestine, Tzachi frequently rebuts the simplistic assumptions of his hosts, recalling the dismissive, borderline rude style with which he initially responds to Tammy's comments: 'Welcome to Israel! In Israel, there is no long-term' (80). Tzachi claims that he focuses on 'facts on the ground' and is sympathetic to Palestinian nationhood (81). In this, Tzachi contrasts with the depiction of Israel in *What We Did to Weinstein*, which emphasizes the brutality of lived experience 'on the ground' in Israel. As Ruth Gilbert has noted, *Two Thousand Years* 'signals the complexity of tarnished optimism' regarding Israel, and it accomplishes this by gently satirizing the comfortable assumptions of its British-Jewish characters (2013: 90).

*Two Thousand Years* thus avoids simplistic associations of Jewish identity and Zionist sympathies at the same time as it subverts normative expectations of British-Jewish identity in particular. Josh's interest in religion functions as a challenge to his parents' comfortable secular life, and Tzachi challenges both the sentimentalism of Dave's archaic Zionism and the reductive liberal assumptions of Tammy and her parents. In doing so, the play exposes fault lines running through British-Jewish identity, with a particular focus on secular, urban, financially comfortable Jewish Britons. In this manner, their unsettling in the process of this play represents the decline of the 'self-effacing' quality that David Brauner has previously discussed as a hallmark of British-Jewish identity (2001: 19). As with *Weinstein*, Israel becomes a primary locus of this process of resignification, alongside religious identity. This process of resignification represented a change in direction for Leigh, and it would have a lasting impact on Craig's work – most notably in 2011's *The Holy Rosenbergs*. As was the case with *Two Thousand Years* and *What We Did to Weinstein*, *The Holy Rosenbergs* is a middle-class British-Jewish domestic drama. The plays even have plot details in common: the audience is shown a son whose newfound allegiance to Israel stuns his parents, as well as the revelation of a family secret from an ageing patriarch, which changes the way a younger generation engages with their Jewish identity. There is also a common sense of disparity in constructions of masculinity between British and Israeli Jews, with younger British-Jewish men often seeming to find these differences emasculating.

Craig's plot dramatizes divergent perspectives on Israel within the British-Jewish community by depicting a process of generational change within a single family. David, the family patriarch, is struggling to keep his kosher catering business afloat amid complaints from within the Jewish community. His progeny have spurned his interpretation of Jewishness in favour of several symbolic directions: his older son has died fighting with the Israeli Defence Forces, his daughter is working with a legal team investigating Israeli (and Hamas) war crimes, and his youngest son is angry and disaffected.

Of all the plays discussed in this chapter, *The Holy Rosenbergs* engages most directly with debates around the status of the Israel-Palestine conflict within the British-Jewish community; David's personal crisis, which undergirds the tragic framing of the play as a whole, becomes inextricably linked to his attitudes towards the conflict. *The Holy Rosenbergs* is multivocal insofar as it represents a fragmentation of assumed community dialogue, through grief, into a cacophony in which no one character's opinion can change that of another. The play thus hinges on both a surfeit of unheeded voices and the silence of Danny, the son whose death during military service in Israel has thrust crisis upon the Rosenbergs and forced David to defend his perspectives on the Israeli state. *The Holy Rosenbergs* can be interpreted as dramatizing the process of 'Israelization' within the British-Jewish community. The debates within the play become less productive as the play goes on: by the time Ruth, upset about her family's lack of understanding about her work assisting the investigation of war crimes, complains 'I don't know who you people are', her words could equally have been uttered by any other member of the family (Craig 2011: 108). Craig's use of 'you people' is thus the corollary of the ambiguous use of 'us' in *What We Did to Weinstein* and for a similar purpose – demonstrating the confused loyalties of his characters. At the conclusion of *The Holy Rosenbergs* an uneasy truce has been drawn, but the divisions remain. Given that the play is so keen to make characters emblematic of different perspectives within the same debate, the symbolic resonance of watching a community (in this case, a family) facing an uncertain collective identity at the play's conclusion can be hard to ignore.

## Land Apart: Julia Pascal

While Craig's and Leigh's plays tend to be domestic dramas set in family homes (with the exception of *Weinstein*'s relatively short depictions of Israel), other British-Jewish playwrights have engaged with ongoing debates by locating their plays exclusively in Israel or Palestine, featuring Israeli or Palestinian characters. Julia Pascal's 2003 play *Crossing Jerusalem* explores Israel-Palestine conflict in more direct terms; it is one of the most direct confrontations with the conflict seen on the British stage. Pascal explicitly positions *Crossing Jerusalem* as a non-didactic play, stating in her introduction to the playtext that her intention was 'to reveal some of the complexities of the situation as lived on the day-to-day level, and also to show that Israeli society is not a homogeneous block, rather a constant debate which remains extremely volatile' (2003: 9). The play was first performed at the Tricycle Theatre in Kilburn, London, in March 2003.

*Crossing Jerusalem*, despite predating even *Seven Jewish Children*, still aligns with contemporary trends. Its recent revival is testament to the lingering volatility in debate that Pascal highlights as a reason behind its creation. Set during the Second Intifada, the play tracks the experiences of a dysfunctional Jewish family as they try to maintain their daily lives. Unusually for a British-Jewish play on this topic, the vessel for the play's moral ambiguity comes through a female character – the matriarch Varda, a powerful real-estate developer. In this play, as with many others on the topic, those caught in the middle of the struggles tend to be the younger generation, rendered politically powerless by the scale of external events. The plot sees a family dinner descend into chaos when an Arab cook, Yusuf, challenges Varda for reparations for his father, a domestic worker she unjustly dismissed from his job. One of Varda's children sides with the cook, causing a rift in the family. Another family member struggles with his guilt about returning to fight in a conflict he does not believe in, while Yusuf's younger brother gets caught up in the violence of the Intifada.

*Crossing Jerusalem* is notable for its immersion in its subject material. While many other plays mediate discussion of Israel through the use of either British-Jewish settings or British-Jewish characters, Pascal's play offers a cross-section of characters who show different facets of Israeli society, while avoiding any claim that they are representative. We see a middle-class Jewish family, as we might expect from other plays – but we also see a Russian-Israeli immigrant, a Christian Arab, an Israeli army refusenik and others. Israeli characters in other British-Jewish plays tend to riff off familiar stereotypes. In Mike Leigh's *Two Thousand Years*, for example, Tzachi's gruff assertiveness can feel stilted – even as a voice of brutal pragmatism, he can reflect stereotypes of Israeli brusqueness. In Gail Louw's *Two Sisters*, first produced at Devonshire Park Theatre in June 2010, the rose-tinted idealism of early Zionism (a similar kind to that shown by Danny in *Two Thousand Years*) is proven to hide family secrets, but there is still a hesitancy to approach Israel on its own terms – the focus is on the characters' shared past, not on contemporary lived experience. *Crossing Jerusalem* has much in common with other texts on the subject despite this – there are tropes used within the play that can be detected in other later work: a family secret, a younger generation grappling with its identity and a tragic narrative arc. The play opens and concludes with scenes of violence and its aftermath, giving a pessimistic view on the potential for any lasting dialogue. Even within the family, dialogue becomes difficult.

In *Two Thousand Years*, characters' constant interruptions of one another make dialogue deliberately difficult for the audience to understand, reflecting the tense relationships between the play's characters. *Crossing Jerusalem* employs a similar strategy of adversarial interaction. For example, in one part of the play we hear an innocent or rhetorical question from one character answered by another, only for two more characters to offer mordant riffs on the same topics:

**Serguel** And when did this all start?

**Lee** Nineteen sixty-seven.

**Varda** For how much longer we fight this Six Day War? Forty years? Fifty?

**Serguel** Until there are thirty-six wise men on the earth.

**Lee** What?

**Gideon** You might as well wait for the Messiah. (Pascal 2017: 24)

Characters use the answers of others to their own ends, stretching a simple question into something else entirely. There is discord here, but there is also a unity of perspective; fatalistic assumptions gradually enable a range of numbers to morph a single figure, a symbol of perpetual hope, as the conversation gets bleaker and more hopeless. Though the subject of the play is politically complex, dialogue is often lively, reinforcing the family dynamics at its core. The dinner-party debate seen in later plays on the topic is given additional dynamism by being located in the middle of the conflict itself: the discussions offering symbolic resonances to the conflict as well as addressing the moral ambiguities emerging from it.

Pascal's play also spends a great deal of time grappling with the complexities of debates around Israel and Palestine by depicting conversations between Arab Israelis – however, these debates mostly serve to feed into the broader Jewish family revelation at the play's core. Lee, Varda's daughter, is the conciliatory voice in the novel, arguing that paying compensation to Yusuf would be 'righting a wrong' (2017: 54). However, this never comes across as a practical (or likely) solution to the problems facing the play's characters – the differences are perceived to be insurmountable, which may perhaps explain why Yusuf phrases it as a demand rather than a conversation. As with other plays, this is partly a generational issue; for all Lee's seeking of resolution, the cycle of mutual distrust and misunderstanding continues into the younger generation. As such, Yusuf's demand for money serves to reveal both the cyclicity of the debate and the bind facing those seeking either justice or reconciliation between opposing parties. The violence that culminates the play reflects this sense of futility. Although *Crossing Jerusalem* has character backgrounds and settings different to more explicitly British plays about the Israel/Palestine conflict, the sense of opinion and indeterminacy succeeding over casual assumptions is evocative of the same processes of mediation around the subject within the British-Jewish community. It too is embroiled in a process of 'constant debate which remains extremely volatile' (Pascal 2017: 9); the Kaufmann family's reckoning with debates that it has attempted to repress can be seen as a reflection of the 'Israelization' of the British-Jewish community that Pascal is a member of herself, in a similar manner to Ryan Craig's Rosenberg family.

Pascal's play enacts her desire to connect with the 'the day-to-day level' of life in Israel and Palestine in a manner that built upon the work of non-Jewish writers such as David Hare, whose play *Via Dolorosa* caused controversy when first produced in 1998 and when it was restaged in 2002 (a year prior to the first production of *Crossing Jerusalem*). *Crossing Jerusalem* sits alongside other British-Jewish productions set in Israel or Palestine which have a process of futile debate built into their dramatic structure. For example, the protagonist of Shelley Silas' play *Eating Ice Cream on Gaza Beach*, who attempts neutrality on the debate, concludes that 'Palestinians. Israelis. Semitic people. We look the same, eat the same, argue the same. We just can't agree on the same.' *Eating Ice Cream on Gaza Beach* makes for a useful contrast to Pascal's play, in part because of its use of Gaza as a setting. Unusually, given this setting, Silas opts to place a British-Jewish character at the centre of her play. Adrian is a young British Jew on a gap year, who encounters an ice cream seller called Rami on Gaza beach. Rami is an Arab Christian who is reluctant to protest against Israel. He introduces Adrian to an anti-Zionist firebrand named Muz. Rami and Muz debate the ethics of Israeli policies with Adrian. Alongside these characters, Silas introduces two Israeli border guards, both of whom resent their posting to Gaza. The play ends in violence when these two narrative strands collide at a protest.

Adrian is portrayed as being out of place in the debates and violence that occur around him, as well as the environment itself; he gets sunburn from sitting out on the beach and relies on the kindness of non-Jewish strangers to keep himself fed and sheltered. His conversations with characters on the beach are constantly interrupted by calls from his mother, who (in a nod to Jewish maternal stereotypes) seems mostly concerned about him getting food poisoning. When Adrian is accused of being a 'fence sitter', he can only repeat, almost mechanically, that he 'doesn't have a side'. Adrian's claims that he can 'see both points of view' begin to seem hollow when faced with the realities of everyday life in Gaza, justifying a reviewer's comment that Adrian is 'fatuously naïve'. Adrian's presence in Gaza seems a benign mistake, but Silas does include moments where his own identity becomes relevant; for example, he discusses how his grandfather fought in the 1948 war. His connection to Israel is mostly visible in his willingness to offer a counter argument to the political claims of Muz and Rami, who both express their hostility towards Israel in the course of the play. Adrian's role in the play is instrumental, to the extent that his conversational blunders are often used by Silas for plot exposition. Adrian's instrumentality bears comparison to other characters in the play – the Israeli soldiers whose dramatic purpose is to provide a point of conflict, as well as Rami, a Christian Arab and the titular ice cream vendor who provides the play with its tragic arc. Dramatic tension in *Ice Cream on Gaza Beach* emerges not from inevitability of its eventual violence, but from the subject position of its self-consciously external protagonist.

The manner in which the audience is constantly reminded of both Adrian's Britishness and his Jewishness could be interpreted as a means of gently mocking attitudes towards the Israel-Palestine conflict within the British-Jewish community; the inclusion of Adrian could be interpreted as a challenge to the community to develop a perspective more informed than his. The line 'we just can't agree on the same' (Silas 2008) is a pithy summary of the conflict, but it can also be read as referring to the internal conflicts within communities that are often overlooked. Chief among these is the British-Jewish community that Silas and Adrian came from, and that form a key part of Silas' audience.

## Conclusion: 'We Just Can't Agree on the Same'

Taken as a whole, these plays do not give us a coherent answer about how British-Jewish theatre is approaching the Israel/Palestine conflict. However, there are a few tropes often used by playwrights to express views on the conflict: Many of these plays centre around a family who are facing the exposition of a shattering secret. In many of these plays, the revelation of the secret completes a complicated dramatic arc which exposes fundamental generational differences in attitudes towards the conflict, with rebellion against parents a major theme. Masculinity remains a potent topic, especially when British-Jewish characters are compared to those from other backgrounds. Many of the plays engage in politics that is as contemporary as possible. Their performance histories are varied, almost all receiving mixed critical reviews. Some have been revived; others have been performed widely; still others await revival.

There is no common way for British-Jewish writers to approach the conflict, though many of the plays discussed in this chapter are concerned with enhancing the range of debate on offer in contemporary theatre. Indeed, what might link these diverse works is their determination to include the process of debate within their dramatic structure. These plays offer a challenge to John Nathan's claim that the conflict is 'a subject that many feel should be dramatised only if the play reflects their views' (Nathan 2008), internalizing the process of argumentation to develop a sense of the difficulties of consensus and agreement. While this disagreement may superficially seem to evoke the embedded ideological divides of the conflict itself, this is complicated by the unique mechanics of British-Jewish identity. Even in plays where the confrontation is implied more than explicitly suggested – plays like *Crossing Jerusalem* – there is an awareness of audience expectations around the subject.

At the same time, these plays demonstrate similar processes of 'Israelization' identified by Green and Shain: they explore topics such as communal identity, political affiliation and religion. This is not to say that the British-Jewish community has become more pro-Israel, so much as Israel has come to play a bigger part in ongoing debates around community identity. The majority of these plays are concerned with debate between Jewish characters – but due to their specific cultural origins, this debate becomes diluted into the transmission of opinion. There is no possibility of persuasion, and the Aristotelian standards of successful rhetoric ('the ability to see what is possibly persuasive in every given case') are roundly ignored (Rapp 2010). However, it is this representation of dynamic rhetorical uncertainty emerging from apparently fixed ideological states that makes these plays so characteristic – and which can also be traced in more recent works such as *One Jewish Boy*.

The reaction to *One Jewish Boy* also highlights another important mode of analysis. This chapter has discussed British-Jewish identity chiefly through analysis of authorial description and a close reading of debates within the plays themselves, but it is also worth noting that a large proportion of these plays' audiences will come from the same community as them – perhaps a consequence of what Ryan Craig has identified as non-Jewish British theatre audiences being 'stubbornly resistant' to viewing explicitly Jewish plays as giving insights into universal phenomena (2014: 52). This does leave the question of what happens when these plays leave this audience community behind – as, for example, when Mike Leigh's play was performed in New York City. If we agree with Craig's observation about universalism, then they might, for example, seem to become anthropological examinations of the British-Jewish community more than anything else. Regardless, the debate and disharmony around the conflict in the British-Jewish community underlies all of the plays discussed in this chapter. None of them are optimistic about what this means for the future of the community itself.

## Notes

1  On 25 July 2018, for example, three of Britain's major Jewish periodicals (*The Jewish Chronicle*, *Jewish News* and *The Jewish Telegraph*) published an identical editorial and front page, warning the community of the 'existential' threat they faced from antisemitism. They argued this was enabled by the increased presence of far-left critics of Israeli policy in the Labour Party.
2  For an overview of the more high-profile responses, see Mackey (2009).
3  These plays have also been chosen due to the existence of supplementary material in which the authors discuss their uncertainties about representing aspects of their own Jewish identities on stage.
4  For more information, see Julius (2010) and Alderman (1992).
5  Although *Two Thousand Years* had a longer run, the plays opened within a day of each other (Leigh's on 20 September 2005, Craig's on 21 September 2005).
6  As Tony Whitehead notes, Leigh had been given

> carte blanche to follow his usual working methods through a six-month rehearsal period, with the unusual result that until a matter of days before it opened, the piece could only be advertised as a 'New Play by Mike Leigh', since he was still evolving it with his chosen cast. Not that

this lack of information seemed to worry anyone, since Two Thousand Years, as it was eventually titled, was sold out for its entire run – some 16,000 advance tickets – over two weeks before the opening night.

(Whitehead 2007: 196)

## References

Alderman, G. (1992), *Modern British Jewry*, Oxford: Oxford University Press.
Brauner, D. (2001), *Post-War Jewish Fiction: Ambivalence, Self-Explanation and Transatlantic Connections*, Basingstoke: Palgrave.
Churchill, C. (2009), *Seven Jewish Children*, London: Nick Hern Books.
Craig, R. (2011), *The Holy Rosenbergs*, London: Oberon.
Craig, R. (2012), *What We Did to Weinstein*, London: Oberon.
Craig, R. (2014), 'Wesker's Dream', *Jewish Quarterly*, 61 (1): 52–3.
Craig, R. and J. Thompson (2017), 'Play Talk: Ryan Craig on Writing about Jewish Identity and Exposing Yourself in Your Writing', *Evening Standard*, 21 March.
Gaonkar, D. P. (2004), 'Contingency and Probability', in W. Jost and W. Olmsted (eds), *A Companion to Rhetoric and Rhetorical Criticism*, 5–21, Oxford: Blackwell.
Gardner, L. (2005), 'Review of *What We Did to Weinstein* at Menier Chocolate Factory, London', *The Times*, 28 September.
Gilbert, R. (2013), *Writing Jewish: Contemporary British Jewish Literature*, Basingstoke: Palgrave Macmillan.
Gilbert, R. (2014), '"Genes, Shmenes": Jew-ish Identities in Contemporary British Jewish Writing', *European Judaism*, 47 (2): 12–20.
Greene, T. and Y. Shain (2016), 'The Israelization of British Jewry: Balancing between Home and Homeland', *The British Journal of Politics and International Relations*, 18 (4): 848–65.
Julius, A. (2010), *Trials of the Diaspora: A History of Anti-Semitism in England*, Oxford: Oxford University Press.
Kingston, J. (2008), 'Review of *Eating Ice Cream on Gaza Beach* at Soho, W1', *The Times*, 29 August.
Laughton, S. (2018), *One Jewish Boy*, London: Nick Hern Books.
Leigh, M. (2006), *Two Thousand Years*, London: Faber and Faber.
Leigh, M. and A. Sierz (2006), '"All My Work Has a Certain Jewishness in It": Interview with Mike Leigh', *The Telegraph*, 17 April.
Louw, G. (2015), *Collected Plays*, London: Oberon.
Mackey, R. (2009), 'Is a Play about Gaza Anti-Semitic? Read the Script', *The New York Times*, 18 February.

Malkin, J. R. and E. Voigts (2018), 'Wrestling with Shylock: Contemporary British Jewish Theatre and Shakespeare's *The Merchant of Venice*', *European Judaism*, 51 (2): 175–85.

Marowitz, C. (1978), *The Marowitz Shakespeare*, London: Marion Boyars.

Miller, S., M. Harris and C. Shindler (2015), *The Attitudes of British Jews towards Israel*, London: City University London, Available online: https://www.city.ac.uk/__data/assets/pdf_file/0008/295361/Israel-Report-FINAL.PDF (accessed 11 July 2019).

Nathan, J. (2008), 'In Theatre, Likening Israelis to Nazis Is Trendy', *The Jewish Chronicle*, 3 October.

Nathan, J. (2015), 'Interview: Julia Pascal', *The Jewish Chronicle*, 6 August. Available online: https://www.thejc.com/culture/theatre/interview-julia-pascal-1.68043 (accessed April 2020).

Pascal, J. ([2003] 2017), *Crossing Jerusalem and Other Plays*, London: Oberon.

Rapp, C. (2010), 'Aristotle's Rhetoric', in E. N. Zalta (ed.), *The Stanford Encyclopedia of Philosophy*. Available online: https://plato.stanford.edu/archives/spr2010/entries/aristotle-rhetoric (accessed 11 July 2019).

Sherwood, H. (2018), 'Life Imitates Art as Play about Antisemitism Faces Wave of Abuse', *The Guardian*, 9 December.

Silas, S. (2008), *Eating Ice Cream on Gaza Beach*, unpublished manuscript.

Stähler, A. (2013), 'Antisemitism and Israel in British Jewish Fiction: Perspectives on Clive Sinclair's *Blood Libels* (1985) and Howard Jacobson's *The Finkler Question* (2010)', *Jewish Culture and History*, 14 (2–3): 112–25.

'Three Jewish Papers Take the Unprecedented Step of Publishing the Same Page on Labour Antisemitism' (2018),*The Jewish Chronicle*, 25 July.

Whitehead, T. (2007), *Mike Leigh*, Manchester: Manchester University Press.

# Part Three

# Contemporary British-Jewish Playwrights and Theatres in Britain: Continuities and Departures

# 9

# 'Affiliation and Belonging': Contemporary British-Jewish Women Playwrights

Eckart Voigts and Sarah Jane Ablett

Research on British-Jewish theatre has tended to focus on the first generation of post-war playwrights, such as Harold Pinter, Tom Stoppard, Arnold Wesker and Peter Shaffer. Yet little attention has been paid to the second and third generation of women who have transformed British-Jewish theatre as part of a larger trend of gradually redressing gender relations in the traditionally male-dominated theatre. This chapter will examine how British-Jewish women playwrights have represented, or chosen not to represent, Jewish identity in their work. It will also discuss the contexts and roles women assigned to women in contemporary British-Jewish theatre through the examples of Shelley Silas' *Calcutta Kosher* (2004) and Nina Raine's *Tribes* (2013).[1]

In her excellent book *Feeling Jewish* (2017), Devorah Baum quotes one of Kafka's diary entries on how nearly impossible it is for an individual to identify simply as a member of a specific group: 'What have I in common with Jews? I have hardly anything in common with myself' (7). This statement echoes Freud, Derrida and the discourse of constructed, unstable identities. Baum wryly concludes: 'You don't *have* to be Jewish to feel you have nothing in common with Jews, but being Jewish helps' (7). Is there, indeed, an intricate link between being Jewish, being a woman and being in the theatre? Devorah Baum links Jewishness, women and acting, with reference to the iconic Sarah Bernhardt (238). This link is explored by dramatists such as Deborah Levy, Michelene Wandor, Diane Samuels, Julia Pascal and Gail Louw, who focuses most of her plays on positioning a strong but ambivalent woman figure centre-stage (as in her two-hander on the ageing Marlene Dietrich, *Miss Dietrich Regrets* 2015). This is achieved most successfully in *Blonde Poison* (2015), Louw's award-winning monodrama portrait of Stella Goldschlag, a Jewish Nazi collaborator. Baum also describes a particular experience of being Jewish in Britain, quoting Philip Roth's novel *Deception* (1990): 'In England, whenever I'm in a public place ... and someone happens to mention the word "Jew," I notice that the voice drops a little' (17). While British theatre critic Michael Billington has noted 'modern theatre's heavy dependence on Jewish writers' (2012), playwright and director Julia Pascal told *Haaretz* that she believes British-Jewish artists' reluctance to openly examine their Jewish heritage is due to still prevalent stereotypes and exposure to 'constant low-level anti-Semitism that filters through British Society' (Quinn 2009). Indeed, few contemporary British-Jewish women playwrights have chosen, like Julia Pascal, to focus their playwriting on their British-Jewish identity. If voices do indeed drop in Britain, demonstrating antisemitic undercurrents, then this has presumably given rise to a desire for passing, the desire to transcend the boundaries of one's ethnicity, gender or class (Ginsberg 1996). And passing in this instance may have a special significance, since theatre is considered the most public of the arts. For British-Jewish theatre-makers, this dual identity is ambiguous because it lacks apparent external markers, such as skin colour, making passing seemingly easy. Jewish identity appears to be white, representing the mainstream in British theatre, yet it is not normatively white and therefore notably different from the Englishness of non-Jewish theatre.

Plays by British-Jewish women writers tend to explore multifarious aspects of the British-Jewish relationship and are particularly sensitive to gender issues. However, with very few exceptions, female Jewish playwrights have been largely neglected by the critical discourse. In her book on *Jewish Women Writers in Britain* (2014), Nadja Valman argues that 'historians of British Jewry have paid little attention to gender' (2), and, similarly, the role of Jewish women in British feminist theatre has rarely been in focus. According to 2014 statistics, only 37 per cent of artistic directors of the 179 British theatres and companies that received Arts Council funding were female. And in line with trends that see the number of women in top echelon positions recede, the number falls to 24 per cent in those receiving more than £500,000. In 2016, the National Theatre participated in a survey in order to address its gender imbalance and found that from 2011 to 2015, women made up just 36 per cent of the NT's casts, 27 per cent of its directors, 23 per cent of its writers (see Advance 2016). Overall, the list of significant female British-Jewish theatre managers and directors is not as long as it might be in view of the historical importance of British-Jewish theatre-makers in contemporary British theatre. Compared to the general under-representation of female directors in the British theatre world, however, this list is still substantial.

While the key names of the first post-war generation of British-Jewish theatre artists are mostly those of men, there are many significant women British-Jewish theatre artists and their role in challenging this patriarchal dominance can hardly be overstated. Michelene Wandor is the author of two pioneering studies of women on the British stage, *Carry On, Understudies*

(1986) and *Look Back in Gender* (1987, revised as *Looking Back in Gender* in 2001). Julia Pascal was the first woman to direct a play at the National Theatre (a dramatization of Dorothy Parker's *Men Seldom Make Passes*). Deborah Levy, whose minimalist, surrealist and postmodernist plays invoked the 'Jewish' themes of migration and European history in abstract, universalized settings and from feminist perspectives, also played an important part in the 1980s wave of women writers who followed the lead of feminist writers such as Caryl Churchill or Timberlake Wertenbaker and the Royal Court Theatre (see Macdonald 2000: 247). In the dominant histories of British feminist theatre, however, British-Jewish writers tend to remain a footnote.[2]

Influential theatre directors and producers such as Nancy Meckler and Jenny Topper have an important role in giving British-Jewish women a voice in contemporary British theatre. While not Jewish herself, Topper is closely tied to the British-Jewish theatre community. She has shaped British theatre and the new writing scene for over three decades, first as one of the managing directors of the small but important Bush Theatre (1977–88) and later at the helm of the Hampstead Theatre (1988–2003), one of the central venues for British-Jewish drama, both mentioned among the 'big six' venues for contemporary writing by Aleks Sierz in 2011 (28). In a conversation with Topper in 2003, Sierz characterized the 'Hampstead play' as one 'that appeals to a local audience of intellectuals. It's an unspoken truth that many come from the area's Jewish community' (Sierz 2003). Topper, however, notes that she 'only put on a handful of Jewish plays' (ibid.). In an interview with Jeanette Malkin, she explained her attitude towards 'Jewish-themed' plays at the Hampstead Theatre:

> I had a lot of plays coming across my desk that were Jewish or with Jewish themes. However, I never thought it was my responsibility to do plays simply because they had a Jewish theme – be they about historical events or Freud or Marx or whatever major player from Jewish history. I thought, in fact that it would be patronizing of me. ... These were people who were highly intelligent, highly engaged, who put a high value on their cultural life, were very committed to the larger community. So yes, it would have been patronizing of me to say, 'Ok, let's be a tiny cozy little enclave.' (Topper in Malkin 2018)

Topper's desire to escape from a set of narrowly defined Jewish-themed plays is echoed in Nancy Meckler's work. Meckler has been almost equally influential and is best known for her theatre work with Polly Teale and the production company Shared Experience, founded by Mike Alfreds. Meckler's biography reflects two relevant characteristics shared by British-Jewish women in British theatre. First, many of them have shaped or were born into families involved in theatre.[3] The second significant biographical detail pertains to Nancy Meckler's American roots. Frequently, American émigré writers brought the American-Jewish avant-garde to the attention of the British theatre scene. American Ed Berman is a key figure in British feminist theatre, having established Inter-Action in London in 1968, and the Almost Free Theatre, which championed women's theatre, gay theatre, and the 'Rights and Campaigns' season in 1978. American Jews, therefore, had a key role in first articulating sexual diversity in Britain's theatre. Meckler was born in 1941 in New York and educated at Antioch College and New York University. Her early work was heavily influenced by Joe Chaikin and Richard Schechner.

Prominent British-Jewish women in the directing scene include Abigail Morris who served as the artistic director and chief executive of the Soho Theatre. Nina Raine has both written and directed plays. Julia Pascal runs her own theatre company and is the most vocal and outspoken of women British-Jewish theatre personalities. Roxana Silbert, born in Argentina of Russian-Jewish descent on her father's side, succeeded Edward Hall at the Hampstead Theatre in 2018. American-Jewish Elyse Dodgson worked for thirty years with five artistic directors as international director at the Royal Court Theatre and her influence there continued through cooperation on plays that engage with the situation in Palestine, such as *My Name Is Rachel Corrie* by Alan Rickman and Katherine Viner or David Hare's *Via Dolorosa* (see Viner 2018). Lisa Goldman worked for the Red Room Theatre Company and headed the Soho Theatre from 2006 to 2010. Sonja Linden founded ice&fire theatre company in 2003 and created a new company, ViSiBLE Theatre Ensemble. Natalie Abrahami, who was born in 1979, represents a new generation of British-Jewish theatre directors. Trained at the Royal Court and Hull Truck theatre, Abrahami served as the artistic director of the fringe Gate Theatre from 2007 to 2012. Since then she has worked as a freelance for renowned theatres such as the National Theatre, the Almeida and the Young Vic. Abrahami has made a point of collaborating with women and fostering women's talent in the theatre. Like Abrahami, activist Lucy Kerbel of Tonic Theatre has sought to promote women in more central decision-making positions in the British performing arts (Kerbel 2017). All in all, however, British-Jewish women directors and playwrights remain mainly on the fringe scene of British theatre-making. Several women British-Jewish playwrights began their career as actresses, such as Tracy Ann Oberman and Alexis Zegerman. Zegerman's career was shaped by her work as an actress, above all with Mike Leigh. *Lucky Seven*, the first full-length play Zegerman wrote, premiered in November 2008 at the Hampstead theatre and was well received. More recently, her play *Holy Sh!t* opened the new Kiln Theatre (formerly the Tricycle Theatre) in 2018. Here, Zegerman explores religious and cultural issues among two middle-class couples in London, the secular Jews, Simone and Sam, and their Anglican best friends, Nick and Juliet.

Several women British-Jewish playwrights have left the insecure, often unstable and perhaps occasionally inhospitable freelance world of theatre. Abigail Morris has become the chief executive of the Jewish Museum London. Samantha Ellis now mainly works as a journalist and in non-fiction. Deborah Levy, a significant writer for the Royal Shakespeare Company in the 1980s (*Pax* 1984), is now a prize-winning novelist (*Swimming Home* 2011, *Hot Milk* 2016). Marion Baraitser, whose fringe plays *Story of an African Farm* (2001) and *Crystal Den* (2002) were published by Oberon Books, has since focused on work in publishing and non-fiction writing. Veteran Jewish feminist theatre scholar, musician and adaptor Michelene Wandor, and renowned novelist, poet and biographer Elaine Feinstein (née Elaine Coolin) have also written plays. Lucy Kerbel (2017) and Rose Lewenstein (2014) have provided some reasons for this exodus or the continuing dominance of male playwriting, such as the traditional dominance of white, able-bodied middle-class men, the prevalent sexist bias, a limiting niche awareness, etc. Given these obstacles, it seems important in the future to make further inroads into theatre managing in the financially lucrative West End Theatre, best exemplified by the high-profile company Sonia Friedman Productions, which provides top positions for women (see Lewenstein 2014). It remains to be seen if emerging British-Jewish playwrights such as Suzette Coon, whose work has been produced, for instance, at the Southwark Playhouse and the King's Head, find a space in the more traditional outlets for British-Jewish theatre on the fringe, chief among them the Hampstead Theatre. Alternatively, they might gravitate towards less-established fringe venues where new voices may be heard, such as the Yard Theatre, the Watford Palace Theatre, the Park Theatre or the Arcola Theatre, where many of Julia Pascal's plays and Suzette Coon's *The Sting* were produced in 2016. Many of these venues are situated in the Jewish terrain of North-East and East London.

The East End that was so crucial for male Jewish writers from Harold Pinter to Bernard Kops, Arnold Wesker and Steven Berkoff (see Jeremy Solomons' chapter in this volume) also features in contemporary British-Jewish playwriting by women. Examples include Diane Samuels' musical play *Poppy + George* (2016),[4] set in the East End after the First World War; Julia Pascal's *Broken English* (2009), which engages with Oswald Mosely's

1930s fascism; and Marion Baraitser's *The Crystal Den*, which confronts Karl Marx's daughter Eleanor and Israel Zangwill. Sometimes, British-Jewish communities outside of London feature in these plays, as in Tracy Ann Oberman's and Diane Samuels' reimagining of Chekhov's classic play *Three Sisters* among the Jewish community in wartime Liverpool in *Three Sisters on Hope Street* (2007).[5] Other examples of British women writers of Jewish descent include Kate Tempest, the successful spoken word performer and poet, and Gillian Slovo, who is best known for her political verbatim plays. While Tempest and Slovo's Jewishness seems to have little contribution to their work, this does not mean that these writers do not engage at all with Jewish themes or politics. Both are, for instance, outspoken critics of the current Israeli government.

Sometimes a play opens up a vista to a specifically British-Jewish perspective that is deliberately feminocentric, such as Diane Samuels' extremely successful, almost all-female *Kindertransport* or Julia Pascal's plays. Not infrequently, these female writers also cover the history of British Jewry, such as Louw's *Blonde Poison* (2011) or Charlotte Eilenberg's success at the Hampstead Theatre, *The Lucky Ones* (2002), set among post–Second World War Jewish refugees in London. Samantha Ellis, a London-based author and the daughter of Iraqi-Jewish refugees, has also written plays that reflect contemporary Jewish life in London and the conflicts of gender and religious identity. In *Cling to Me like Ivy* (2010), Ellis explores the multi-ethnic, multireligious world of contemporary London. While some of the plays mentioned here address the contrasting worlds of secular and more orthodox Jewry in Britain, British-Jewish women writers' ongoing engagement with the Holocaust is best represented by plays such as *Kindertransport* (1993) by Diane Samuels. This is probably the most internationally successful play written by a woman British-Jewish dramatist. Other examples include Gail Louw's *Blonde Poison* (2012), which addresses Jewish collaboration with the Nazis, and Julia Pascal's *The Holocaust Trilogy* (2000).

Beyond these specifically Jewish themes, we ask, what a 'certain Jewishness' or covert 'discernible subtext' from a specifically female perspective, even in British-Jewish writers who do not write in 'conspicuously Jewish' ways, might be composed of (Meyerowitz 1995: 3)? Might the 'inherited sense of exile, loss and isolation' that Billington (2012) suggests as a possible key to British-Jewish dramatists' work – clearly with writers like Pinter and Stoppard in mind – be intensified by an intersectional feminist perspective of female loss and isolation within the legacy of patriarchal rule? Perhaps Valman's list of possible preoccupations of British-Jewish writers may be of help here. Valman names several typical topics: 'subjectivities produced by dislocation' (3), 'questions of affiliation and belonging' or the 'thoroughgoing interrogation of Jewish domestic life' (4). It is therefore no coincidence that the plays that will be discussed below are both set at the dinner table, the very heart of domestic life. Indeed, many British-Jewish women writers address dislocated subjectivities as well as questions of affiliation and belonging – the children torn from their parents in Diane Samuels' *Kindertransport* being the most visible example.

Devorah Baum proposes a list of specifically Jewish structures of feeling, namely self-hatred, envy, guilt, being 'over the top', paranoia, motherly love and affection. Baum, however, understands these structures to transcend the limits of Jewishness. She follows the historian Yuri Slezkine to regard them above all else as 'model modern' (in Baum 2017: 11), because in her view contemporary Jews' 'situation of marginality has come to encompass more or less everyone' (Baum 2017: 249). Baum calls these structures of feeling Jew-*ish* as they transcend narrowly defined notions of being Jewish. In the remainder of this chapter, we will pursue these Jew-*ish* dimensions of, for example, food in Silas' *Calcutta Kosher* (2004) or deafness in Raine's *Tribes* (2010).

Shelley Silas' *Calcutta Kosher* complicates the prevalent idea of white Ashkenazi Jewishness because it is set in the postcolonial small Jewish community in Calcutta, India. Silas is a playwright of British-Jewish origin, born in Calcutta and raised in North London. In our interview, the author noted that culturally, she was brought up as an Indian and that she received racist comments from Ashkenazi Jews in secondary school. This outsider perspective on British-Jewishness may in part explain her statement that 'most of the stuff I write about has nothing to do with Jewry at all' (2017). Her perspective is clearly at odds with the work of Diane Samuels, Gail Louw or Julia Pascal, who are outspoken about Jewish influence on their work that engages with the eastern European Jewish Diaspora and the twentieth-century history of persecution. In Silas' *Calcutta Kosher*, the daughters of a British-Jewish-Indian family return to their birthplace Calcutta when they hear of their mother's illness. The Western-influenced daughters Esther and Silvie represent various types of Western Anglo-American Jewish diaspora: both daughters attended British boarding schools, but while Esther stayed in London – the seat of Anglo-Jewish conservatism – Sylvie lives in LA, representing the glamourous West Coast lifestyle. The youngest daughter, Maki, is the illegitimate love child whose father is Hindu, embodying ethnic and national hybridity. Their mother, Mozelle, both protests and affirms the diversity within the Jewish communities: 'We are all different. The Bombay Jews. The Bene Israel Jews. The Cochin Jews. We have our own ways, our own rituals. You must preserve them' (Silas 2004: 89). Esther and Sylvie's secularized Western lifestyle is contrasted with Maki's more pronounced and traditional Jewish practice: Maki and Mozelle wear kippahs, and Maki – unlike Sylvie – can pray in Hebrew. While perhaps more traditional, the characters of Mozelle and Maki are, however, placed in a less traditional, dominant and powerful and typically patriarchal setting.

*Calcutta Kosher* includes most of the 'Jew*ish*' structures of feeling according to Baum: Mozelle is stereotypically portrayed as crushing her daughters with love and behaving passionately 'over the top' in a sharp contrast with her stand-offish, 'English' daughter Esther. At the dinner table, the conflicts between the family members escalate, and emotions fly high concerning sibling rivalry and Maki's secret relationship with a Muslim man named Faisal (Silas 2004: 91). At the height of tensions, when her daughters confront Mozelle about her secret love affair with Ravi, the Hindu man, and their half-sister Maki, Mozelle works herself into an excited trance repeating 'Shema Israel' while the non-religious Esther tries to stop her (78). Despite unresolved conflicts, the family finally comes together at the matriarch's deathbed. This resolution seemingly celebrates the affection between the family members, contrasting the prevalent crass humour and cynicism throughout the play. One such example is when Mozelle accuses Esther of having 'a disgusting mouth' (66) or when Sylvie asks Mozelle why she had Maki instead of having a 'back street abortion' (70).

Mozelle's character embodies the themes common in these confrontational scenes – self-hatred, envy, guilt, being 'over the top', paranoia, motherly love and affection. Indeed, as a Jewish mother, Mozelle is in danger of being read as a stereotype when we consider Baum's description of the Jewish mother as 'a double whammy' that 'best distills within a single stereotype the contradictory motifs informing both misogynist representations and anti-Semitic ones' (Baum 2017: 192). But then none of these supposedly Jew*ish* structures of feeling are exclusively Jewish. In her interview, Silas revealed that her play *Calcutta Kosher* was apparently a long time in the making because people argued she should decide on *one* ethnic scenario, either Indian *or* Jewish, and finally the Kali Theatre Company decided to stage the play in spite of its hybridity. Even more fascinating is that Silas complicates the idea of a definitive, singular (Jewish) core identity in her play. Echoing Valman's list of thematic preoccupations, in the interview our research group conducted with her, Silas said: 'Actually, you know, it's just about family and belonging' (2017). Mixing two kinds of un-English 'ethnic' foods in its title, *Calcutta Kosher* explores the un-Englishness of both Indian and Jewish cultures, and the inevitable joke about the blandness of English food contrasts sharply with the rich cultural heritage of the Indian and Jewish food in the play. At the very moment the Indian-Jewish mother Mozelle admonishes the Anglicized Esther, complaining about Esther's 'disgusting' mouth – that is, her sacrilegious exclamation 'Jesus fucking Christ' (Silas 2004: 66) – Mozelle begins to choke on her food. The mouth, both as an organ involved in food consumption and language production, is the play's key metaphor for cultural exchange and generational conflict. Language and food then both indicate loss or retrieval of identities.

Language is also central in Nina Raine's breakthrough play *Tribes* (2010).[6] Raine is best known for *Tribes*, which premiered at the prestigious Royal Court and subsequently played in New York City in 2012 as well as in many other countries, and for *Consent* (2017).[7] *Tribes* is a play about family (mis-)communication, deafness and sign language. Its overt themes of communication and disability, and cultural identities' subtext make it highly relevant to our discussion. The domestic setting in *Tribes* is strikingly similar to *Calcutta Kosher* although it is set in England. *Tribes* deals with the everyday fights and conversations of a highly literary and unconventional family that has the family patriarch Christopher – a witty, cynical, caustic and politically incorrect man – at its head. The favourite son, Billy, who remains to an extent excluded from the family by their refusal to converse in sign language, is deaf and is bringing his new girlfriend, Sylvia, to dinner. Sylvia uses sign language, Billy doesn't. Billy's male relatives, his father Christopher and his older brother Daniel, fear losing Billy to Sylvia and what Christopher calls the 'bloody deaf community' (Raine 2013: 31). Christopher accuses the deaf community of tribalism and exclusion, comparing them to a cult and finally calling them 'the fucking Muslims of the handicapped world' (31) who wallow in their own persecution. The title *Tribes* refers to cultural group loyalty. The ideological boundaries of belonging and lack of belonging can be set up along the ability/disability binary, as well as along ethnic identities.

The first names in the family originate in the Hebrew Bible (with Beth, the mother, and the siblings Daniel and Ruth). At one moment, in fact, Jewish identities in the family scenario come to the fore:

**Christopher** Hayley [Daniel's ex-girlfriend] comes from Leeds, she needed to be told. And I enjoyed telling her. And, if you ask me, that's what signing is like. Northern.
**Ruth** Northern? Signing?
**Beth** My God, a confluence of two prejudices! Fantastic.
**Christopher** Yes. Northern. From what I can see. A lot of fake joviality. A construct of a personality.
**Daniel** Really? I always thought the signing persona was a bit *Jewish*. (*He does a bit of cod signing.*)
**Beth** Dan. That is not nice.
**Daniel** We're Jewish, I'm allowed. (Raine 2013: 32)

In this passage, the markers of a Jew*ish* structure of feeling as proposed by Baum appear: most of the family members in *Tribes* are precluded from success by neurotic self-hatred; envy and guilt between them abound. Their behaviour is constantly 'over the top'; affection is clouded by cynical repartee. That Christopher might not be Jewish – if we take the character's names as cue – illustrates that Raine appears to agree with Baum that Jewishness is above all a shorthand for an urban modernity which easily transcends ethnic borders. It is indeed the too strict identification of Billy as a member of a 'tribal group' (i.e. deaf sign-language users) that is seen as threatening the dysfunctional family.

In the passage quoted above, three markers of group identity – Northern, deaf, Jewish – are juggled, and only the non-specified Jewishness, cast here as manic, intellectualized verbal fencing, seems to be allowed into the family. The Northernness of Daniel's former girlfriend, Hayley, excludes her from the family. In abrasive and even sexist language typical of the family discourse, Christopher calls her 'a Northern twat' with 'all the charisma of a bus shelter' and 'as thick as two *tits*' (Raine 2013: 22). While Christopher may not be Jewish, he still fits perfectly into the family. Here, the family discourse is similar to the confrontational style of conversation in *Calcutta Kosher* but painted in even harsher brush strokes. While the family members in *Tribes* are all intellectuals, they are also insecure and prone to failure: Ruth is a failed opera singer; Daniel is addicted to medication and has a stutter. When the mother Beth in *Tribes* asks in exasperation, 'Why can't you move a step without an argument in this house?' and Christopher replies, half ironically, 'Because we love each other!', his daughter Ruth adds, 'Yeah. Like a straitjacket' (21). Indeed, the central final image in *Tribes* is the sign-language gesture for love, crossed arms, performed by Daniel 'miming being in a straitjacket' (65). Thus, to be a member of a family is like being confined in a straitjacket, extending to the group identity of being Jewish, deaf or using sign language. Whether group identities are enabling or disabling is a matter of perspective, and while the inability to hear is clearly marked as a lack of ability, the dysfunctional family communication in *Tribes* suggests the failure of uttered words. Loud confrontational exchanges take turns with signed language that is captioned for the non-signing audience. At the end of Act One, in a poignant moment, Sylvia confronts her loss of hearing and her increasing inability to play the piano, and when he starts playing Debussy, the musical notation comes up for the audience, and everybody congregates while Billy remains separate (44). This scene, among others, makes the audience aware of the various inclusions and exclusions through different kinds of utterances and notations. *Tribes* does not just employ surtitles in theatrically interesting ways and the emotional language of music, signing and words to make points about dis-ability, access and exclusion; it is also a somewhat covert discussion of Jewishness that takes the ability to hear and listen beyond its physical and physiological dimensions to be a communicative competence.

Compared with the Jewish avant-garde theatre in the United States and its articulate and pronounced Jewishness, British-Jewish women writers have largely not been part of the English directing and playwriting mainstream. Nor do they exhibit any sense of a group identity or common thematic concerns that may be found in the kind of theatre now generally – and very problematically pigeonholed as BAME theatre (i.e. Black, Asian and Minority Ethnic theatre). The work of published and produced playwrights such as Pascal, Raine and Silas, but also Diane Samuels, Gail Louw, Samantha Ellis, Tracy Ann Oberman, Amy Rosenthal or Alexis Zegerman transcends any narrowly defined British-Jewish thematic interest. Just as their non-Jewish women counterparts, British-Jewish women dramatists have been marginalized and obscured but are gradually making inroads into the male dominance of theatre-making. Since the 1980s, but increasingly in the twenty-first century, British-Jewish women writers have brought fresh perspectives to contemporary British as well as Jewish culture, even if they continue to be relegated to the theatrical fringe to some extent. Specialists in domestic drama and memory plays, British-Jewish women dramatists nevertheless transcend the sphere of the domestic, loading their family scenarios with a fascinating discourse on intersectional identities, and explore the cultural specificity of the role of Jewish identity within British society.

## Notes

1 *Tribes* was first performed in 2010.
2 In Aston (1995, 2003) or Aston and Reinelt (2000), only Levy and Wandor are mentioned. The essays collected in Farfan and Ferris (2014) also have little to say on British-Jewish women theatre. In contrast to 'Black British', the category 'British-Jewish' is missing.
3 Meckler is married to film producer David Aukin; her sons are director Daniel Aukin and actor Jethro Aukin.
4 *Poppy + George* was first performed at Watford Palace in 2016.
5 *Three Sisters on Hope Street* was first performed at Everyman Theatre Liverpool/Hampstead Theatre in 2007.
6 Raine was born in 1975 to a Jewish mother, Ann Pasternak Slater (novelist Boris Pasternak's grand-niece), and the acclaimed poet Craig Raine.
7 *Consent* focuses on the legal debate of a rape case and is therefore highly relevant in the wake of the Harvey Weinstein scandal and the #MeToo movement.

# References

Advance (2016), 'Gender Equality in England's Performing Arts Organisations'. Tonic Theatre and Royal Central School for Speech and Drama, University of London. Available online: http://www.tonictheatre-advance.co.uk/ (accessed 30 April 2020).

Aston, E. (1995), *An Introduction to Feminism and Theatre*, London: Routledge.

Aston, E. (2003), *Feminist Views on the English Stage: Women Playwrights, 1990–2000*, Cambridge: Cambridge University Press.

Aston, E. and J. Reinelt, eds (2000), *The Cambridge Companion to Modern British Women Playwrights*, Cambridge: Cambridge University Press.

Baum, D. (2017), *Feeling Jewish*, New Haven, CT: Yale University Press.

Billington, M. (2012), 'J Is for Jewish Dramatists', *The Guardian*, 14 February. Available online: https://www.theguardian.com/stage/2012/feb/14/jewish-dramatists-modern-drama (accessed 30 April 2020).

Ellis, S. (2011), *Cling to Me Like Ivy*, London: Nick Hern Books.

Farfan, P. and L. Ferris, eds (2013), *Contemporary Women Playwrights: Into the 21st Century*, London: Palgrave Macmillan.

Ginsberg, E. K., ed. (1996), *Passing and the Fictions of Identity*, Durham, NC: Duke University Press.

Kerbel, L. (2017), *All Change Please. A Practical Guide to Achieving Gender Equality in Theatre*, London: Nick Hern Books.

Lewenstein, R. (2014), 'Hey British Theatre, Where Are All the Women?' *Vice*, 28 October. Available online: https://www.vice.com/en_uk/article/av9zbe/where-are-the-women-in-british-theatre-028 (accessed 30 April 2020).

Louw, G. (2015), *Collected Plays. Blonde Poison, Miss Dietrich Regrets, Shackleton's Carpenter, Two Sisters*, London: Oberon Books.

Macdonald, C. (2000), 'Writing Outside the Mainstream', in E. Aston and J. Reinelt (eds), *The Cambridge Companion to Modern British Women Playwrights*, 235–52, Cambridge: Cambridge University Press.

Malkin, J. (2018), Personal interview with Jenny Topper, London.

Meyerowitz, R. (1995), *Transferring to America: Jewish Interpretations of American Dreams*, New York: SUNY Press.

Pascal, J. (2000), *Theresa; A Dead Woman on Holiday; The Dybbuk*, London: Oberon Books.

Quinn, B. and T. Forward (2009), 'New Depiction of Fagin on London Stage Sparks Fears of Anti-Semitic Stereotypes: Critics Question Whether Portrayal of Jewish Street Thief Fagin in Dickens' "Oliver!" Is Acceptable', *Haaretz*, 29 January. Available online: https://www.haaretz.com/1.5069031 (accessed 30 April 2020).

Raine, N. (2017), *Consent*, London: Nick Hern Books.

Raine, N. ([2010] 2013), *Tribes*, New York: Nick Hern Books.

Samuels, D. (1995), *Kindertransport*, London: Nick Hern Books.

Sierz, A. (2003), 'Hampstead Theatre: Curtain Up for Act I', *The Independent*, 12 February. Available online: https://www.independent.co.uk/arts-entertainment/theatre-dance/features/hampstead-theatre-curtain-up-for-act-ii-118663.html (accessed 30 April 2020).
Silas, S. (2004), *Calcutta Kosher*, London: Oberon Books.
Silas, S. (2017), Interview with Eckart Voigts and Jeanette R. Malkin, London. Available online: britishjewishtheatre.org.
Valman, N., ed. (2014), *Jewish Women Writers in Britain*, Detroit: Wayne State University Press.
Viner, K. (2018), 'Elyse Dodgson Obituary', *The Guardian*, 2 November. Available online: https://www.theguardian.com/stage/2018/nov/02/elyse-dodgson-obituary (accessed 30 April 2020).
Wandor, M. (1986), *Carry On, Understudies. Theatre and Sexual Politics*, London: Routledge and Kegan Paul.
Wandor, M. (2001), *Post-War British Drama. Looking Back in Gender*, London: Methuen.

# 10

# Three Ways of Being a Contemporary British-Jewish Playwright: Tom Stoppard, Patrick Marber, Ryan Craig

Jeanette R. Malkin

London's theatre is endlessly rich. It is the theatre-heart of Britain, the home of the Royal National Theatre, of the West End, of multiple fringe venues. Among those riches, as this book argues, is a contingent of plays and performances we call British-Jewish theatre: plays and/or performances that reflect Jewish lives in Britain, specific Jewish interests or themes (such as Israel or antisemitism), or a voice sustained by a playwright who identifies as British-Jewish. Within the space of this theatre, imagined here as consisting of some combination of both British and Jewish identities, there is also a British-Jewish audience whose interest in seeing their 'tribe' onstage is evidenced by the many reviews of such plays and playwrights and directors found in journals which cater to British Jews – such as the *Jewish Chronicle*, *Jewish Renaissance*, *Jewish News* or *Jewish Quarterly*.

Among the dozen or so contemporary British-Jewish playwrights we have spoken to during our research, three are perhaps the most prominent: the internationally renowned Tom Stoppard (b. 1937), whose Jewish identity was, until recently, known mainly through two autobiographical essays he published in 1999, occasional biographies and news articles. With his 2020 'Jewish' play *Leopoldstadt*, produced at a West End theatre, Stoppard has publicly declared himself a British Jew. Stoppard's foreign birth, exile, acquired English, the secrets and lies of his family history, the late discovery – and acceptance – of his Jewish provenance: all of these mark Stoppard as a European immigrant in the image of the post-Holocaust 'fathers' of British-Jewish theatre who tended to be influenced by European drama and theatre.[1] Patrick Marber (b. 1964), who has worked with Stoppard over the last few years as a director of his plays, reached celebrity status during the turn of the century with his two hit plays *Dealer's Choice* (1995) and *Closer* (1997) which was turned into a successful movie in 2004 with Marber's screenplay and under Mike Nichols' direction.[2] These two successes were followed by Marber's only play to deal explicitly with his Jewish identity, *Howard Katz* (2001); it was directed by Marber and was a theatrical failure. Marber, who claimed in interview that he considers himself 'a Jew first and an Englishman second' (Nathan 2015), regards all of his work as 'Jewish' since it all flows from this firm identity. The third playwright, Ryan Craig (b. 1972), is the youngest of the three. He has written six Jewish-themed plays, three of which were produced at London's Royal National Theatre. Craig is the only one of the three whose plays reflect the singularity of British-Jewish lives in London today and the consequences of feeling nowhere 'at home'.

My assumption in this chapter is that English theatre is aimed at various memory communities. *Rosencrantz and Guildenstern Are Dead* assumes a memory of *Hamlet* in its viewing audience, just as Caryl Churchill's *Cloud 9* assumes a remembrance of British history, and as S. Ansky's play *The Dybbuk*, originally written in Russian, and then Yiddish, will be incomprehensible to those unacquainted with European Jewish lore. Following Stanley Fish's definition of 'interpretive communities' (Fish 1980), I will discuss the communities at which these playwrights' Jewish plays are aimed and how they have been received.

Interpretive communities, according to Fish, are discrete groups who tend to interpret texts in a similar manner because they share similar social positions and cultural experiences. Meaning resides in the readers and audiences of texts, claims Fish, and the readings, like the audiences, are culturally constructed (Fish 1980: 147–74). Within these parameters I will claim that Stoppard's texts, including his most recent *Leopoldstadt*, are aimed broadly at a cultured Anglo-European audience interested in his literary/historical subjects and who enjoy his unique style. Ryan Craig's *What We Did to Weinstein*, as well as his *Holy Rosenbergs*, will be more attractive and intelligible to an English-Jewish audience than to a non-Jewish audience, despite Craig's claim that 'I believe such plays can redefine what it is to be British'. Craig also admits that, 'the British theatre [remains] stubbornly resistant to this idea when it comes to Jewish characters' (Craig 2014). As for Patrick Marber, despite his repeated claims of being first and foremost a Jew, his lack of explicit Jewish characters – except in one play – means his plays require intentional interpretation, founded on biography and interviews, if one is seeking a Jewish layer of meaning. This move can be theorized through Edmund Husserl's pre-phenomenological concept of the *Lebenswelt*, the Lifeworld, which, he posits, is fundamental for all epistemological enquiries (Husserl 1936/1970: 139ff). Just as interpretive communities share social positions and cultural experiences, lifeworlds can be analysed and compared in terms of experience *within* the pre-existing bio-eco-socio-cultural ground.

A lifeworld is subjective; it is the world as directly experienced in everyday life and is sharply distinguished from the objective 'worlds' of science. As Husserl claimed, the 'lifeworld' is already-always there; it precedes us and is the 'ground' for all shared human experience (Husserl 1936/1970: 139ff); this 'ground' is thus intersubjective. 'Life conditions', writes Björn Kraus, a German social philosopher, 'mean a person's material and immaterial circumstances of life. Lifeworld means a person's *subjective construction* of reality, which he or she forms under the condition of his or her life circumstances' (Kraus 2015: 4). By adopting the concept of the 'Lifeworld', phenomenology was opened up to the study of consciousness and meaning in context, and consciousness was recognized as embedded in pre-existing meanings and judgements constituted through history, culture and social position. Without a consideration of Stoppard's specific and complex lifeworld, it would be difficult to see the ways in which he is a British-Jewish playwright.

## Tom Stoppard: The 'European' British-Jewish Playwright

> I think of myself as 'a British writer of Jewish origin' and – so far – I have not written a play specifically as a Jew, though one might say I have written nothing except as a Jew.
>
> (Stoppard, November 2016, in a private email)

On 26 June 2019, the *Guardian* published a surprising article reporting that Stoppard, then aged eighty-two, 'will return to West End with *Leopoldstadt*, based in the old Jewish quarter of Vienna'. For those who hadn't been following Stoppard for the last thirty years, the article went on to report what it had taken Stoppard most of his life to discover: that he had 'four Jewish grandparents and much of his family from his parents' generation died in Nazi concentration camps'. Tom Stoppard, as he himself wrote, had 'turned out' to be Jewish (Stoppard 1999a, 1999b).[3]

This fact was first known to Stoppard in 1993, when a Czech relative drew a family tree for him and his mother, a tree reproduced in *Leopoldstadt* and projected among the black-and-white images that hover between scenes. In addition to his grandparents from both sides, Stoppard learned, three of his mother's sisters had also died in the camps. Yet already in the early 1970s Stoppard began political activism in support of Soviet 'prisoners of conscience', mostly Jews. From this it would appear that Stoppard had long, perhaps always, known that, in addition to having been born in Zlin, Czechoslovakia, as Tomáš Sträussler in 1937, in addition to having lost his father in Singapore in 1942 and knowing nothing about his grandparents, there was a deep family secret, hidden and yet somehow apparent to him. After all, displaced, uncertain about his family past, a father lost, a new language earned, magnificently earned, yet – the trace of an accent remained: was not this the condition of an entire generation of European Jews?

Stoppard left Zlin with his parents and older brother Peter in March 1939, outrunning Hitler, ostensibly because of one 'wrong' grandparent. The family spent a few years in Singapore, where Dr Eugen Sträussler had been sent by his Zlin employer, for his safety. When the Japanese invaded Singapore in 1941 the family left first for Australia and then for Darjeeling, India; Stoppard's father remained behind to help and was killed in the fighting. In India, his mother, Martha Beckova, met and married a British Army officer, Major Kenneth Stoppard, who subsequently adopted her two sons. Thus, in 1946 the new family, the Stoppards, settled in Bristol; there Tomáš Sträussler, now Tom Stoppard, eight years old, began his new life.

Stoppard's mother never spoke of her Czech family, of his father's death, of any Jewish heritage. One of the reasons for this, Stoppard later understood, 'was that my stepfather wasn't sympathetic' (Stoppard 1999c: 15).[4] Surely this unspoken and fraught history, the displacement and dislocation, as biographer Ira Nadel argues, translated into Stoppard's most recognizable dramatic traits: his ambivalence,[5] the repeated doublings in his plays,[6] and a deep suspicion of history and biography (see Nadel 2000: 157–70). Stoppard's reinventions of historical figures such as Joyce, Byron, Housman and Herzen come from a place in which truth, as Oscar Wilde says in *The Invention of Love*, 'is the work of the imagination' (Stoppard 1997: 92), and biography, as Nadel writes, 'is always a fiction more to be mistrusted than believed' (Nadel 2004: 20).

In a famous 1977 *New Yorker* essay, Kenneth Tynan wrote that in order to understand Stoppard it is essential to remember that 'he is an émigré'. In the early 1970s, this émigré began to quietly work with a number of non-governmental organizations (NGOs) on behalf of Soviet dissidents. This continued for a few years and included sending a letter to British Prime Minister Edward Heath reporting the persecution of Soviet ballet dancers Valery and Galina Panov because of their wish to emigrate to Israel (Hurst 2016). The matter of politically motivated psychiatric abuse – Soviet internment of dissidents such as Vladimir Bukovsky and Victor Fainberg in psychiatric wards – was particularly abhorrent to Stoppard (Gussow 1984)[7] who met Fainberg in his asylum prison during a visit in 1976. In 1977 Stoppard travelled twice to the Soviet bloc: in February, he met with some of the most influential dissidents of this period, including Andrei Sakharov. Then in June 1977 Stoppard visited Czechoslovakia where he met Vaclav Havel, the Czech playwright who figure-headed Charter 77 and later became Czechoslovakia's first post-Soviet President (Hurst 2016).

Two of Stoppard's plays reflect these activities: *Every Good Boy Deserves Favour*, first performed at the Royal Festival Hall in July 1977, is set predominantly within a psychiatric hospital and explores the (comi-tragic) situation of a sane dissident known as Alexander Ivanov, who shares a cell with a schizophrenic patient, also called Ivanov. Bernard Levin, in the London *Sunday Times*, termed the play 'a profoundly moral work' which, writes Tynan, 'rests on the assumption that the difference between good and evil is obvious to any reasonable human being' (Tynan 1977). Stoppard dedicated the play to Fainberg and Bukovsky. The BBC TV drama *Professional Foul*, aired in September of that year, tells an equally comic and acutely political story of a dissent in Prague; it was dedicated to Vaclav Havel. This subject comes up again in 1979 in *Dogg's Hamlet* and *Cahoot's Macbeth*, and in 2006 in *Rock 'n' Roll*, a play about music and revolution in Czechoslovakia.[8] 'What the plays reveal', wrote Billington, 'is Stoppard's ingenuity being put to the service of a moral cause' (2015). Stoppard's 'ingenuity', his well-known Wildean humour, the dramatic puzzles, the riddles and theatrical games have tantalized Stoppard's audiences from the start. But the games were only a part of his art: 'For Stoppard art is a game within a game,' wrote Tynan, 'the larger game being life itself, an absurd mosaic of incidents and accidents in which … "something is taking its course"' (Tynan 1977).[9]

In 2000, a year after Stoppard's new biographical information had been published, Ira Nadel wrote: 'From his earliest to his latest writing, Stoppard has presented biography as a falsifying art. The obscurity of his own past has contributed to this skepticism.' Thus, Nadel suggests, Stoppard's representation of historical figures outside of their actual biographies reflects a view of history (refracted through the lens of *his*-story), as always tentative and incomplete. The dramatist of simultaneous time, of twins and doubles and rearranged life stories, Nadel implies, is *himself* inscribed in his plays. As Stoppard wrote to me in 2016: 'I think of myself as "a British writer of Jewish origin" and – so far – I have not written a play specifically as a Jew, though one might say I have written nothing except as a Jew.' Or, as Stoppard put it elsewhere, 'You can't help being what you write and writing what you are' (Jaggi 2008).

In that same 2000 article, Nadel continues: 'Recent efforts to re-establish his former history … have met with unexpected success. But … such discoveries have so far not altered Stoppard's view of biographers and their errors. Biographical truth still remains mystifying and suspect.' With *Leopoldstadt*, history falls into place with clarity and remorse. With *Leopoldstadt*, Stoppard has written his first 'straight' family story, an ensemble play which takes place mainly in a grand salon; it is chronological, historically cogent, with a few fully developed, realistic characters, and borders on the tragic. The only games being played here are played by history. It is a portrait of four generations of the intermarried Merz and Jakobovicz clans, Austrian Jews who belong to 'the prosperous end of Viennese bourgeoisie' (Stoppard 2020: 3). The forty-plus characters (including fifteen children) who fill the stage for two and a half hours move from prosperity, assimilation and the illusion of social acceptance, through *Kristallnacht* and the Holocaust. It takes place in a well-researched Vienna between 1899 and 1955 and is partially autobiographical. There is the sense of an abundance of life during the first five scenes of the play, which take place at the turn of the twentieth century when '[a] Jew can be a great composer. He can be the toast of the town,' says one of the characters, 'But he can't *not* be a Jew' (Stoppard 2020: 23). The words 'Jew' and 'Jewish' are spoken over a hundred times in the play and on the stage, quite naturally, since the fact of their Jewishness is central to every facet of their lives. 'It's a lot to do with being Jewish, knowing you are Jewish, acknowledging you are Jewish, acting like you are Jewish … or not,' Stoppard explained about the characters; 'And that's the area where I felt I was looking inward rather than outward' (Nathan 2020).

Scene 8, November 1938, brings *Kristallnacht* into the Merz apartment. In it we meet Leopold Rosenbaum, son of Aaron (who has died) and Nellie, who is now married to the British journalist Percy Chamberlain. Leo, Stoppard's stand-in character, is aged eight and will soon leave Europe for England with his mother and new British father. In the final scene, set in 1955 in the same apartment, Leopold Rosenbaum, now named Leonard Chamberlain, is aged twenty-four. He is on a visit to Vienna from England and has returned to the Viennese apartment of his childhood with two other family survivors – Rosa, who has lived in New York for years and is also visiting, and her nephew Nathan, the only survivor of Auschwitz in their family. The apartment is almost bare and has been abandoned for years. The scene shows us Leonard coming to 'know', though not yet understand, who he is. A young British man with little historical imagination, he angers Nathan when he quips, unthinkingly – 'I'm sorry you had a rotten war' (Stoppard 2020: 92). Nathan tries to make him understand that this war was his as well: 'No one is born eight years old. Leonard Chamberlain's life is Leo Rosenbaum's life continued. His family is your family. But you live as if without history, as if you throw no shadow behind you' (Stoppard 2020: 99). Billington wrote, incisively, 'What makes the play so moving is the sense that it is an act of atonement for Stoppard's belated recognition of his Jewish inheritance' (Billington 2020). That 'inheritance' is one of historical continuity, of remembering who you are and where you come from. This is clearly signified in the memory interlude that occurs directly before the play's final litany. The 'ghosts' of Passover past (from Scene 6) reappear, seen through the eyes of Rosa, then a child. Passover is an ancient Jewish holiday whose major injunction is: remember.

On Passover it is the parents duty to tell their children the story of their escape from Egypt, from slavery, to invoke in them a sense that 'we' ourselves had been there. As the memory bubble acts itself out, Hanna, often at the family piano during the first scenes, plays quietly during the following. Leo is looking at the family tree drawn for him by Rosa. He asks about the fate of those listed. Leo will not completely understand what he's told, since he barely knows the persons involved. But the audience, or the reader, who have lived through parts of their lives, will:

| Leo | Ernst. |
| Rosa | Auschwitz. |
| Leo | Hanna |
| Rosa | Auschwitz |
| Leo | Kurt |
| Rosa | Dachau, 1938 |
| Leo | Zacharia |
| Nathan | Death march. Nowhere |
| Leo | Sally |
| Rosa | Auschwitz |
| Leo | Mimi |
| Rosa | Auschwitz |
| Leo | Bella |
| Rosa | Auschwitz |
| Leo | Hermine |
| Rosa | Auschwitz |
| Leo | Heini |
| Rosa | Auschwitz |

The play ends in this act of remembrance, in this despairing elegy. Through it Stoppard integrates Leo's – and his own? – biography into the history that was long written out of his life.

## Patrick Marber: British-Jewish Playwright

I'm a Jew. Proud. That's what I am. It's deep in me. I'm also patriotic and love my country. But it's my race. It's my being. It's what I am.

(2015, interview with John Nathan)

Patrick Marber has known almost only success as a playwright, an adapter, a theatre director. His early work, beginning in 1994 with Steve Coogan on sketches for *On the Hour* and for the iconic character of Alan Partridge, drew a large audience of cognoscenti that included Richard Eyre, the then new artistic director of the Royal National Theatre. Eyre offered Marber the opportunity to participate in an NT Writer's Workshop that led to a formal commission – unheard of for an untested playwright – to produce Marber's first play, *Dealer's Choice*, which he was also allowed to direct. Set in a London restaurant and presenting a group of small-time gamblers (partly inspired by Marber's own dark experiences with gambling addiction), the play's huge success instantly put Marber on the map. *Dealer's Choice* won the *Evening Standard* Theatre Award for Best Comedy of 1995 and the Writer's Guild award for best West End play. Harold Pinter sent Marber a letter of praise (Thompson 2017). That same year, *After Miss Julie*, based on the Strindberg play, was broadcast on BBC television, Marber's first of many successful play adaptations. Marber set the action during the Labour Party's victory in the general election of 1945, with Miss Julie the daughter of a Labour peer. In 1997 the Royal National Theatre produced Marber's second original play, *Closer*, again with Marber as director. This explosive play about four lovers, focusing on sex, betrayal and the pain of warped intimacy, 'secured his reputation as one of the most scintillating, daring writers of his generation', wrote Isobel Thompson in *Vanity Fair* (Thompson 2017). This play too won the *Evening Standard* award for Best Comedy, the Critics Circle award for best play, the Laurence Olivier award for Best New Play of 1997 and, when transferred to Broadway, won the New York Drama Critics' Circle Award for best foreign play of 1998–9. It may have won other awards as well, since the play was translated into thirty languages. Marber's third original play, produced at the National Theatre as well, under his direction, was *Howard Katz* (2001); it was his first play to receive a large proportion of negative reviews.

*Howard Katz* is Marber's 'Jewish' play, his only play thus far with Jewish characters; its theme is redemption, hardly a specifically Jewish subject. Katz, a fifty-year-old theatre agent who represents mainly floozies and losers, is Marber's very personal mid-life crisis stand-in, written when he was thirty-six. It tells the story of a self-centred, self-destructive, very unhappy man. The play begins and ends on a park bench, with Katz wearing a yarmulke, contemplating suicide and trying to get God's opinion on the matter. In between these framing scenes we follow Katz during a year or so as his career, marriage and family relations all fall into irreparable ruin. Formally, *Katz* is a departure from Marber's former carefully structured plays. It is an almost expressionist series of short scenes, a 'picaresque mess' (Brown 2001) in which, at various moments, the stage and the characters other than Katz 'freeze', indicating the play's radical subjectivity. 'Most of all', writes Stephen Brown (2001), '*Howard Katz* is hobbled by a kind of structural, and peculiarly male, narcissism.' There seems to be no outside to the play's interiority.

When asked in 2001 about the Jewish dimension of *Howard Katz*, Marber answered that this was not new in his writing; that Stephen, the disappointed father and restaurant owner in *Dealer's Choice*, as well as his son Carl, are both Jewish (they were inspired by himself and his own father), as is writer Daniel Woolf in *Closer*. 'But [the Jewish] elements are not important to those plays,' Marber explains, 'Howard's Judaism is important' (Greene 2001).[10] When asked again by theatre critic John Nathan in 2015, by which time Marber himself was fifty, whether his own midlife has a Jewish 'flavour in the way Howard Katz's does', Marber answered: 'My whole life has a Jewish flavour. I'm a Jew. I think of myself as a Jew first and an Englishman second.' Nathan is surprised by this declaration, surprised 'that this in some ways *very English kind of Jew*, expresses his identity so emphatically'.[11] This is perhaps the key to understanding Marber as a British-Jewish playwright. Unlike Stoppard, whose unknown life as a 'Jew' is unknowingly expressed in his work, or Craig, whose Jewish world is the explicit subject of many of his plays, Marber is saying: everything I do, I do as a Jew. There is no turnstile separating my English and Jewish identities. Thus the question of whether he has written Jewish-themed plays, or not, is somehow irrelevant. 'I consider myself a Jewish writer,' he has said, 'like all my heroes: Tom Stoppard, David Mamet, Philip Roth, Arthur Miller, Woody Allen' (Forrest 1997). Of these, only Stoppard is British.

Patrick Marber was born in 1964 and grew up with an older brother in the London suburb of Wimbledon – not a particularly Jewish neighbourhood. His parents were not religiously observant but were very aware of their Jewish heritage and Patrick had a bar mitzvah. His father, Brian Marber, was a leading and highly regarded technical analyst in the city. Brian's own parents' families had emigrated from Poland and Russia via Antwerp to London. Patrick Marber's mother, Angela, he said in interview, is 'kind of more Golders Green Jewish'. She spent some years, from 1956, caring for orphaned Jewish children 'of color' (meaning of North African or Indian origin) for Norwood,[12] 'because no one else wanted to' (Doherty 2020). Marber was educated at St. Paul's, London, later at a boarding school in Surrey, and he read English at Wadham College, Oxford. He has said that he encountered antisemitism and bullying in school. 'I grew up in the Seventies, anti-Semitism was always there' (Harvey 2020). This however has never deterred Marber from insisting on his Jewish identity: 'I'm a Jew. Proud. That's what I am. It's deep in me. I'm also patriotic and love my country. But it's my race. It's my being. It's what I am' (Nathan 2015).

While this identity is not always clearly inscribed in his plays, those interested in such things might have read some twenty articles, reviews and interviews with or about Marber published in the *Jewish Chronicle*, England's foremost British-Jewish newspaper, over the past five years. Long reviews and interviews can also be found in the *Jewish Renaissance*. Marber's Jewish provenance is found as well in articles published in most English newspapers and especially in the *Guardian*. As a premiere theatre director as well as a playwright, a screenwriter and occasional actor, Marber is often in the news. This is especially true for the last five years (2015–20); in 2015 Marber wrote his first original play since *Howard Katz* – *The Red Lion*, ostensibly about football (one of Marber's passions) though dealing as well with moral issues. 'For me', Marber has said, 'it's really nothing to do with football, it's to do with parenting, with being a father' (Appleyard 2017). This subject is central as well in *Dealer's Choice*, and Howard's father in *Howard Katz* is a heartbreakingly tragic figure. *The Red Lion* premiered at the National Theatre at the same time that Marber's *Three Days in the Country*, a version of Turgenev's 1850 play (which Marber also directed), was running there. That same year, Marber's *Closer* was revived at the Donmar Warehouse, directed by David Leveaux, again to excellent reviews. The following year Marber directed a revival of Tom Stoppard's *Travesties* at the Menier Chocolate Factory which 'broke box office records ... becoming the first play in the company's history to sell out ahead of its first preview' (Bowie-Sell 2016) and which soon transferred to the West End Apollo theatre. The revival was nominated for five Olivier Awards. In 2018 the production transferred to Broadway and was nominated for four Tony Awards among many others.

Work on *Travesties* brought Marber and Stoppard closer together and it was during this period that Stoppard began work on *Leopoldstadt*. Marber was chosen to direct the play but, as Stoppard writes in his 'Author's Note' to the published edition, he did much more than that: 'Patrick Marber was my first reader at every stage. His notes had a beneficial effect on *Leopoldstadt* from first to last' (Stoppard 2020). Critics all mention the family tableaux Marber created in many of the onstage scenes and in photos projected on the rear wall. The family, a subject never before found in a Stoppard play, is at the heart of *Leopoldstadt* and it reverberated with Marber. His own father too had years before drawn a family tree, putting an asterisk by those who had been 'murdered by the Nazis'. Since working with Stoppard on *Leopoldstadt*, this chart has become very important to him. 'There's a whole bunch of Marbers who came from Poland and Russia and were in the Warsaw Ghetto and died in camps,' he has said (Harvey 2020). While working on *Leopoldstadt* 'I was suddenly powerfully moved and, like Tom, appalled that I hadn't taken enough notice of this' (Kellaway 2020).

## Ryan Craig: 'Diasporic' British-Jewish Playwright

The real nub of it for me ... is that Jewish characters [Shylock, Marlowe's Barabas, Dickens' Fagin], are never allowed any *nobility of purpose*. ... To me that's what has been so unspeakably damaging, and, in my opinion, still impacts, consciously or otherwise, on people's attitudes today.

(Craig, personal email 2016)

In October 2000, Jewish theatre critic David Jays published an article in the *New Statesman* bemoaning the lack of contemporary Jewish characters on the British stage, despite the popularity of plays by Pinter, Wesker and Deborah Levy. Since then many Jewish-themed plays have been written, five of them by Ryan Craig. Two of these plays were performed at the Royal National Theatre (2009, 2011) and two at the Hampstead Theatre (2006, 2017). A fifth, early play, *What We Did to Weinstein* (2005), performed at the off-West End Menier Chocolate Factory, was nominated for the Most Promising Playwright Award of the *Evening Standard*. All five plays, performed between 2005 and 2017, were well received and widely discussed in the media making him, I would contend, the potentially best-known contemporary British-Jewish playwright. As he writes in his *ars poetic* essay 'Wesker's Dream', 'I've written a couple of plays about the British Jewish experience in the twenty-first century and, for better or worse, it's what I'm known for, if I'm known at all, in the British theatre' (Craig 2014).

Born 1972 in London, near Hampstead Heath, Craig is a third-generation British Jew and the youngest of our three playwrights. He and his brother were brought up in the up-and-coming suburb of Mill Hill in North West London as culturally Jewish, which included a bar mitzvah but 'I was never forced to go to *shul* [synagogue] after that and we never ate kosher.' As a boy, Craig recalled in interview, non-Jewish children threw bacon and spouted slurs at him as he walked to Hebrew school. For his twelfth birthday, Craig has said, a school friend bought him the text of Harold Pinter's *The Caretaker*, of which he writes: 'It blew my mind. The language, the anger, the humour. So close to the rhythms of my East End Jewish family.'[13] He has in fact described Pinter's cutting, menacing style as, to him, 'hyper-realistic.'[14] Craig's family background is unusually diverse: His paternal grandmother was Irish Catholic and converted to Judaism during the Second World War when she married his grandfather, whose father had come to Britain to escape pogroms near Bialystok, Poland. His maternal grandmother's side were Sephardic Dutch Jews, religiously observant and numerous, who fled Nazi-occupied Holland for London. His maternal grandfather stemmed from a mixture of German Jews and French Huguenots. Craig describes his family as 'loud, talkative, argumentative, and possibly too close for its own good'. This, he explains, is very different from the non-Jewish English with whom they live. 'When I was growing up, my father always said, "Don't be a *shtummer*," [Yiddish for a silent bystander]. That's terrible advice in England .... The Jewish personality doesn't compliment the English personality. The English are reserved ... They're not open about things. And the Jewish personality doesn't complement that, so it rubs up against it' (this volume, p. 241).

Despite the diversity of Craig's immediate family, his Jewish characters are homogenized as secular, middle-class, London-based, much like their author. These characters undergo generational conflict, ethical disagreements about Israel and the meaning of their Judaism; they have secrets and suffer from guilt and the alienating effects of antisemitism. There are no religious ceremonies in his plays and almost no references to faith or a Jewish God. Unlike Stoppard, whose 'Jewish' play is anchored by history, or Marber, whose *Howard Katz* is a subjective, almost private play, Craig is repeatedly drawn to write about his 'lifeworld', the *world* of his Jewish identity – the family, the community, the problems and customs common among his people. Craig at one point said that he can only write about what he knows, and even his non-Jewish-themed plays contain the embryo of his British-Jewish world. He readily admits to being influenced by Ibsen (this volume, p. 242), and his plays too might be considered 'problem plays' in the sense that they deal seriously with real social and ethical problems.

*What We Did to Weinstein* (2005), his first Jewish-themed play, has all of these elements. It takes place in a holding cell in the Israeli West Bank, where Josh, British-born and Hendon-raised, who had left England to become a citizen and soldier in Israel, is being interrogated by an army officer after 'losing' a West Bank Arab, Yusef, he had arrested for being out after curfew. This space transforms into a variety of sites in West London, a bar, a wedding hall, an apartment, his father Max's hospice room. 'There should be a liquidity to the piece,' read the stage instructions; 'Scenes should run into each other' (Craig 2005: 13) – this is after all a memory play, taking place between 1994 and 2002. Max, Josh's dying father, is a famous British writer, a leftist and anarchist, vociferous and anti-Israel whose philosophy is to forget the past and live for a communal, egalitarian future. His own past includes having been sent to England as a child through the *Kindertransport* and fighting Mosley and his Union of British Fascists together with his friend, later his literary agent, Sam. Max is horrified by Josh's decision to seek his 'tribal identity' (as he puts it) in Israel and the two don't get along. Sam has a similar problem with his daughter, Sara, at one time Josh's girlfriend, a journalist who takes an anti-Israel view in her political writing. This has caused Sam much grief within the Jewish community. He, unlike

Max, is a Jew who can't forget the past, supports Israel, and believes that Jews are and will always be hated and alone. Additional characters include Yasmin, Max's lovely Muslim nurse, and Tariq, her belligerent, alienated brother. British (non-Jewish) minorities appear frequently in Craig's plays; here, a clear parallel is drawn between Josh and Tariq, who similarly leaves England for Pakistan, seeking his own 'tribal identity'. De Jongh wrote of the play in the *Evening Standard*, 'There is no more compelling or politically significant drama in town than Ryan Craig's *What We Did to Weinstein*. Nothing matches its scope or ambition. Craig writes with psychological astuteness about Jews and Arabs caught in the close bind of hatred and guilt' (2005).

The play ends with the officer again interrogating Josh about Yusef, and with the penultimate line: 'You know I never approved of having foreigners in the army. This can never truly be your country.' Craig clarified in interview: 'It's kind of a key moment in the play. I guess what I'm saying is – we diaspora Jews can be in a lot of places, we have the freedom to be here in the UK, to live in America, in Israel. But we are nowhere. We feel like we belong nowhere' (this volume, p. 242).

The following year, 2006, Craig's play *The Glass Room*, about Holocaust denial, was performed at the Hampstead Theatre, a theatre with a traditionally large Jewish audience.[15] 'Sian Thomas who played the denier, was incredibly brave,' Craig said in interview. 'That first Saturday night, a surprising proportion of the audience had *kippot* [head coverings worn by religious Jewish men]. You could feel the hostility. I mean, they knew she was acting, but the hostility!' (this volume, p. 244). The crux of the play is the confrontation between Elena, a revisionist historian whose recent book claims that gas chambers were a fiction created by Jews, and Myles, her lawyer. Myles, a reluctant half-Jew (his mother is Irish Catholic, much like Craig's own grandmother), tries to hide his Jewish identity while exploring the extent to which it is meaningful to him. His real agenda is to prevent the case from going to trial in order to deny Elena the status of a free-speech martyr. It is only when she finally falls into an antisemitic rant that he understands his own position.

> **Elena** [Jews] should never be allowed to feel safe here. Why should they? They think they're cleverer and funnier and holier than everyone else. They take power, they twist facts to their own advantage. They flash their money, the money they squeezed out of the tolerant England that rescued them from destruction yet again. No they must never be allowed to feel safe. To take root. Never.
>
> (Craig 2006: 92)

At the end of the play Myles admits that 'I never felt Jewish until I met her. I never felt anything much. She attacked something that was in my core. She activated it. What I do with it now ... I have no idea' (Craig 2006: 114). What is activated for Myles is a new form of knowledge. The abstract idea of Jew-hatred has become specific, real. For Craig, antisemitism is a core Jewish inheritance; 'Jews have changed in modern times,' he said, 'but they still have the vestige of thousands of years of persecution in their bones' (Nathan 2009).

Craig's later plays continue this line of ideological division among secular Jewish – diasporic – families. 'Diasporic' describes a subjective sense of being. All immigrant communities are, potentially, diasporic: living outside of their 'mother' country. Traditionally, diasporic groups hold onto a myth or collective memory of their homeland and regard it as their true home, to which they will eventually return (Safran 1991). For millennia, Jews considered themselves to be in *galut*, in exile from their true home, Zion. But today, Israel is a country that divides the Jews rather than unite them. Jews who consider England their true and only home will not define themselves as diasporic. But the desire for a place without antisemitism, where one does not need to feel self-consciously *different* and judged, reverberates in most of Craig's Jewish plays. While Israel is not a perfect option (as we see in *Weinstein*), it is still an option.

This option returns, again tragically, in Craig's 2011 play *The Holy Rosenbergs*,[16] a play loosely structured along the lines of Arthur Miller's *All My Sons*. It was performed at the Cottesloe theatre as a theatre-in-the-round and evoked mixed reviews. The play centres on the North London Rosenberg family, kosher caterers with business problems, on the eve of their son's funeral. Danny, a pilot in the Israeli air force, was killed in action over Gaza. The family's immediate problem centres on his sister Ruth, a human rights' lawyer on the UN legal team, investigating alleged abuses by the Israeli Defense Forces in Gaza. The family has been informed that if Ruth – considered a traitor by the community – speaks at Danny's funeral, the community will protest against her instead of attending. Patriarch David Rosenberg is doubly burdened since he is wracked by the fear that advice he recently gave his son may have convinced him to stay in the army (rather than return home), leading indirectly to his death. Critics compared *The Holy Rosenbergs* to Arthur Miller's *All My Sons* in terms of the plot secret, but also in terms of the ethical clarity that Craig pursues.

Pat(mat)riarchal inheritance is the explicit subject of Craig's latest Jewish-themed play – much as it is also in Mike Leigh's *Two Thousand Years* and Patrick Marber's *Howard Katz*, both performed as well at the Cottesloe. *Filthy Business*, Craig's fourteenth and most personal play, deals head-on with his own family's experience of being immigrants and of negotiating the British class system. It ran in 2017 at the Hampstead Theatre, starring the much-praised Sara Kestelman as the matriarch Yetta Solomon, who still oversees the successful rubber retail business she founded fifty years ago, and which is now being run by her sons and grandchildren. 'She makes the average tigress look lackadaisical in her fierce determination to keep her cubs together,' writes Paul Taylor in the *Independent*; 'But it's the 1960s now and the young folk have ideas of their own' (Taylor 2017). The play is a comedy of sorts – a comedy of family and time. On the stage a sign reading SOLOMON RUBBER Co Ltd. places us within the family business. The sign and Yetta's Yiddish-accented diction might mark the family as Jewish and as immigrants, but in every other way this is a story about the grip of family, any family, and of distorted love. As in almost all of Craig's plays, *Filthy Business* contains an ethical dilemma and a secret. It also, again, contains other minorities, especially a Nigerian employee newer to England but no less desperate to succeed than Yetta. Unlike his previous plays, this autobiographical portrait of three generations is less markedly Jewish and more epic – the word 'Jew' never appears in the text, but only, at one point, as graffiti. The play spans over two decades of political and economic change and portrays the loosening of family ties that Yetta, 'a superbly modern Mother Courage' figure, in Billington's words, cannot accept (2017). So she takes action.

In this play Craig leaves his diasporic position behind. This is the world of his English family, no less violent than the Israeli option that is not really an option in his plays, but rather the illusion of an option. With this play Craig places himself among the many immigrants who have had to fight for their place and who have made England their imperfect home.

\*\*\*\*

These three contemporaneous British-Jewish playwrights live and work in the same city, grew up in the same country and have more than one joint identity: as British Jews, as secular men from bourgeois homes, as playwrights and theatre people. Despite the very different ways they give expression to their identities – their styles are different, their voices speak in different idioms – they also have much in common. All three seek the same cultured audiences; indeed, all three have aimed at and been included in the National Theatre repertoire. Marber and Craig write, for the most part, about the lives of middle-class figures; Stoppard usually writes about figures who might fascinate a cultured middle-class audience. All have known antisemitism, all three are often concerned with ethical dilemmas, and they all seem to have a libertarian or a left-of-centre world view. Their diversity shows the breadth within what, in many ways, is a seemingly similar lifeworld – or, we might say that each has left his own particular warp within their common woof.

## Notes

1   See the Introduction in this volume for a discussion of this usage of 'European'.
2   Mike Nichols (1937–2014) was one of the most prominent Jewish-American voices in the mainstream film and Broadway theatre in the United States, emerging as a key film director of the 1960s with movies such as *Who's Afraid of Virginia Woolf* (1966) and *The Graduate* (1967). He is the Jewish grandson of the German-Jewish socialist theorist, pacifist and advocate of 'social anarchism', Gustav Landauer.
3   Stoppard published two nearly identical articles, in 1999, updating his biography: *'On Turning Out to Be Jewish'* and *'Another Country'*.
4   It is clear that Kenneth Stoppard did not approve of Martha's Jewish identity and they had agreed not to mention it.
5   'Ambivalence means survival in Stoppard's universe.' Nadel (2004): 22.
6   Ira Nadel called his 2002 biography of Stoppard *Double Act: A Life of Tom Stoppard* and writes: 'The repeated doublings in his work, not only of *Rosencrantz and Guildenstern* but the twins in *Hapgood* and the divided Housmans in *The Invention of Love*, mirror his own double identity as an Englishman and Czech, non-Jew and Jew.' (Nadel 2004: 21–2).
7   As David Hare said of Stoppard: 'On any libertarian issue, he tends to distinguish between those countries that use censorship and torture as systems of state and those who use it more randomly' (Gussow 1984).
8   The text of *Rock 'n' Roll* opens with a disclaimer, explaining that while the play's leading man, Jan, was born like Stoppard in Zlín, there the parallels end.
9   'Something is taking its course', Tynan is quoting from Samuel Beckett's *Endgame*.
10  Marber told me in interview that Stephen and Carl were inspired by his father and himself.
11  Emphasis added.
12  Norwood is the UK's largest Jewish charity supporting children, families and people with learning disabilities and autism. https://www.norwood.org.uk/
13  A personal email from Ryan Craig, 8 March 2018.
14  Ibid.
15  See the chapter by Garson in this volume.
16  In interview Craig explained that Nick Hytner, artistic director of the National Theatre, offered to produce *The Holy Rosenbergs* there after Craig's very successful adaptation of Tadeusz Słobodzianek's polemical play *Nasza klasa*, *Our Class*, for the National. The play presents a small nameless village in the northeast of Poland where up to 1,600 local Jews were rounded up by their neighbours, locked inside a small barn and burned to death – the well-known story of the pogrom in Jedwabne. Traditional Polish

historiography attributed the guilt for the now infamous pogrom to the Nazis. But Jan T. Gross' 2001 study, *Neighbors: The Destruction of the Jewish Community in Jedwabne*, proved it was done by the Polish people of the village themselves. The production was a huge success.

## References

Appleyard, B. (2017), 'Interview: Patrick Marber on How Football Cured His Writer's Block', *The Sunday Times*, 22 October.
Billington, M. (2015), 'Tom Stoppard: Playwright of Ideas Delivers a New Problem', *The Guardian*, 17 January.
Billington, M. (2017), 'Filthy Business Review – a Superbly Modern Mother Courage', *The Guardian*, 17 March.
Billington, M. (2020), 'Life, Love and *Leopoldstadt*: Don't Be Surprised if Tom Stoppard Gets Emotional', *The Guardian*, 27 February.
Bowie-Sell, D. (2016), 'Tom Hollander to Star in *Travesties* West End Transfer', *What's on Stage*, 28 October.
Brown, S. (2001), 'No Hidden Depths', review of *Howard Katz*. *Times Literary Review*, 22 June.
Craig, R. (2005), *What We Did to Weinstein*, London: Oberon Books.
Craig, R. (2006), *The Glass Room*, London: Oberon Books.
Craig, R. (2014), 'Wesker's Dream', *Jewish Quarterly*, 61 (1): 52–3.
De Jongh, N. (2005), 'The Bonds of Hatred', *Evening Standard*, 27 September.
Doherty, R. (2020), 'Norwood Orphan Is Reunited with Her Carer after 60 Years', *Jewish Chronicle*, 24 January.
Fish, S. (1976), 'Interpreting the Variorum', *Critical Inquiry*, 2 (3): 465–85.
Fish, S. (1980), *Is There a Text in This Class?*, Cambridge, MA and London: Harvard University Press.
Forrest, E. (1997), 'Patrick Marber: "I've Written a Play about Sex That People Quite Like – That Doesn't Make Me Dr Ruth"', *The Guardian*, 1 December.
Greene, R. A. (2001), 'British Playwright Makes Use of His Judaism', *Jewish Telegraphic Agency* (JTA), 6 September.
Gussow, M. (1984), 'The Real Tom Stoppard' *New York Times Magazine*, 1 January.
Harvey, C. (2020), 'Patrick Marber Interview: "Possibly Every Jew on the Planet Has an Exit Strategy – I Do,"' *Telegraph*, 24 January.
Hurst, M. (2016), '"Slowing Down the Going-Away Process" – Tom Stoppard and Soviet Dissent', *Contemporary British History*, 30 (4): 484–504.
Husserl, E. (1936/1970), *The Crisis of European Sciences and Transcendental Phenomenology*, trans. D. Carr, Evanston: Northern University Press.
Jaggi, M. (2008), 'You Can't Help Being What You Write', interview with Stoppard, *The Guardian*, 6 September.

Kellaway, K. (2020), 'Patrick Marber: "I'll Be in Therapy for the Rest of My Life – If I Can Afford It"', *The Guardian*, 7 March.

Kraus, B. (2015), 'The Life We Live and the Life We Experience: Introducing the Epistemological Difference between "Lifeworld" (*Lebenswelt*) and "Life Conditions" (*Lebenslage*),' *Social Work and Society*, 13 (2). Available online: http://www.socwork.net/sws/article/view/438

Nadel, I. (2000), 'Tom Stoppard and the Invention of Biography', *Modern Drama*, 43 (2): 157–70.

Nadel, I. (2002), *Double Act: A Life of Tom Stoppard*, London: Methuen.

Nadel, I. (2004), 'Writing Tom Stoppard', *Journal of Modern Literature*, 27 (3): 19–29.

Nathan, J. (2009), 'Ryan Craig Owns Up: I Have to Write about Jews', *Jewish Chronicle*, 1 October.

Nathan, J. (2015), 'Interview: Patrick Marber', *The Jewish Chronicle*, 30 July.

Nathan, J. (2020), 'Stoppard on *Leopoldstadt*: "I Think about the Holocaust, It Feels Like Every Day"', *Jewish Chronicle*, 23 January.

Safran, W. (1991), 'Diasporas in Modern Societies: Myths of Homeland and Return', *Diaspora: A Journal of Transnational Studies*, 1 (1): 83–99.

Stoppard, T. (1997), *The Invention of Love*, London: Grove Press.

Stoppard, T. (1999a), 'On Turning Out to Be Jewish', *Talk*, September: 190–4.

Stoppard, T. (1999b), 'Another Country', *Sunday Telegraph Magazine*, 10 October: 14–19.

Stoppard, T. (1999c), 'The Heart in the Closet', interview by Lyn Gardner, *Guardian Weekend*, 16 January: 15.

Stoppard, T. (2020), *Leopoldstadt*, London: Faber & Faber.

Taylor, P. (2017), 'Filthy Business, Hampstead Theatre, London, Review: Sara Kestelman Left Me Feeling as Weak with Laughter as Dame Edna Does', *The Independent*, 20 March.

Thompson, I. (2017), 'Patrick Marber: "When I Couldn't Write, I Felt Like a Zombie"', *Vanity Fair*, 21 March.

Tynan, K. (1977), 'Withdrawing with Style from the Chaos', *New Yorker*, 19 December.

# 11

# Staging Jewishness in the Twenty-First Century: Reflections on Key London Venues

Cyrielle Garson

That's my ... sense of what it was to be Jewish, it was definitely to be an outsider, but to be a kind of cowering outsider.

(*Listen, We're Family*, 2013)[1]

The English have never understood why anyone should be concerned with the mystery of identity. That's because they're so certain of their own. The notion of belonging or not belonging is alien to them because they belong.

(Harwood 2008: 62–3)

Is there such a thing as a Jewish influence in contemporary British theatre, and if so, where does it begin and end? And how might it be defined? While British-Jewish playwrights such as Harold Pinter, Tom Stoppard, Patrick Marber and Arnold Wesker are often recognized for their specific voices within the rich diversity of contemporary British theatre, this chapter posits that British-Jewish theatre directors are in comparison less visible or rather that they are paradoxically both central and unidentified. A good example of this is Julia Pascal, who became the first woman director at the National Theatre in 1978, paving the way for many other women directors. Another example is the late Braham Murray, who became the youngest artistic director in the country when he took over Century Theatre, a theatre company based in Manchester, in September 1965 at the age of twenty-two. Indeed, as this chapter will seek to demonstrate, household names who have led key London theatre venues such as Dominic Cooke (Royal Court Theatre) and Nicolas Kent (Tricycle Theatre) are seemingly more prudent when it comes to the foregrounding of their Jewish background. This begs the question as to whether this intricate state of affairs may have had any bearing on the trajectory contemporary British theatre was to ultimately take in the new millennium. But what I want to consider here are, more specifically, the actual possibilities for the staging of Jewishness and how the politics of place and representation intersected in the twenty-first century, at an unprecedented time when five British-Jewish directors occupied some of the most coveted roles in the industry.

## British-Jewish Theatre and Venues in Context: Setting the Scene

In 2011, two prominent British-Jewish artistic directors – Nicholas Hytner and Dominic Cooke – were named the second top movers and shakers of the theatre industry by *The Stage* newspaper (Shenton 2011). That same year, Nicolas Kent received the prestigious Liberty Human Rights Award for his extraordinary political theatre work at the Tricycle Theatre in North London.[2] In neither Hytner nor Cooke's case was there any mention of their Jewish background; thus, although such mention is rarely expected, outside of Jewish journals or newspapers, it allows no apparent way to engage publicly with Jewishness or to acknowledge the considerable role of Jewish figures in the UK theatre industry. Thus Jewish theatre artists are simply seen as 'white', upholding the liberal fiction of a monolithic white Britishness.[3] Indeed, as Tanika Gupta argues in an interview with Lyn Gardner: 'Nobody goes round describing Harold Pinter as a Jewish white playwright' (Gardner 2006).[4] It thus seems that the discretion with which British Jews supposedly carry, or rather whisper, their Jewishness and minimize their 'difference' is still publicly favoured. Strikingly, in the introduction to his first explicitly Jewish play, Mike Leigh confesses that he spent most of his adult life 'keeping quiet about [his] Jewishness' (2006: v). Perhaps the fullest expression of this self-depreciation, prompted by a marginalizing British society, can be seen in the fact that Tom Stoppard only wrote his first openly Jewish play – *Leopoldstadt* – in 2019.[5]

Although Jewishness is an uncontested staple of New York City theatre, Jewish involvement in contemporary British theatre is significantly harder to read. A century ago, London's East End acquired a notable reputation for its Yiddish theatre scene, which became a lifeline for the displaced Jewish community post–First World War. In this context, Yiddish theatre helped sustain the Jewish community's roots and values, as well as their dreams and aspirations for a better future. More recently, as this chapter will demonstrate, the 2000s saw an unprecedented and little-documented surge of artistic directors with a Jewish background heading some of London's most prestigious venues, including the National Theatre and the Royal Court Theatre. At this juncture, it is particularly interesting to observe that while the Jewish community – one of Britain's oldest minority groups – represents less than 0.5 per cent of the total UK population, numerous talented Jewish personae, such as Sir Nicholas Hytner, Sam Mendes CBE, Mike Leigh OBE FRSL, Peter Brook CH CBE and the late Elyse Dodgson, have all played pivotal roles in contemporary British theatre history.

Most famously, in 1968, Jewish politician George Strauss secured the seismic abolition of theatre censorship; in 1997, Jewish-American actor and director Sam Wanamaker brought the Globe Theatre – the most popular theatre in London – back to life on the south bank of the Thames. One of the best-loved playhouses in London, the Shakespeare Globe, commemorates this work, now boasting the indoor Sam Wanamaker Playhouse. In addition to the National Dorfman Theatre, both the Clore Learning Centre and the Rayne Centre are also named after philanthropist members of the same West London synagogue.[6] What is more, some of the most luminous landmark performances that graced the contemporary British stage took place under five visionary directors of Jewish background: Nicolas Kent at the Tricycle Theatre (1984–2012), Sam Mendes at the Donmar Warehouse (1992–2002), David Lan at the Young Vic (2000–18), Nicholas Hytner at the National Theatre (2003–15), and Dominic Cooke at the Royal Court (2006–13). Their productions include David Hare's *The Blue Room* (1998) starring Nicole Kidman, *The Colour of Justice* (1999) by the Tricycle Theatre, *Elmina's Kitchen* by Kwame Kwei-Armah (2003), Jez Butterworth's *Jerusalem* (2009), Alecky Blythe and Adam Cork's *London Road* (2011), Tim Crouch's *The Author* (2009), and Arthur Miller's *A View from the Bridge* in a version directed by Ivo van Hove (2014). These, taken together, have well earned their place in the ever-expanding canon of contemporary British theatre, and the latter, conversely, would be unthinkable without them.

If most critics and commentators argue that the strand of work known as contemporary British theatre is the result of a productive cross-fertilization (Billington 2002; Haydon 2013; Sierz 2005), its Jewish influence has to this day seldom been considered in mainstream discourse. Twenty years into the twenty-first century and at a time when antisemitism has disturbingly resurfaced in British public life, it is especially important to acknowledge the impact of Anglo-Jewish artists on British theatre. The staging of Stephen Laughton's *One Jewish Boy* (2018), which explores rising antisemitism in the UK, posed a challenge and was itself met with antisemitism. As these lines are being written, more posters of the play have been found with swastikas drawn over the word 'Jewish' in London, and Palestinian flags have been posted online in response to mentions of the play. Undoubtedly, British-Jewish theatre-makers respond to a much wider spectrum of artistic simulation than their Jewishness alone. However, such works importantly help remedy an industry-wide blind spot by tackling prevalent societal stereotypes and prejudices.

As we have seen, the more one observes the contemporary pairing of Britishness and Jewishness in British theatre, the more one must consider the politics of place, the abstract and the systemic designs one lives within and labours under. This particular state of affairs will be described in detail in the next section.

## The Challenges of Representation and the Paradoxical Position of Jewish Artistic Directors in the UK

Looking at the available body of theatre criticism, I argue that British-Jewish directors have been relatively overlooked in comparison to their fellow playwrights. Jewish directors in the UK must contend with both inclusion and exclusion from the mainstream of British cultural life: they typically occupy a paradoxical position as both established and hidden from view, being ubiquitous and marginal presences at the same time. According to the title of Nathan Abram's collection of essays on Jews and Jewishness in British film, television and popular culture, it is largely a case of being 'hidden in plain sight' (2016). While it is impossible to give full justice to the entirety of these five artistic directors' work within this chapter, it may be useful to chart some of their major accomplishments.

First, Nicolas Kent decidedly put the Tricycle Theatre, a small 235-seat theatre in North London, on the map during his pioneering twenty-eight-year tenure (1984–2012). Among his many achievements in the realm of political theatre, Kent's tribunal plays[7] inspired a new generation of theatre-makers to create verbatim works. These plays also reached a global audience of 25 million people, thanks to BBC television and radio adaptations.

Let us also recall that British-Jewish director Sam Mendes ran the small 250-seat Donmar Warehouse in Convent Garden for ten years (1992–2002). Under Mendes' memorable tenure, this Off-West End venue largely exceeded its former function as a studio space for the Royal Shakespeare Company to become an extremely successful and award-winning London playhouse, whose lively productions often crossed the Atlantic. Notably, during Mendes' tenure, *Assassins* won the Best New Musical Award in 1992 (Critics' Circle). Mendes also won *The Evening Standard* Theatre Award for best director the same year for *The Rise and Fall of Little Voice* and was awarded the Best Director Award at the 1995 Critics' Circle and the 1996 Laurence Olivier Award (Best Director) for *The Glass Menagerie*, and productions such as

*Cabaret* (1993), *The Blue Room* (1998) and *The Real Thing* (1999) successfully transferred to the United States.

As for David Lan, he markedly defined the Young Vic in Waterloo as a dynamic place for experimentation and innovation, to the point that this Off-West End venue was sometimes deemed to be the 'UK's most influential theatre' (Jays 2017) and one of the most admired theatres in the world (Lefkowitz 2018). More specifically, during his eighteen-year tenure, Lan acquired a reputation for developing the careers of young theatre-makers, reaching out to bold directors from across the globe, and challenging 'the way that emerging (English) directors think about their arts' (Boenisch 2015).[8]

Nicholas Hytner's remarkable twelve years at the helm of the National, Britain's most iconic theatre (2003–15), were characterized by spectacular successes, such as *The History Boys* (2004), *War Horse* (2007) and *The Curious Incident of the Dog in the Night-Time* (2012). His tenure included the introduction of National Theatre Live cinema broadcasts around the world, opening the National's doors to a broader audience than ever before and a mainstream redefinition of the role of contemporary theatre.[9] Andrew Haydon cogently observed that 'here was an NT regime with its sights clearly trained on the twenty-first century' (2013: 89), most notably through its unexpected collaborations with independent companies such as Kneehigh and Punchdrunk. The National was also determined to reflect the nation and commissioned Black British and South Asian plays, as well as plays directed at young people.

Finally, Dominic Cooke presided over one of the Royal Court's most dazzling periods (2006–13), with more than 130 plays staged, bringing an exciting new generation of playwrights to the stage, including Bola Agbaje, Mike Bartlett, Alia Bano, Anya Reiss and Polly Stenham.[10] To mitigate a culture constantly gravitating towards the new, Cooke also worked to nurture the next step of emerging writers such as Lucy Prebble and Laura Wade, while also welcoming established writers such as Richard Bean, Jez Butterworth, Caryl Churchill, Martin Crimp, David Eldridge, Simon Stephens and Roy Williams.

Having briefly reviewed the voluminous and substantial work of these five British-Jewish artistic directors, I argue that their role in contemporary British theatre has been to create repertoires and shape contemporary theatre.[11] For all that, I contend that the first decade of the twenty-first century was not necessarily a particularly fertile ground for the staging of Jewishness and that the quality, quantity and volume of conversations on British-Jewishness in multicultural Britain did not significantly increase as a result of the work of these five driven and innovative directors. Mendes' tenure at the Donmar, for instance, was not exceptionally marked by an abundance of Jewish plays, apart from the aforementioned award-winning *Cabaret* and *The Blue Room*.

Clearly, for the attentive observer of contemporary British theatre, for all the presence, success and creativity of Jewish practitioners on either side of the footlights, few have openly expressed their Jewish identity or shown a particular concern with Jewish issues in their work. Even Hytner, who openly calls himself a 'Jewish director' (2017), said in a recent interview with Jewish theatre critic John Nathan: 'I don't think I've gone out specifically to look for material of Jewish interest' (2011). Indeed, if the new millennium is widely held to be a golden period, with one of the latest reports from the British Theatre Consortium concluding that 'for the first time since records began, new work has overtaken revivals in the British theatre repertoire (new work constituted 59 per cent of all productions)' (2015), the representation of British-Jewishness on stage did not necessarily follow suit, making overtly Jewish characters the exception rather than the norm.[12] Writing in 2003, Julia Pascal explained that it is rather difficult for British artists to receive public funds to support such plays: 'We are told quite plainly by the Arts Council that "Jews are not a priority"' (2003: 74). Put another way, the theatre establishment does not consider British Jews a minority group worthy of exploration, pointing to a more or less tacit censorship that almost systematically silences their voices within the subsidized and mainstream sector. Arguably, within the current system, British dramatists can only write obliquely about their experience of Jewishness, should they wish to be produced on the main stages and circumvent the existing institutional blocks.

Crucially on one level, the overall lack of British-Jewish voices and the continuing absence of their representation is linked to the convenient forgetting of earlier immigration to Britain in the surge of interest and concern in much more recent arrivals. In *Rewriting the Nation*, British critic Aleks Sierz calls this forgetting the 'cult of the new' (2011: 15). Contemporary British theatre is often described as political, referring to its dutiful voicing of minority groups such as South Asians and Black Britons, as well as refugees and asylum seekers. However, putting the British-Jewish experience on stage could decidedly reveal some of the hidden dynamics of British society as a whole, another fascinating way of seeing within Britishness. While it would be wrong, I think, to imply that one particular minority by virtue of its 'outsider' (Wandor 2001: 141) position can offer better insights into British identities, Jewish Britons can be said to uniquely inhabit a liminal space in British society, and, as such, their work participates in the ongoing exploration of British culture(s) and their fault lines.

The simultaneous ubiquity of Jewish practitioners is thus paralleled by a relative absence of Jewish voice on the British stage. In other words, it is a contemporary history that is marked by both the visibility and camouflage of Jewish material. Yet, on closer examination, there is also cause for optimism regarding British-Jewish representation on stage in the twenty-first century. For one, the Hampstead Theatre firmly occupies a central position in this new history, due mostly to the fact that 'its core audience is Jewish' (Sierz 2011: 66). As a result, more explicitly Jewish plays, or what Aleks Sierz calls the 'Jewish-issue play' (Sierz 2006) and John Nathan terms the 'Jewish-interest play' (Nathan 2011), appear to be thriving, with plays like Charlotte Eilenberg's *The Lucky Ones* (2002), Alexis Zegerman's comedies *Lucky Seven* (2008) or *Holy Sh!it* (2018) and Ryan Craig's continuous exploration of the problematics of Jewish identity in *The Glass Room* (2006) and *Filthy Business* (2017). Something similar seems to have been happened at the National. Most memorably, filmmaker Mike Leigh produced his first self-declared 'Jewish play', *Two Thousand Years*, which sold out within days in the fall of 2005 and subsequently moved from the Cottesloe to play at the larger Lyttleton auditorium.[13] There were also, among others, Ryan Craig's *The Holy Rosenbergs* (2011), Tadeusz Słobodzianek's Holocaust play *Our Class* (translated by Craig in 2009) as well as both Nicholas Wright's *Travelling Light* (2012) and Richard Bean's East End play addressing immigration, *England People Very Nice* (2009) featuring hora-dancing Hassids.

An Off-West End theatre venue also deserves a special mention here. As a local theatre with a strong interest in its community, the formerly named Tricycle Theatre produced Jewish-interest plays such as Richard Norton-Taylor's *Nuremberg War Crimes Trial* (1996), just like it produced Black and Irish plays. Supported by the Pears and One to One Children Foundations, the Tricycle Muslim Jewish Youth Theatre Group (MUJU) was created in 2004 to encourage young Muslims and Jews to meet for weekly drama workshops to allow their members to express themselves creatively and explore themes of interest (e.g. issues of race, religion, poverty, social justice and youth culture). As for the Royal Court Theatre, it would seem to have taken a comparatively different path in contemporary British history despite the presence of Dominic Cooke at its helm and a celebrated revival of Arnold Wesker's *Chicken Soup with Barley* in 2011, especially due to the infamous controversy surrounding Caryl Churchill's *Seven Jewish Children: A Play for Gaza* in 2009.

Similarly at the Young Vic, the revival of the late Alan Rickman and Katherine Viner's *My Name Is Rachel Corrie* in 2017 was met with hostility in some quarters. It should be noted here though that since Harold Pinter's 2005 Nobel Prize in Literature and Arnold Wesker's knighthood for services to drama the following year, there are ample signs that the situation is beginning to change for this hyphenated minority.[14] In this respect, JW3, 'the new postcode for Jewish life' – whose website claims to have transformed the British-Jewish landscape in London since its opening in September 2013 (Sherwood 2017) and timely 'point[s] to a new confidence and visibility among British Jews' (Abrams 2016) – is an interesting case in point. Indeed, with its 200-seat hall and a smaller 60-seat studio on Finchley Road in North West London, Britain's first Jewish community centre seeks to offer a much-needed and authentic picture of the complexities of British-Jewish identity to a general audience.[15] More implicitly, its aim is also to help revitalize the British-Jewish community and maintain a strong sense of shared Jewish community in Britain.

Based on extensive interviews with dozens of Jewish Londoners from all parts of the city – Hendon, Enfield, Ruislip, the East End and Essex – and among spouses, parents and offspring, on the topics of family, identity, religion and relationships, JW3's first theatrical commission, Kerry Shale and Matthew Lloyd's *Listen, We're Family* (2013), the first British-Jewish verbatim play, compellingly set out to explore with four actors on stage playing a handful of characters in ninety minutes sharp, what it means to be both British and Jewish in the twenty-first century.[16] Through a poignant tapestry of successive (hilarious at times) real-life characters ranging from a middle-aged man sitting in his communal garden, a barber in his nineties with a love of Yiddish slang, and a gay man in his twenties from St Albans to a freelance academic, broadcaster and writer in his forties, a divorcee at odds with her son, and a woman in her eighties who grew up in the old East End talking about their variously loving or troubled home lives, the play also touches on more serious issues including Israeli politics, immigration and antisemitism in Britain. As Carol Martin reminds us, verbatim theatre 'has the ability to portray Jewish people apart from the typical representational strategies and stereotypes' (2012: 165). In other words, this strand of theatre practice forcefully enables more authentic and complex intersectional British-Jewish experiences to be represented on stage, including those of British-Jewish women who are otherwise almost entirely absent in new writing.

Cleverly juxtaposing humour and reflection, JW3's second commission *Making Stalin Laugh* (2014) was also a brand new piece of British-Jewish theatre purposefully avoiding the more obvious topics of the Holocaust and Israel. This time, it took a non-verbatim approach to tell the unique true story of the Moscow State Yiddish Theatre (known as GOSET) and its charismatic and world-renowned artistic director Solomon Mikhoels under Stalin, before the company was eventually closed and its actors executed. However, it should also be noted that there are some limitations inherent in the viability of the theatre model proposed by JW3. Its main role may be conflated with an act of compensation – in the second case giving Jewish writer and comedian David Schneider a chance to write a piece of Jewish theatre rather than tackling contemporary issues endemic to the British theatre industry today.[17] Notwithstanding this last point, JW3, like the newly formed Jewish Artists' Collective, is a step in the right direction, however small a step it may be.[18]

## Conclusion: Thinking Contemporary British Theatre Anew

I have argued that there is an almost untold story about Jewish participation in contemporary British theatre, which can be attributed to both an ambivalent attitude towards Jewishness in the contemporary moment and the widespread illusion of inclusion within society more broadly. Indeed, more often than not, the assumption of white privilege overrides any consideration of challenge or vulnerability. Arguably, this cultural invisibility or camouflage can have particularly damaging consequences for the British-Jewish community, which has repeatedly witnessed an erasure of authentic Jewish representation despite the important work of numerous venues in London, including our last example, JW3. Indeed, each of the examples presented in this article revealed that the theatre establishment had (knowingly or not) underrepresented the experience of British Jews.

Not only have the five aforementioned Jewish household names – Cooke, Hytner, Kent, Lan and Mendes – helped shape contemporary British theatre, but their work also has had important and transformational implications for other practitioners and theatres in the UK and further afield. While it may be too early to meaningfully assess the full legacy of these British-Jewish artistic directors, they have left their mark on the theatre industry both nationally and globally and on public discourse. As such, it is no longer tenable to read contemporary British theatre as a purely gentile narrative, and such a reading must be challenged accordingly.

## Notes

1   The play text being unpublished, this quotation was written using my notes while attending the show at JW3.
2   The Tricycle Theatre underwent a change of name last year and is now known as the Kiln Theatre. Although Nicolas Kent rarely mentions his Jewish background in interviews (his father was a Jewish-German refugee who arrived in Britain in 1936 and changed his name from 'Kahn' to the

more English-sounding name 'Kent' during the war), he admitted in one of them that his political vision for the Tricycle was a direct consequence of the antisemitism he suffered at school: '[T]hose experiences made me empathise with those on the receiving end of Islamophobia, and it made me empathise with being black' (Jeffries 2012). Nicolas Kent is also mentioned in *The Palgrave Dictionary of Anglo-Jewish History* (Rubinstein and Jolles 2011: 512–13).

3  The same year, the Jewish Museum in London began to address this gap by hosting an exhibition entitled 'Entertaining the Nation: Stars of Music, Stage and Screen', celebrating the role of Jewish immigrants in shaping Britain's popular culture. More recently, the Jewish Museum in London launched a new and ambitious project called 'Jewish Lives' (with the help of the Kirsh Charitable Foundation and including a book series, an interactive digital platform and a visual display at the museum) in six parts that tells the stories of the remarkable Jewish men and women in British society, with one of the books entirely dedicated to their role in the arts with over 250 notable Jewish figures.

4  Harold Pinter's upbringing as an East End Jew was clearly important in his development, but it was rarely reflected in his plays as an overt theme. See Mark Taylor-Batty's chapter in this volume for a deeper consideration of this aspect in Pinter's work.

5  British-Jewish writer Naomi Alderman partly accounts for this British specificity by stating in her novel *Disobedience* that there is a vicious circle 'in which the Jewish fear of being noticed and the natural British reticence interact [and that] [t]hey feed off each other so that British Jews cannot speak, cannot be seen, value *absolute invisibility* above all other virtues' (2007: 50). Similarly, in Stoppard's *Leopoldstadt*, Leo, a British-Jewish character, confesses at the end of the play that he knew he was Jewish, but in England 'it wasn't something you had to *know*, or something people had to know about other people' (2019).

6  Importantly, British-Jewish men have also been involved in building several West End theatres, such as Sidney Bernstein and the Phoenix Theatre in the late 1920s, and distinguished Jewish architect Sir Denys Lasdun was the man behind the Royal National Theatre on the Southbank in 1976.

7  Tribunal plays are single-sourced verbatim plays scrupulously based on the transcripts from high-profile legal cases. Kent's first tribunal play, *Half the Picture* (1994), became the first play ever to be performed in the Houses of Parliament and won a Freedom of Information Campaign Award. The video recording of *The Colour of Justice* (1999) has also notably been used in the context of racial awareness training by some of the police forces.

8  Since the theatre reconstruction in 2006, Lan added two new spaces: the Maria and the Clare. And since winning an Olivier Award in 2003 for the whole season, the Young Vic has won every other major London and New York theatre award, several times over. David Lan finally received the Special Award at the Critics' Circle Awards in 2018 for his role in British theatre, which also includes his work within the local community around the theatre.

9   According to the Society of London Theatres, the NT became responsible for approximately a third of the entire play-going public in London in 2009, and in 2012 it achieved its highest ever income.
10  The Royal Court also received the award for 'London Theatre of the Year' in the first ever Stage 100 Awards in 2011. Not surprisingly, Dominic Cooke was awarded a CBE in the 2014 New Year's Honours List for services to drama.
11  It is important to acknowledge that artistic directors do not work in isolation and that the success of one venue during a given period is unquestionably a collective effort. I also contend that a particular director's vision is instrumental in shaping the artistic direction(s) pursued by a given institution.
12  When there are British-Jewish characters, such as in Alan Bennett's *The History Boys* (2004), Mark Ravenhill's *Shoot/Get Treasure/Repeat* (2008), or David Eldridge's *The Knot of the Heart* (2011), they tend to be peripheral or incidental, rather than central.
13  Leigh saw Kwame Kwei-Armah's *Elmina's Kitchen* at the NT in 2003, and its portrayal of a Black community inspired him to revisit his own roots (Carlson 2018: 205). However, the play's structure relied heavily on the presumed gentile audience's incomprehension of Jewishness, rather than a confident assertion of its distinctiveness (Vice 2016: 43).
14  In October 2017, Nicholas Hytner opened the Bridge Theatre, a new and promising theatre building, seating 900 people with former NT executive director Nick Starr. This was the first large-scale commercial venue to open in central London since 1973. In his *Balancing Acts* (2017), Hytner also hints at the possibility of building other theatres in the future.
15  By early 2015, JW3 completed a merger with the London Jewish Cultural Centre (LJCC), with the latter moving its operations from its former site at Ivy House in Hampstead to JW3's prominent site in North-West London (Cohen 2014).
16  More specifically, the play used the 'headphone verbatim' technique – a 'paperless form of performance featuring the faithful reproduction of speech patterns whereby actors are required to wear headphones and speak along to a sequence of carefully edited audio interviews' (Garson 2014: 51) – popularized in the UK by the mainstream work of Alecky Blythe. Following on from this, the running time of the show was exactly fifty minutes for Act One and forty minutes for Act Two.
17  British-Jewish theatre is only one of the numerous missions of West Hampstead's impressive JW3 cultural centre and whatever the merits of offering a home for such a worthy excavation with sporadic reviews in the national press, its reach is rather limited (no planned publication of the play texts or public subsidy, no access to bigger stages, current resources making the creation of cutting-edge work particularly challenging, a rarity of second productions, and the impossibility at times to offer more than a staged reading, as was the case with Eva Hoffman's *The Ceremony*, discussed at length by Phyliss Lassner in this volume).

18  The Jewish Artists' Collective was formed in 2019 following a row over cultural appropriation and misrepresentation in a recent production of *Falsettos*. Their main aim is to encourage a broader conversation about engagement with Jewish stories and representation in the British theatre industry (Lenson 2019).

## References

Abrams, N., ed. (2016), *Hidden in Plain Sight: Jews and Jewishness in British Film, Television, and Popular Culture*, Evanston, IL: Northwestern University Press.
Abrams, N. (2017), 'Jews Go Pop', in The Jewish Museum London, *Jewish Lives Project. Arts*, 325–36, London: The Jewish Museum.
Alderman, N. (2007), *Disobedience*, London: Penguin Books.
Billington, M. (2002), 'The Players', *The Guardian*, 6 July.
Billington, M. (2012), 'J Is for Jewish Dramatists', *The Guardian*, 14 February.
Boenisch, P. (2015), *Directing Scenes and Senses: The Thinking of Regie*, Manchester: Manchester University Press. Kindle Edition.
British Theatre Consortium (2015), 'Project: British Theatre Repertoire', BTC, 14 May.
Carlson, M. (2018), *Affect, Animals, and Autists: Feeling around the Edges of the Human in Performance*, Ann Arbor, MI: University of Michigan Press.
Cohen, J. (2014), 'Exclusive: JW3 and LJCC to Merge', *Times of Israel*, 17 September.
Gardner, L. (2006), Interview with Tanika Gupta 'Write about Arranged Marriage? No Way!' *The Guardian*, 25 July.
Garson, C. (2014), 'Remixing Politics: The Case of Headphone-Verbatim Theatre in Britain', *Journal of Contemporary Drama in English*, 2 (1): 50–62.
Harwood, R. (2008), *An English Tragedy*, London: Faber & Faber.
Haydon, A. (2013), 'Theatre in the 2000s', in D. Rebellato (ed.), *Modern British Playwriting 2000–2009: Voices, Documents, New Interpretations*, 40–98, London: Methuen Drama.
Hytner, N. (2017), *Balancing Acts: Behind the Scenes at the National Theatre*, London: Vintage. Kindle Edition.
Jays, D. (2017), 'The Secret of David Lan's Success as the Young Vic's Artistic Director', *The Times*, 30 July.
Jeffries, S. (2012), 'The Saturday Interview: Nicolas Kent', *The Guardian*, 18 February.
Laughton, S. (2018), *One Jewish Boy*, London: Nick Hern.
Lefkowitz, A. (2018), 'Former Young Vic Artistic Director David Lan to Receive Special Award', *Broadway News*, 6 April.
Leigh, M. (2006), *Two Thousand Years*, London: Faber and Faber.
Lenson, A. (2019), 'If Not Now, When?: Falsettogate, and What It Teaches Us about Meaningful Minority Inclusion', *Exeunt Magazine*, 2 September.

Martin, C. (2012), 'Apart from the Document: Jews and Jewishness in Theater of the Real', in E. Nahshon (ed.), *Jews and Theater in an Intercultural Context*, 89–118, Leiden and Boston, MA: Brill.

Nathan, J. (2011), 'How Nicholas Hytner Made the National a Jewish Theatre', *The Jewish Chronicle*, 1 December.

Pascal, J. (2003), 'Creating Space for Jewish Theatre', *Jewish Quarterly*, 50 (3): 73–6.

Rubinstein, W., and M. A. Jolles, eds (2011), *The Palgrave Dictionary of Anglo-Jewish History*, London: Palgrave Macmillan.

Shenton, M. (2011), 'ATG's Top List of 20 Most Influential People in the U.K. Theatre Announced', *Playbill*, 6 January.

Sherwood, H. (2017), 'Ultra-Orthodox Rabbis Call for Boycott of Jewish Arts Centre Over LGBT Support', *The Guardian*, 3 December.

Sierz, A. (2005), 'Beyond Timidity', *PAJ: A Journal of Performance Art*, 27 (3): 55–61.

Sierz, A. (2006), 'Playwright Ryan Craig on Holocaust Denial', *Theatre Voice*, 11 December. Available online: http://www.theatrevoice.com/audio/interview-ryan-craig-the-playwright-talks-to-aleks-sierz-ab/ (accessed September 2019).

Sierz, A. (2011), *Rewriting the Nation: British Theatre Today*, London: Methuen Drama.

Stoppard, T. (2019), *Leopoldstadt*, London: Faber and Faber. Kindle Edition.

Vice, S. (2016), '"Becoming English": Assimilation and Its Discontents in Contemporary British-Jewish Literature', in A. Reiter and L. Cairns (eds), *Jewish Identities in Contemporary Europe*, 100–11, London and New York: Routledge.

Wandor, M. (2001), *Post-War British Drama: Looking Back in Gender*, London and New York: Routledge.

# Part Four

# Television Drama

12

# British-Jewish Television Drama: Jack Rosenthal to the Present

Sue Vice

Television drama is sometimes thought to fall between the genres of theatre and cinema and to offer pale imitations of both. However, the genre has moved far beyond the efforts of its early days to replicate in visual and narrative terms the conventions of staged plays and is customarily now approached as an art form with its own techniques, distinct from those of cinema. Such critics as Christine Geraghty (2003) and John Caughie (2000) argue for television drama's distinctive institutional and aesthetic history as well as its public and political significance. While its broad appeal and ephemeral nature have been regarded as television's liabilities, these features are, rather, its great strength and the reason for its influence and significance. Such a medium offers the chance to represent and reflect upon contemporary cultural trends as they occur, summed up by Daniel Reast (2017) as changes in how 'social class, race and racism, and women' are shown. The present chapter will focus on a version of these very features as they appear in British-Jewish television drama: class as it intersects with, or is expressed by means of, Jewish social life; Judaism in the form of cultural and religious difference; and gender, taking the form, in the examples here, of representations of Jewish masculinity.

Within such an established tradition of critical legitimation, the role of television drama in relation to British-Jewish cultural production has been less widely studied. Some critics, including James Jordan (2012), Ruth Gilbert (2014), Rachel Garfield (2016) and Isabelle Seddon (2020), have begun the work of emphasizing the long legacy of a specifically Jewish strand in British television history. Drawing on this critical heritage, it is clear that, although British-Jewish drama on television has a long and coherent lineage, it is one that is rarely acknowledged in accounts of this art form. Even the best-known examples of television drama of a British-Jewish kind are not usually brought together under such a rubric and are seen instead in the more generic terms of such categories as generation gap, culture clash or work-based situation dramas. Thus, for instance, the comedy series *A Little Big Business* (1963–5), in which the Jewish owner of a furniture business, the Latvian-born Marcus Lieberman (David Kossoff), works alongside his son Simon (Francis Matthews), fits the first and third of these sitcom categories, its friction arising from the younger man's wish to modernize his father's old-fashioned work practices. The popular series *Never Mind the Quality, Feel the Width* (1967–71), about a Jewish (John Bluthal) and a Catholic tailor (Joe Lynch) who go into business together, falls into the second and third categories as a culture clash comedy set in a tailor's shop. The series *My Son Reuben* (1975) follows the pattern of the earlier dramas by presenting a hybrid of British with Jewish cultural detail, as is evident for instance in the form of the Catholic tailor's Irish background in *Never Mind the Quality*. In *My Son Reuben*, the notion of an 'apron strings' comedy about the eponymous 35-year-old bachelor Reuben Greenberg (Bernard Spear) who lives with his mother Fay (Lila Kaye) draws on the detail and anxieties of a specifically British version of Jewish life. Reuben reluctantly works in his late father's dry-cleaning shop, is attracted to a non-Jewish woman and tries to take his mother on holiday to Israel instead of her usual destination of Bournemouth. The generic British sitcom scenarios of generation gap, cross cultural and workplace drama all cohere around the comic trope of a devoted and demanding mother, who is constructed in this case as Jewish.

As these examples suggest, Jewish-related material in British television drama is often subsumed by, or read in relation to, mainstream British concerns. This is the case even for the works of a Jewish-identified scriptwriter such as Jack Rosenthal, among whose plays are those based on his own biography as the Manchester-born member of a working-class Jewish family, notably the television dramas *The Evacuees* (directed by Alan Parker in 1975) and *Bye Bye Baby* (directed by Edward Bennett in 1992). While the BBC Play for Today *The Evacuees* is a fictionalized version of Rosenthal's own unhappy experience of wartime evacuation with his older brother David, *Bye Bye Baby* represents his post-war experience of national service as 'the only Jew … in the Navy' (Rosenthal 2005: 85). The third of Rosenthal's works which centres on Jewish concerns is his Play for Today *Bar Mitzvah Boy* (directed by Michael Tuchner in 1976). Despite the prominence in his oeuvre of the two Plays for Today, on which the discussion here focuses, neither the Jewish content of Rosenthal's work, nor his influence as a Jewish writer has been fully acknowledged or explored (for analyses which have begun this exploration, see Dunn 2011; Garfield 2016; Vice 2009, 2013). Rosenthal's writing is most commonly identified instead in the terms of the medium's historiography as a central example of British television drama's 'golden age' of the 1960s and 1970s. This epoch arises from these mid-century decades in which, as Catherine Johnson puts it, 'the funding structures and ideological values of public service television were seen to provide the space for aesthetic innovation and socio-political purpose' (2007: 56). It is also a generic term, invoking a sense of the era's writing as predominantly of a gently comic social-realist kind.

Yet Rosenthal's contribution to the British-Jewish literary canon is evident on his own account and in relation to his influence on such contemporary television drama as Simon Amstell's *Grandma's House* (directed by Christine Glennon), co-written with Dan Swimer, and Robert Popper's *Friday Night Dinner* (directed by Steve Bendelack and Martin Dennis). This influence can be perceived in relation to shared themes and tropes, as well as the distinctive technique used by all three writers by means of which the Jewish context is taken for granted rather than being glossed or explained. The elements held in common include a focus in each case on the construction of masculinity within the family, a comic clash between material and spiritual attitudes, relations with the non-Jewish world, and a visual and cultural setting which displays details of the sociology and history of both Britain and British-Jewish life. In each case, a central means by which such elements are brought together, offering occasions for comic discord among the characters, is that of the dinner table, as shown by each of the examples that follow. As Lez Cooke argues, in a study which includes a chapter on *Bar Mitzvah Boy*, dinner table scenes in television drama are valuable in allowing the sustained representation of domestic intimacy, requiring particular kinds of camera work and editing in order to show the spatial and emotional relationships between individuals (Cooke 2013: 2–3). The argument in the present chapter is that these domestic scenes bring into close proximity not only members of the dramatis personae, who are forced into close quarters in a confined space, but the features of British and Jewish life in relation to food, ritual and dialogue.

## *The Evacuees* (1975)

Although Rosenthal's play *The Evacuees* is, on the one hand, autobiographical, it is also highly constructed and symbolic. Most obviously, *The Evacuees*' title refers to the plot's centring on Neville (Stephen Serember) and Danny Miller (Gary Carp) being evacuated from their urban Manchester home to seaside Blackpool when war breaks out in 1939. The boys are taken in by a childless non-Jewish couple, Mr and Mrs Graham (Ivor Roberts, Margery Mason), whose middle-class status and Victorian approach to child-rearing contrasts with that of the boys' loving, working-class Jewish family. Eventually, the younger boy Danny, whose character is based on Rosenthal, lets his mother (Maureen Lipman) know how unhappy they are, and she takes the boys back to bomb-damaged Manchester. Beyond this, *The Evacuees* uses the historical concept of evacuation and return as a metaphor about the journey out of childhood. In order to do so, it unites British and Jewish tropes. The promise of Vera Lynn's celebrated wartime song 'We'll Meet Again',[1] which forms the soundtrack to the boys' setting off on the evacuation train, is fulfilled when they make the return journey home in time to celebrate Chanukah, and Neville gives a heartfelt account of the festival's meaning as 'the return of the Israelites to the Temple, after forty years in the wilderness' (Rosenthal 1978: 138).

The dinner table scene at the Grahams' house immediately after the boys' arrival places their Jewish habits into conflict with those of their non-Jewish foster parents. The camera movement is important to allow the audience to follow the boys' viewpoint: we enter the dining room as they do, to the sound of one of Hitler's speeches on the radio. Reassuringly, despite his Hitlerian moustache, Mr Graham tuts his disapproval on hearing the speech. However, the camera's pan across the room away from Mr Graham suggests something more sinister: Mrs Graham comes into view as we hear the shouts of 'Sieg Heil!', followed by evidence of her dictatorial behaviour at the table, where the boys have to stand to eat food whose appearance disconcerts them:

> **Danny**  I don't like cold sausage, Mrs Graham.
>
> **Mrs Graham**  Of course you do! It's real pork. [*Danny and Neville exchange frantic glances of panic ...* ]
>
> **Danny**  We've never had pork sausage, Mrs Graham. We're not allowed it.
>
> **Mr Graham**  [*with consummate wisdom*] How do you know you don't like it then, eh? Mmmm? Can't answer that one, can you? (Rosenthal 1978: 106)

The Grahams' insistence that Danny and Neville eat the food provided arises from their attitude to children, who must 'respect their elders and betters' (139), in Mrs Graham's words, but also their obliviousness to the possibility of cultural difference. The rueful comedy of the dinner table scene is enhanced by close-ups on the boys' distressed faces, accompanied by the exaggerated sound of their efforts to gulp down the forbidden food. In the screenplay, the boys are described as each uttering a 'short Hebrew prayer' (106) before eating, but in the film, the disjunction is amplified since the blessing Neville 'whispers' is the one for bread. Such comedy relies on an audience who does understand the significance of Danny's phrase, 'We're not allowed it', and that this is indeed '*the biggest crisis [the boys have] ever had to face*', as the stage direction has it (106). While the boys are away in their Blackpool exile, Danny acquires such traits of conventional masculinity as how to hold back his tears and to take an interest in girls. The play starts with his grandmother (Margery Withers) urging him to sit up straight, 'like a mensch' (Rosenthal 1978: 109) and ends with the ironic fulfilment of this wish. When he arrives back home, Danny physically assaults another boy for being an evacuee in Manchester who talks with a cockney accent, in just the way he was attacked in Blackpool for his Mancunian one. It seems that returning home entails this ambiguously presented assertion of a local norm, so that, rather than being a victim of the war, Danny has assumed warlike behaviour in turn. We learn that he has lost his childhood nickname 'the little rabbi', suggesting that his future lies outside religious Judaism. This makes the play into a variety of *künstlerroman*, in which we witness the journey of Rosenthal's fictional counterpart towards his adult destiny of comic playwright.

## *Bar Mitzvah Boy* (1976)

Rosenthal's Play for Today *Bar Mitzvah Boy* follows *The Evacuees* in portraying the detail of a British-Jewish milieu in realist fashion while also using that detail for symbolic purposes. In Rosenthal's words, the significance of the bar mitzvah ceremony around which the play revolves lies in its marking the moment when, at the age of thirteen, 'a Jewish boy "becomes a man", and takes on a man's responsibilities' (2005: 217). The ceremony offers a formalized version of the transition into adulthood, and one that the eponymous boy, Eliot Green (Jeremy Steyn), tries to resist by bolting from the synagogue during his bar mitzvah ceremony. As Eliot tells his older sister Lesley (Adrienne Posta), this is because of his dissatisfaction with the models of masculinity that he witnesses in the form of his narcissistic father Victor (Bernard Spear), infantile grandfather (Cyril Shaps) and supine future brother-in-law Harold (Jonathan Lynn), portraits which the play develops in comic detail to support his verdicts. The tension here does not arise from a confrontation with the gentile world, as it does in *The Evacuees*. However, the role of Eliot's non-Jewish schoolmate Denise (Kim Clifford) at the film's opening acts to draw attention to the play's central dramatic conceit of the bar mitzvah. Her puzzlement at the conversation between her fellow pupils Eliot and Squidge

(Mark Herman) about the impending bar mitzvah is itself presented with humorous indirection:

> **Eliot**  You know what tomorrow is, don't you? ... Only the day that marks my passage, isn't it! ...
>
> **Denise** [*to* **Squidge**]  What is it? What passage? ... Is it rude?
>
> **Squidge**  It's something Jewish. What Jewish boys do. You wouldn't understand. (Rosenthal 1978: 9)

The function of this exchange is to ally the viewer with Eliot rather than Denise. It is a narrative effect that makes familiarity with Jewish practice the norm, as was the case in *The Evacuees* and which, as we will see, also forms a prominent strand of comic meaning in the later plays.

The Friday night dinner table scene in this play, which runs for a crucial five minutes, takes place on the evening before the bar mitzvah and prepares us for Eliot's decision to flee the synagogue. The attitudes of the adults become clear through the vehicle of dialogue about the impending bar mitzvah, as well as the camera's movements. We see significant close-ups on individuals' faces, particularly Eliot's expressions as he silently judges everyone around him. The family's apparently shared focus on trivial and social detail rather than the religious elements of the bar mitzvah is given a strict gender division, one hinted at in Squidge's remark to Denise that the rite is one for 'Jewish boys'. Eliot's father Victor's self-absorption and irascibility, and Harold's efforts to please everyone, are viewed by Eliot more harshly than his mother's (Maria Charles) concern with her newly styled hair or his sister's impatience at Harold's romantic attentions.

The presence of British alongside Jewish concerns is represented here in the form of the signifiers of class stratification which take on a Jewish content. Thus Rita's distress about Stan and Dora Clyne's failure to reply to their dinner-dance invitation reveals what could be described as a lower-middle-class concern for propriety and social status, yet in the Jewish context of a bar mitzvah and expressed in Yiddish:

> **Rita**  The seating plan, though! It'll make ashenblotty of the seating plan! They should be on the second table and it's full!
>
> **Lesley**  They're not relations.
>
> **Rita**  He's a doctor. He expects it. [*Sighs*] They'll give him a beautiful present. (Rosenthal 1978: 23)

In this setting, Eliot's rebellion falls into the well-established pattern of a young man impatient with his family's reducing to a material level what is of importance to him in an intellectual sense. In this way, he is a version of Richard Hoggart's 'scholarship boy' (1957: 242), whose educational achievements and exposure to a middle-class world place him at odds with his family. Such a pattern is evident in Eliot's sudden outburst at the dinner table, provoked by a conversation about getting his hair cut, as he berates his family for what he sees as their trivial concerns:

> **Eliot**  I thought it was a *bar mitzvah* tomorrow! ... The Torah doesn't mention it's a hairdressing contest! (Rosenthal 1978: 25)

What Hoggart describes as the scholarship boy's finding himself 'at the friction-point of two cultures' (1957: 225) is exemplified by *Coronation Street*'s Ken Barlow, who is shown in the television series' first-ever episode returning home from university for a fraught dinner with his working-class parents. Such 'friction' is made more complex in Eliot's case by the presence of a third cultural allegiance, outside the mainstream. The extra element of Judaism means that British class structures are dramatized in Eliot's case in the terms of Jewish ritual and vocabulary.

Rosenthal's interest in rites of passage in men's lives continues to characterize contemporary British-Jewish television drama, as can be seen in the examples of *Grandma's House* and *Friday Night Dinner* which follow. In these later examples, we continue to encounter young men whose temporary return to the family home prompts a clash between spiritual or intellectual concerns and material ones, arising from the family's Jewish-inflected adherence to a lower-middle-class realm of propriety and respectability. Such a norm is disrupted in the home not only by the ethos of the educated, middle-class returnees, but by elements not present in Rosenthal's writing. These take the generic forms of self-reflexivity in *Grandma's House*, and the absurdist slapstick with which Jonny and Adam are represented in *Friday Night Dinner*, as well as more explicit thematizing of issues relating to gender and sexuality.

## *Grandma's House* (2010–12)

The series *Grandma's House* centres on Simon's (Simon Amstell) return visits to family gatherings at his grandmother Lily's (Linda Bassett) suburban home. Its hyper-realism possesses a postmodern self-consciousness, since the series' fictional protagonist is, like the actor, a television personality called Simon, played by Amstell as 'a slightly skewed version of himself' (Dantzic

2012). As Ruth Gilbert argues, one of the effects of this autofictionality is that Simon is presented as a gay man, one who is 'neither boyish nor effeminate, but sexualized in a way that ... re-inscribes Jewish masculinity as queer' (2014: 193).

In Rosenthal's *Bar Mitzvah Boy*, we both sympathize with Eliot and also distance ourselves from his thirteen-year-old extremity of judgement. In *Grandma's House*, the question of identification is even more uneven, and each episode's denouement presents Simon for comic critique. For instance, at the dining table in the series' first episode (9 August 2010), we witness events at first from Simon's viewpoint when his grandmother presents him, as a vegetarian at a chicken dinner, with a dish consisting entirely of two unadorned halves of an avocado, and he is then treated by his mother's boyfriend Clive (James Smith) not only to advise about how to cook 'succulent lamb', but to the details of the latter's job in a box-manufacturing company. Yet the episode's conclusion appears to reverse this allegiance, since it is Clive who offers to drive Simon's grandfather Bernie (Geoffrey Hutchings) to a doctor friend for an emergency check-up.

The structuring conflict in *Bar Mitzvah Boy* between unthinking materiality and dogmatic insistence on the spiritual is repeated in *Grandma's House*, with the same effect that this binary is itself subverted. Simon's apparently estimable efforts at transcendence and emotional honesty are shown to be fruitlessly self-deluding. Thus the series' first episode opens with Simon talking at cross-purposes with his family. His wish to leave his job as a 'mean' television presenter in order to 'live! breathe! find some love!' is met with his mother's asking in genuine bafflement, 'What more do you want from life? ... why do you need to breathe all of a sudden?', and his grandfather's literal-minded recommendation that he take the Knowledge and become a taxi driver, since 'The new TX4 cabs are air-conditioned'. In another subversion of Simon's plea for spiritual values and 'healing', in this instance his wish to 'complete with the past' by inviting his estranged father, Richard (Allen Corduner) to grandma's house, Tanya declares of her ex-husband:

**Tanya**    He's already complete – a complete prick! (*Pause*) That was a good one, no?

**Simon**   Yes, very good.

Following the series' self-reflexive ethos, Simon and Tanya break off from the argument here to comment both intra- and extra-diegetically on their performances. However, this clash of the earthly with the spiritual does not take the form of British class anxiety versus Jewish religious observance, as it does in Rosenthal's play. Indeed, one of the possible solutions Simon imagines for his disenchantment is to 'go to Thailand and become a Buddhist monk', suggesting that it is his family's lower-middle-class Jewishness from which he wants to flee. Likewise, Tanya tries to deflect her son's wish to heal past rifts with Richard by reminding Simon that his father has 'become a frummer – and you hate religion!'

Judaism is the all-encompassing backdrop to *Grandma's House*. We learn that the eponymous house is in Gant's Hill, historically the north-east location of an early stage in Jewish Londoners' migration away from the East End, one followed by younger and more affluent individuals – such as Simon, who lives in Hampstead – moving north-west. The series' lower-middle-class setting is thus established in the terms of British-Jewish history as well as the mise en scène and characterization. The series' characters read the *Jewish Chronicle* and discuss circumcision, shivahs and bagels, while almost no gentile characters appear or are mentioned. Yet the plot does not turn on such material, omnipresent though it is.

In the case of Richard, the now orthodox ex-husband, Jewish religious affiliation is represented for the sake of comic irony. Simon's inviting Richard to the house against everyone's wishes ends up bringing his efforts at reconciliation and transcendence bathetically down to earth. Richard's newly acquired habit of religious observance is seen by Lily simply as an additional hypocrisy, as she berates him for his infidelity: 'Gone frum! You think God didn't see you screwing that whore in a canoe?', and his attempt to invoke religious judgement in the form of the Talmud is quickly interrupted by Tanya's scathing 'Piss off!'. Simon's initially urging others to leave acrimony behind serves only to expose his own adherence to the petty affronts of the past. Such an effect is clear in Simon's angry response to his 'controlling' father's unchanged domestic habits, such as demanding that his son use a coaster on the table to 'protect the woodwork'. Jewishness here is not so much an element of the plot as it is a means of exaggerating the comic irony of situation and character.

## *Friday Night Dinner* (2011–)

The conceit of *Friday Night Dinner* is the weekly return home by the Goodman brothers Adam (Simon Bird) and Jonny (Tom Rosenthal) for dinner with their parents Martin (Paul Ritter) and Jackie (Tamsin Greig). As Simon does in *Grandma's House*, the boys regress to childhood roles 'once they close the front door', as the series' writer Robert Popper puts it (Popper 2011). Although this establishes a contrast to Rosenthal's plays, where the boys are younger and on the cusp of an adulthood they are ambivalent about, Popper describes Jonny and Adam 'revert[ing] to being 13 again' (Popper 2011), the very age of *Bar Mitzvah Boy*'s Eliot.

The Jewish content of *Friday Night Dinner* is increasingly boldly represented over its long span, despite Popper's initial ambivalence about foregrounding it in a comedy that is identified in terms of the 'classic British humour' of a sitcom (Curtis 2019). The Jewish meaning is frequently mediated through the figure of Jim (Mark Heap), a gentile neighbour whose ignorance about Jewish life makes him a hapless figure from whom spectators must distance themselves in order to get the joke. Jim's errors about Jewish religious practice arise from his wish for acceptance by the family, particularly Jackie. This approach is a version of Rosenthal's practice of immersing the viewer in the unexplained detail of Jewish life, which has to be worked out contextually. In this instance, Jim's errors are encouraged by the sons and turn into comic set pieces. Thus, for example, in the first episode of series five, 'The Other Jackie' (4 May 2018), Jim mistakes Martin and Jackie's aspirational installation of a hot tub in the garden, a development scorned by their sons, for a ritual practice:

**Jim**　Do Jewish people not take baths indoors?

**Jonny**　Not on Friday nights.

**Jim**　Ah, of course … shalom!

As is the case with Jim's other errors, which centre on eating habits and Yiddish or Hebrew phrases, a garbled version of a real Jewish practice is apparent here, and we might imagine that he is thinking of a *mikveh* (ritual bath). In this episode, Jim inveigles an invitation to dinner for himself and his date (Rosie Cavaliero). She is also called Jackie, but the first name she shares with Jackie Goodman is shown to be all they have in common. The details of the mise en scène, which make clear in every episode the ritual nature of the eponymous dinner, are exaggerated here. A menorah is constantly visible behind Jim on the dining-room sideboard, and a deep-focus perspective emphasizes the shiny and prominent presence of a challah loaf at the end of the table. Yet 'Jackie 2', as she is called in the cast list, remains oblivious to these signs. Jim's confiding his happiness to the family when she is out of earshot prompts Martin's sarcastic reference to Jackie 2's unnerving habits, including her incessant laughter:

**Jim**　This might be the greatest day of my entire life … she might be *the one*!

**Martin**　The one that murders us all!

The episode's denouement makes Martin's riposte appropriate in relation to more than Jackie 2's off-putting manner. Just at the moment when it seems that she reciprocates Jim's affection, the extent of her non-Jewish status is revealed as she describes why she left her job as a legal secretary:

**Jackie 2**   I didn't like the people.

**Jackie**   Oh, why not?

**Jackie 2**   They were Jews!

The generic requirements of a situation comedy like *Friday Night Dinner* mean that everything will return to the status quo at the episode's end. In this way, the unsuitability of Jackie 2 as Jim's romantic partner is necessary to ensure that his position as eccentric bachelor is resumed. After this utterance, Jackie 2, described as 'a Nazi' and 'Mrs Goebbels' by the sons, is unceremoniously ejected from the Goodmans' house, trying vainly to retrieve the situation as she is hustled out of the door by claiming that she was not referring to 'all Jews'. The episode concludes in a version of its beginning, as Jim offers to 'say a few extra shaloms in penance', this time appearing to give a confused version of Catholic practice along with his all-purpose use of the Hebrew greeting. For good measure, he adds a glancing reference to the entire history of Jewish persecution in his wish to 'make amends to your poor, poor people'. Notwithstanding debates about increased antisemitism at the time of this episode's release, the generalization sounds hyperbolic in this British context, where Jackie 2's behaviour has taken the form of a giant social faux pas. Typical as such an instance might be of extreme dramatic irony as befitting a sitcom, the way in which Jackie 2 is revealed to be unsuitable as Jim's mate arises from the drama's British-Jewish content. In the context of the Friday night dinner itself, there is little else she could have said to make herself so comprehensively ineligible.

## Conclusion

While the influence of genre and medium is inescapable in these examples of British-Jewish television drama, the precedent set by Jack Rosenthal's writing of the 1970s is also clear in relation to the artistic detail of this hybrid genre in the twenty-first century. The Jewish content is entwined with awareness of status and class, that constant source of British anxiety and humour, in these dramas which present characterizations of contemporary British-Jewish men in domestic and dinner-table settings. The detailed attention to mise en scène, dialogue, accent and clothing allows us to identify the home setting as a lower-middle-class one in each case, a class formation that 'hovers between the proletariat and the bourgeoisie' (Marx and Engels, quoted in Burris 1995: 19), its in-between status prompting a fearful adherence to the 'mainstream and respectable' (Felski 2002) against which we see the young men rebel.

There are uncomfortable lessons about both gender and religious assimilation in each of the dramas discussed here. In *The Evacuees*, Danny turns into the kind of young man who terrorized him as a child; Eliot must compromise his principles to be accepted; Simon's therapeutic impulses are self-deceptive; Adam and Jonny are wrong-footed by their parents. Even if the 'emancipation contract' (Endelman 1990: 74; Vice 2016: 228), by means of which the freedom to practise Judaism in a British context comes at the price of lying low and remaining unidentified, is not evident within the dramas' plots, such a contract could be invoked as the explanation for the scarcity of such televisual representation and the susceptibility of *Friday Night Dinner* in particular to have its Jewish content overlooked. Nonetheless, rather than an assimilatory 'Englishing' of Jewish practice, in David Ruderman's phrase, the class- and gender-related humour in all these examples of Jewish households relies, more subversively, on a 'Jewishing' of hegemonic Britishness (2000: 215ff).

## Note

1   'We'll Meet Again' is a 1939 song made famous by Vera Lynn. Music and lyrics by Ross Parker and Hughie Charles.

## References

*Bar Mitzvah Boy* (1976), [TV programme] BBC Play for Today, 4 September.
Burris, V. (1995) [1986], 'The Discovery of the New Middle Classes', in A. J. Vidich (ed.), *The New Middle Classes: Life Style, Status Claims and Political Consciousness*, 15–54, Basingstoke: Palgrave.
*Bye Bye Baby* (1992), [TV programme] Channel 4.
Caughie, J. (2000), *Television Drama: Realism, Modernism and British Culture*, Oxford: Oxford University Press.
Cooke, L. (2013), *Style in British Television Drama*, London: Palgrave.
*Coronation Street* (1960), [TV programme] ITV, 9 December.
Curtis, L. (2019), '*Friday Night Dinner* 2020 Release Date Confirmed', Available online: https://www.realitytitbit.com/channel-4/friday-night-dinner-2020-release-date-confirmed-for-march-everything-you-need-to-knowfriday-

night-dinner-is-confirmed-for-a-series-6-but-are-all-of-the-cast-returning-11-03-2020

Dantzic, T. (2012), 'Television Preview: *Grandma's House*', *Telegraph*, 9 May.

Dunn, K. (2011), 'Responses to Rosenthal: A Comparison of Audience Reaction to Jack Rosenthal's *Bar Mitzvah Boy* and *Eskimo Day*', *Journal of British Film and Television*, 8 (2): 272–82.

Endelman, T. (1990), *Radical Assimilation in English Jewish History, 1665–1945*, Bloomington, IN: Indiana University Press.

*The Evacuees* (1975), [TV programme] BBC Play for Today, 5 March.

Felski, R. (2002), 'Why Academics Don't Study the Lower Middle Class', *Chronicle of Higher Education*, 25 January. Available online: https://www.chronicle.com/article/Why-Academics-Dont-Study-the/3283 (accessed 7 January 2020).

*Friday Night Dinner* (2011–), [TV programme] Channel 4.

Garfield, R. (2016), 'From *The Evacuees* to *Grandma's House*: Class, Sexuality and Jewish Identity on British Television, 1975–2012', in N. Abrams (ed.), *Hidden in Plain Sight: Jews and Jewishness in British Film, Television and Popular Culture*, 130–48, Evanston, IL: Northwestern University Press.

Geraghty, C. (2003), 'Aesthetics and Quality in Popular Television Drama', *International Journal of Cultural Studies*, 6 (1): 25–45.

Gilbert, R. (2014), 'My Big Fat Jewish Wedding: Representing Jews on Contemporary British Television', *Jewish Film and New Media*, 2 (2): 181–200.

*Grandma's House* (2010–12), [TV programme] BBC Two.

Hoggart, R. (1957), *The Uses of Literacy: Aspects of Working-Class Life*, London: Essential Books.

Johnson, C. (2007), 'Negotiating Value and Quality in Television Historiography', in H. Wheatley (ed.), *Re-viewing Television History*, 55–66, London: I.B. Tauris.

Jordan, J. (2012), 'Assimilated, Integrated, Other: An Introduction to Jews and British Television, 1946–1955', in T. Kushner and H. Ewence (eds), *Whatever Happened to British Jewish Studies?*, 259–74, London: Vallentine Mitchell.

*A Little Big Business* (1963–5), [TV programme] ITV.

*My Son Reuben* (1975), [TV programme] ITV.

*Never Mind the Quality, Feel the Width* (1967–71), [TV programme] ITV.

Popper, R. (2011), 'The Sound of Young America: Robert Popper, British Comedy Writer of *Look around You* and *Friday Night Dinner*'. Interview by X. Jardin. *Bullseye with Jesse Thorn*, Maximum Fun [podcast platform], 31 August. Available online: https://www.maximumfun.org/sound-young-america/robert-popper-british-comedy-writer-look-around-you-and-friday-night-dinner-inte (accessed 7 January 2020).

Reast, D. (2017), 'New Approaches to the "Golden Age" of British Television Comedy'. Available online: https://think.iafor.org/new-approaches-golden-age-british-television-comedy/ (accessed 7 January 2020).

Rosenthal, J. (1978), *Three Award-Winning Plays: Bar Mitzvah Boy, The Evacuees, Spend, Spend, Spend*, Harmondsworth: Penguin.

Rosenthal, J. (2005), *By Jack Rosenthal: An Autobiography in Six Acts*, London: Robson Books.

Ruderman, D. (2000), *Jewish Enlightenment in an English Key: Anglo-Jewry's Construction of Modern Jewish Thought*, Princeton, NJ: Princeton University Press.

Seddon, I. (2020), *East End Jews and Left-Wing Theatre: Alfie Bass, David Kossoff, Warren Mitchell and Lionel Bart*, London: Vallentine Mitchell.

Vice, S. (2009), *Jack Rosenthal*, Manchester: Manchester University Press.

Vice, S. (2013), 'Jack Rosenthal's Family Romances', in C. Bainbridge and C. Yates (eds), *Television and Psychoanalysis: Psycho-Cultural Perspectives*, 91–110, London: Karnac.

Vice, S. (2016), 'Christmas Trees and Hanukah Bushes: The "Emancipation Contract" in the Contemporary British Television Dramas *Hebburn* and *Friday Night Dinner*', in N. Abrams (ed.), *Hidden in Plain Sight: Jews and Jewishness in British Film, Television and Popular Culture*, 227–51, Evanston, IL: Northwestern University Press.

# 13

# 'It Was F***ing Biblical, Mate': The Maturing of British Television Drama

Nathan Abrams

A revolution is happening on British television right before our eyes. It is, however, so subtle that many viewers have missed it. The revolution is not simply that there is an increasing number of Jewish characters on mainstream British television: indeed, recent years have witnessed a veritable explosion of Jewish characters on the television. Nor is it that a wider range of these characters – well rounded, subtle, shocking even – are now appearing on screen. Rather, surprisingly, these Jewish characters seem virtually indistinguishable from their non-Jewish counterparts. The result is that these new Jewish TV characters are depicted as not only being born and bred in Britain, but also sound like they are. They are now, at least in terms of their accents, harder to distinguish from their gentile co-characters. Indeed, they have become visually indistinctive – not bearing the physical markers of Jewishness, whether in terms of clothing (kippot, peyot, shtreimels and the like) or 'looks', that is, physiognomy.[1] Indeed, as viewers, we sometimes must be explicitly told that they are Jewish. There is a key reason for this: Jewish actors are typically not playing these televisual Jews. This phenomenon encompasses a range of shows set in various historical eras. This is a sign of the maturing of British television drama.

## Past Stereotypes

In the past, explicitly Jewish fictional characters were relatively rare on television in the UK. For decades, Jews were hidden on British television screens. One had to look hard to find an explicitly Jewish character beyond the odd Holocaust documentary or religious programme. Jews frequented our television screens, but not always playing Jews or playing Jews in disguise (think Warren Mitchell as Alf Garnett); consequently, for the uninitiated they were not always easy to spot. This includes such British-Jewish actors, not just on television, but also drawn from the world of film and theatre, as Miriam Margolyes, Peggy Ashcroft, Maureen Lipman, Anthony Sher, Stephen Fry, Helena Bonham-Carter, Claire Bloom, Miriam Karlin, among others. This has continued into the modern era, where Jewish actors of the younger generation such as Daniel Radcliffe, Jason Isaacs, Sacha Baron-Cohen, Rachel Weisz, Sophie Okonedo inter alia are not always decisively marked as Jewish for British audiences. Furthermore, because Jews are a tiny percentage of the overall British population, non-Jews are very unlikely to meet or have any connection with a Jewish person. Consequently, when British-Jewish characters did appear, in order to render them visible to a general audience, they tended to be overly coded on screen, conforming to a limited set of visual clichés and stereotypes such as the overbearing Jewish mother, the Hasid, or literary figures like Shylock and Fagin.

To ensure the British audience knew the characters were Jewish, they were costumed stereotypically (sporting ear-locks, ultra-Orthodox-style shtreimels or other easily identified symbols). If they were not distinguishable through dress, they possessed a clear Eastern European accent that demarcated them from the gentiles around them. Thus, they often had a marked tendency to sound like they just arrived from Eastern Europe. It did not matter whether the programme was set in 1919 or 2019, or if the characters in question were fifteen or fifty. Furthermore, such recognizably Jewish actors as Maureen Lipman, Henry Goodman and Miriam Margoyles usually played them. The archetypal example of this is the series of adverts (1987–) for the national telecommunications provider, British Telecom, featuring Lipman as the anxious Jewish grandmother, 'Beatrice Bellman' ('Beattie/BT'). In heavily accented English, Beattie chats on the phone to her grandson Anthony (Jacob Krichefski). He informs her that he has failed almost every subject in his exams but has passed pottery and sociology. A relieved Beattie responds, 'You get an 'ology, you're a scientist.'

Today, by contrast, because Jews have become a relatively frequent presence on our screens, the situation has changed. Jewish characters appear in a variety of dramatic shows, as detailed by Sue Vice in the preceding chapter. Recent examples in the last decade, as Vice points out, include *Grandma's House*, in which Jewish comedian Simon Amstell plays himself; *Friday Night Dinner*, in which the Jewish Goodman family which meets every Friday night for Shabbat dinner and which is portrayed by Simon Bird, Tamsin Greig, Paul Ritter and Tom Rosenthal respectively; and in *Hebburn*, with Kimberley Nixon as Sarah. These are joined by such documentary shows such as *Jews*, *Two Jews on a Cruise*, *Strictly Kosher*, *Jews at Ten*, *Jewish Mum of the Year*, and the long-running series, *The Apprentice*, helmed by openly Jewish businessman, Lord Alan Sugar, now airing in its fifteenth season at the time of writing.

## Jewish Police

Writing in the *Jewish Chronicle* in 2018, journalist David Aaronovitch asked, '[H]as there been a Jewish detective yet on television?' This televisual absence reflects, in part, the real world. As I have written (2012), stereotypically, the world of the police is perceived by Jews as one that excludes Jews. German-Jewish philosopher, Hannah Arendt, wrote of 'the traditional Jewish fear of the "cop" – that seeming incarnation of a hostile world' (1944: 11). Many Jewish immigrants hailed from countries, like Tsarist Russia, where the police acted as agents for anti-Jewish governments and when they settled in Britain, the British police hardly opened its arms to the new arrivals. What is more, there is a perception that the police force is a very anti-intellectual and *goyische* (gentile) profession given that it overwhelmingly drew from the unskilled and semi-skilled working class. Policing was not seen as a viable profession for British Jews. As Jenni Frazer has written, '[P]olicing as a career is considered an arcane choice among Britain's Jews. But for years, becoming a police officer has not been on the radar of the Jewish community' (Frazer 2020). James Yaffe famously asked of the profession, 'Is this any job for a nice Jewish boy?' The other side of the coin is that since policing embodies *goyim naches* (Yiddish, meaning non-Jewish joy or enjoyment or pleasure for the gentiles), Jewish self-hatred becomes the price of acceptance into the police 'family'. Denial of one's Jewish self, even self-hatred, therefore, is the price to be paid for acceptance into the *goyische* police 'family'. Alternatively, the idea of the Jewish police officer is considered as an oxymoron and often treated as a fertile subject for humour, especially in American drama. Series three of the BBC One television drama series, *WPC 56* (2015), by contrast, takes a middle route between these two poles in its character of Detective Inspector (DI) Harry Sawyer (Oliver Rix).

*WPC 56* is set in a fictional police force in the West Midlands, circa 1956. It revolves around the first female police – WPC stands for Woman Police Constable – to join the fictional Brinford Constabulary. DI Harry Sawyer is not exploited for humorous purposes nor depicted as a self-hating Jew. His creator, screenwriter Dominique Moloney, described him thus:

> Born 1925. Harry is charming, with rakish good looks, and a jocular disposition. He doesn't come from money but has a middle-class sensibility and can hold his own amongst intellectuals. He has a hint of darkness about him that makes him irresistible to women, especially of the vulnerable variety. Ironically it is Harry's own damage that keeps him from finding true intimacy – he has a habit of sabotaging good relationships by cheating or simply dropping them when things get too

serious. His one true passion is his career; his intelligence, diligence and ambition have helped him rise in the ranks impressively quickly, but it is entirely deserved, and his elders soon learn not to underestimate him.

(2014)

As befitting this description, Oliver Rix's portrayal of Harry is a breath of fresh air. Born in Birmingham, England, he naturally has an English accent. As his creator, Dominique Moloney revealed to me, 'Yeah, I absolutely wouldn't have him speak with any kind of accent, he's a Brit basically, born in Birmingham, as is his mother' (ibid.).

Harry is handsome, with dark good looks, clearly attractive, and is a compulsive womanizer. Most significant, from my perspective, is that his Jewishness is incidental to his characterization, not the main reason for it. Certainly, his ethnicity is no barrier to his entry into, or promotion within, the ranks of the police force. In fact, Harry keeps his Jewishness strictly private. We do not know if he even practises anything and we only learn of Harry's Jewishness because, in various domestic scenes with his family, we meet his mother and dying grandmother. According to Moloney:

> Harry's kind of young and sexy and dynamic. ... What I like about Harry is he's a conventional British hero, who just happens to be Jewish. If we didn't have those domestic scenes with his family, you'd never know it. We've made him Jewish (or half Jewish) for a few reasons. In the first series our DI Jack Burns (or Jacob Bernstein) was going to have a whole story about his Jewish background, and how he hides it because of the anti-Semitism of the time – WPC 56 always tackles the racism, sexism and homophobia of the 50's and I wanted to explore anti-Semitism too, especially in the years after the war, I thought it would be dramatically interesting. And we had a crime story that tied in to it all (about Holocaust survivors) but there just wasn't room for it in Series 1. Anyway, we then lost our first DI, and always intended to make the next one Jewish so we could play this out, which is what we've done – our main crime story is about a Nazi war criminal.

In contrast to the Beattie character, Harry's mother, June, is also non-stereotypical. Born in 1908, she grew up in Brinford in a stable Jewish family but was always something of a wild child who never saw eye to eye with her mother Lily. June was gifted with beauty and had ambitions of being a movie star from an early age. She was pregnant at sixteen (she refused to say who the father was) and gave birth to Harry. His early years were secure and loving as Lily cared for him while June studied acting. June showed little interest in her son but resented her mother's bond with him. When June decided to move to London to pursue her acting career, she took four-year-old Harry with her, despite a fierce row with Lily. In line with the tradition of Westernizing Jewish-sounding surnames, June changed hers from Krajnik to Sawyer. However, there any comparison to typical Jewish practice ends. She was (and still is) an actress of moderate talent – beautiful, vain and utterly selfish. As a child, Harry was dragged from pillar to post as June took up with various men and lived an itinerant lifestyle in show business. To June, Harry was a fun distraction, as long as he didn't whine or cry or get in the way of what she wanted. As he got older and more demanding, she took him home to her mother, promised she would be back for him, but never was. He was ten. She saw him from time to time over the years; she took him to some of her shows when he was a teenager, but Harry never forgave her. In another twist, Harry is investigating a crime which has its roots in the Second World War and involves Nazi medical experiments and avenging Jewish twins. *WPC 56*, in naturalizing the Jewish police officer within the world of the police, is a sign of the maturing of British-Jewish television drama.

Much more recently, an even more unusual incarnation has emerged: a British-Jewish female police officer. In the 2019 BBC drama, *Giri/Haji* (Duty/Shame), Sarah Weitzmann is a detective constable played by non-Jewish actor, Kelly Macdonald. Hailing from Glasgow, the character has a similarly identifiable Scottish accent. Even if her name was not instantly recognizable as Jewish to viewers, Weitzmann is openly Jewish. She even takes part in a Yom Kippur ritual of sorts. As befitting the hostile world of the police officer, as outlined by Arendt above, Weitzmann feels alienated within the Metropolitan Police. But this is not because she is Jewish; indeed, this is shown to be of no concern to her fellow officers. It is because she has broken the informal police code by informing on her partner (also a police officer) who had rigged a police investigation and has been ostracized by her fellow police officers. Arguably, it is her *menschlikayt* (Yiddish for being a fine, decent upstanding human being, an exemplar of integrity and honour) that motivates her to do the right thing (although she is also in part hurt by her partner's affair with another police officer). DI Harry Sawyer and DC Sarah Weitzmann demonstrate, on television at least, that 'the traditional Jewish fear of the "cop" – that seeming incarnation of a hostile world' (Arendt 1944: 11) is beginning the slide into obsolescence.[2]

## Gangsters and Criminals

*McMafia* was an eight-part British crime drama television series created by Hossein Amini and James Watkins and directed by Watkins, focusing on the exploits of one expat Russian-Jewish crime family living in London and their Jewish associates across the world. *McMafia* was co-produced by the BBC, AMC and Cuba Pictures. It was first broadcast on BBC One from 1 January 2018 and then premiered on AMC on 26 February 2018.

While this series focuses on Jews, the casting for *McMafia* ironically largely excludes Jews. Only one member of the Godman tribe, Uncle Boris, is played by a Jewish actor, David Dencik. The lead role is played by an actor who went to a Catholic school, James Norton. Writing in the *Jewish Chronicle*, David Aaronovitch opined, 'The Godman family, transitioning from Russian mobsters to London financiers are supposedly Jewish, though heaven knows how you would tell. The paterfamilias seems more Glaswegian than Odessian, the kids are pure Bedales [an independent British boarding school] and they wish each other a long life when making toasts. Next, they'll be lighting their Passover dreidels' (2018). British-Jewish Comedian David Baddiel added to the chorus, tweeting on 5 January 2018, 'No sign so far of the enormous woke outcry over James Norton playing a Jew in *McMafia*', and then, 'So you'd be OK with a white man playing Othello?'

The second complaint about *McMafia* is its portrayal of Jews on television as gangsters. The non-fiction book by Misha Glenny entitled *McMafia: Seriously Organised Crime* (2008) inspired the series. The cover blurb describes itself as 'a journey through the new world of international organised crime, from gunrunners in Ukraine to money launderers in Dubai, by way of drug syndicates in Canada and cyber criminals in Brazil'. Significantly, nowhere does this mention either Israel or Jews, although at least one chapter entitled 'Aliyah' does focus on Jewish gangsters in Israel. Glenny recounts how, following the murder of a Russian pimp, Oleg 'Karpits' Karpachov in September 1996, Israeli police unravelled an invisible Russian-speaking network of pimps, brothels, protection rackets, counterfeit documents and kidnapping that kept itself strictly divorced from the rest of Israel society as if in a parallel world. The single largest business was prostitution.

It is from this milieu, as well as the 1 million Jews who left the FSU to emigrate to Israel from 1989 onwards, that the creative team behind *McMafia* drew inspiration. In so doing, by contrast to the book, the television series vastly reduces its scope to focus on the Godman family as well as an Israeli businessman and Knesset member called Semiyon Kleiman (played by the non-Jewish American actor, David Straithairn). Kleiman also leads a shadowy existence as an international sex trafficker, drug runner and money launderer in the show. This leads to the obvious question: why produce a drama about global organized crime only to reduce it to the story of one Jewish family? Furthermore, especially when in reducing it to several key Jewish characters, the series taps into and hence propagates stereotypes of Jews, money and international conspiracies that lie at the heart of the *Protocols of the Elders of Zion*? The group known as the UK Lawyers for Israel, for example, accused the show of gratuitous slurs against Israeli businessmen in making references to Israel that were not mentioned in the original book (Harpin 2018).

The BBC's own interviews with the writer, director and cast are curiously silent on the subject of the centrality of Jewishness to the drama, mentioning Jews only once, but not explaining the focus on them. However, when confronted with the criticism, Hossein Amini was reported to claim that the depiction was not intended to be offensive (Kraft 2018). One of the few Jewish actors in the show, Yuval Scharf, who plays Kleiman's assistant, Tanya, stated,

> I don't feel that Israel is presented in a more negative way than Russia or England or any other country condemned for corruption. The show is not about Israel, it's about the way crime touches the core of everything. It's not about Israel, it's not about London, it's about the bad people there. It's talking about the globalized world of organized crime and all the globalization of the mafia, and we live in a global world now. And all the accents and all the different people from all over the world – a lot of extras from Russia, India, a lot of accents come together on set.
>
> (Spiro 2018)

David Aaranovitch concludes, 'In some ways having unstereotypical Jewish villains is a sign of progress. We should be pleased. Maybe.'

BBC's *Peaky Blinders*, the fifth season of which aired in 2019, is a period gangster drama, based on fact, about the (non-Jewish) eponymous gang (so-called because they hide razor blades in their caps) in Small Heath, Birmingham, in the 1920s, trying to become legitimate bookmakers. In a strategic manoeuvre, the Peaky Blinders clan decided to team up with 'the Jews' of Camden Town, North London (which is incidentally, where this writer went to school). Thus, they meet with Alfie Solomons, memorably played by Tom Hardy (previously Bane in *The Dark Knight Rises*), the leader of a gang of Jewish 'bakers', who smuggle rum.

Alfie is based on a real-life individual. Solomon, along with his brother Harry, provided protection for Jewish bookmakers at the track where they became both 'famed and feared'. 'Holding hands with history', as *Peaky*

*Blinders* writer, Steven Knight put it, he transformed Solomon into Solomons with the help of non-Jewish actor Tom Hardy (Round 2014). While instantly recognizable as Jewish by the garb he wears in the series, Solomons again has an accent more befitting Camden Town than Hamburg. Rather than sticking to stereotype or slavishly following history, Knight explains, '[W]hen you have an actor of the standard of Tom Hardy you want to make the most of him so we have portrayed him as funny but with an edgy character.' The result is a character that is as tough as nails, violent and full of expletives. Indeed, it is from this character that the title of this chapter is drawn: describing some violence he has committed, Solomons explains how, 'I shoved a 6 inch nail up his fucking nose and hammered it home with a duckboard. It was fucking biblical, mate.' Previously, if one thought of Jewish gangsters, one might have considered New York or Odessa. But now with Tom Hardy as Alfie Solomons, British television is beginning to represent the British-Jewish past in a more realistic light.

## Why the Change?

What explains this change in Jewish representation? I argue that factors external to the Jewish communities of Britain provoked this transformation among a younger generation of British Jews who are not, in the words of Howard Jacobson, simply content to 'stay shtumm', a Yiddish phrase meaning 'stay quiet'. Jacobson (2007) explains how '"Stay shtumm," was the advice given to me when I was growing up. Don't draw attention to yourself'. The arrival in the UK of a significant number of non-white immigrants from the former colonies and other commonwealth countries removed the spotlight that shone on the majority of Ashkenazi Jews because, to all intents and purposes (*haredim* aside), in racial terms, Jews appeared *white* to the British mainstream (Stratton 2000, 2008). In response to this new type of mass non-white immigration, legislation such as the Race Relations Act of 1976 was passed and anti-discrimination policies enacted, from which Jews undoubtedly benefited. Not only did the law now protect the observance of certain religious practices, it also recognized that the media was required to cater for an increasingly ethnically and religiously diverse population. Thus, by the end of the twentieth century, open hostility and active discrimination towards Jews in the UK were on the decline.

Jewish self-confidence in the UK was boosted by Margaret Thatcher's accession to power as prime minister from 1979 until 1990. This period saw both the rise of multiculturalism in the UK and the broader visibility of Jews in public life (Stratton 2009). This can be attributed in particular to Thatcher's anti-Establishment and pro-Jewish stance (Jews were both a 'model minority' but also classic exemplars of non-Establishment figures), as manifested in Thatcher's disproportionate appointments of Jews to the Cabinet and the reactions to it. While they promoted Jewish assurance, they also attracted snide, backhanded remarks. Former prime minister, Harold Macmillan, is known to have remarked, 'The thing about Margaret's Cabinet is that it includes more Old Estonians than it does Old Etonians.' The use of the term 'Estonians' was clearly a pun on the term 'Etonians' – the leading independent school where much of the British elite political class were educated – but also a euphemistic reference to the Eastern European origins of many British Jews of whom many traditional Conservatives thought Prime Minister Thatcher overly favoured.

Meanwhile, greater awareness because of increased education about the Holocaust, combined with the acceptance of the inescapability of Jewishness, convinced British Jews that a low profile was useless when antisemites are not so discerning in their discrimination. This awareness was also caused by curriculum changes, the growth of modules and degree programmes at all levels in the subject at higher education level, the setting up of museums and memorials (Beth Shalom, the Imperial War Museum and the new UK Holocaust Memorial and Learning Centre) and finally the establishment of an annual and national Holocaust Memorial Day from 2001 onwards. At the same time, the growth of Holocaust education has surely affected non-Jewish British perception of Jews. It is now, for example, all but impossible in mainstream British political discourse to deny publicly the Holocaust anymore. As evidence of this, the far-right British National Party in the UK has removed open Holocaust denial as a plank in its platform (see 'Countering' 2007).

Together, the results of improved Jewish education, the distancing from the Holocaust, and the growth of the notion that neither was the *Shoah* going to happen again nor in Britain, combined to convince Jews that being Jewish openly was no longer a barrier to full entry into British public life. That is, Jews no longer had to stay in the background and not draw attention to themselves as they had done for decades previously. A new generation of British Jews has rejected the timidity of the Jewish establishment, together with its anxiety that conspicuously Jewish behaviour might spark antisemitism. This generation either recognizes, or does not care, that how Jews act and appear is not in itself a direct cause of antisemitism. And if it is, then they might ask: why act differently when those who hold antisemitic views will always find some ammunition, however dubious, to legitimate their spurious claims?

Other Jewish cultural production attests to this change in climate. New groups, *minyanim* and organizations unrelated to the traditional religious denominations and synagogues have sprung up, particularly in London, as exemplified, above all, by Limmud. It is possible now to lead a varied and spiritually/intellectually fulfilling post-denominational Jewish existence outside of and unrelated to the mainstream organizations and their institutions. One does not need to go to a synagogue to be Jewish anymore. Most notably, there has been a flowering of new Jewish literature: Naomi Alderman, David Baddiel, Linda Grant, Howard Jacobson, Reva Mann, Charlotte Mendelssohn, Suzanne Portnoy, Francesca Segal and Adam Thirlwell, to mention just a few, write on all sorts of Jewish topics. Jews can thus be seen as one branch of hyphenated multicultural Britain.

At the same time, as mentioned above, although Jews were never 'whitened' in the UK as they were in the United States, to all intents and purposes they looked *white*. Karen Brodkin (1998) explains how immigrant Jews from Eastern Europe were classified as 'non-white' in the United States. However, following the Second World War, American Jewish intellectuals instigated a process of whitening by which they stressed the quintessentially 'American' characteristics of immigrant Jewish culture and by defining it in opposition to Blackness. Consequently, Jews moved from 'non-white' to becoming 'more or less, accepted as white' in the United States (Brodkin 1998: 10). By contrast, as Jon Stratton has argued, the 'imperative to whiten the Jews', owing to a lack of large-scale immigration and economic need, did not occur in the UK (Stratton 2008: 198). There was no process. Rather, coupled with the perception of Jewish success (which concomitantly ignores any indication to the contrary such as working-class or poor Jews, or any non-white *Mizrahi*, Indian or Ethiopian Jews), Jews have now been absorbed into the largely *goyish*, white establishment in Britain, passing or flying under the radar.

No longer perceived as an oppressed minority, it thus becomes possible not to treat Jews as a protected characteristic within the UK cultural industries. This means that Jews now become available for a form of what has been called 'Jewface'. Miriam Margolyes et al. (2019) describe 'Jewface' as

> a heightened and characteristic (mis)representation of Jews built on a secondary understanding of tropes, ticks, mannerisms and vocal affectation that has no awareness of the primary factors such as psychology, geography, culture and history that have framed these outward signifiers of Judaism. Jewishness is easy to caricature and this seems all the more disappointing when Jewish representation is absent and the ability of Jews to tell or contribute to their own stories is dismissed. Caricatures feed into stereotypes and stereotypes feed into prejudice. This is not to say that non-Jewish actors cannot accurately and sensitively represent Judaism on stage, but rooms that appropriate and erase Judaism are unacceptable; there is an obvious correlation

between reduced representation in the creative process and increased misrepresentation in the product.

This is precisely the accusation that David Baddiel, among others, has thrown against the makers of dramas like *McMafia*. However, the irony here is that while it is correct that Jewishness and Judaism are easy to caricature, this caricaturing has been carried out by Jewish actors themselves who, in building upon a primary understanding of tropes, ticks, mannerisms and vocal affectation combined with awareness of the primary factors such as psychology, geography, culture and history that have framed these outward signifiers of Judaism, have fed into stereotypes and hence into prejudice. Thus, one could certainly make the argument (*pace* Margolyes) that over the years it is precisely the type of Jewish actors who signed the above open letter that has neither accurately nor sensitively represented Jews, Jewishness and Judaism on British television. Rather, the opposite is the case: it is and has been non-Jewish actors who are producing the more accurate and sensitive portrayals of Jews on screen by not playing them as stereotyped or caricatured Jews but by playing them as themselves.

## Conclusion

David Ben Gurion memorably said, 'When Israel has its own prostitutes and thieves, it will be a state like any other.' He saw the existence of such types as a sign of Israeli/Jewish maturity. Appropriating Ben Gurion's observation, and applying it to Britain, now that British television has Jewish police officers, gangsters and others, who sound and can pass as gentile, we can see that this points to a maturity in Jewish television drama. What is more, if I had more space, I could further mention the upper-class Atticus Aldridge (played by Matt Barber) in *Downton Abbey* or the odd character such as Baron Nahum (Julius D'Silva) that crops up in *The Crown*. Furthermore, Paul Spector (played by actor/model Jamie Dornan) in the BBC police procedural *The Fall* is a family man and bereavement councillor during the day but a serial-killer psychopath at night (this is not a spoiler; we know this from the very first episode). When confronted by a disgruntled client who questions him about his surname, Spector replies, without shame, 'Russian Jewish'. This Jewish character is highly unusual: good looking, a loving parent, a councillor but also a violent misogynist. Such characters arguably, therefore, represent a landmark change in the representation of Jews in British television. Finally, the long-held British-Jewish tradition of resorting to simplified visual and linguistic stereotypes and clichés to depict such characters seems to have been broken. UK television programming increasingly resembles its edgier American counterpart. Ironically, these new depictions are probably not so much a function of the greater confidence among Jews in the UK in terms of asserting and showing their identity. Rather, it is because, for the most part, it is non-Jews who are creating and playing these characters, and hence it is they who, together with the directors, producers and screenwriters of these shows, are less afraid to push the boundaries of Jewish televisual representation.

## Notes

1. Although physiognomy, along with phrenology, has been widely discredited as racist and pseudo-scientific, being the basis for much antisemitic representation (see Gilman 1991), here I am using the term critically not to endorse the use of physiognomy as a valid means of identification in the Jewish context but rather how older productions have used an approach based on looks to typify Jewishness.
2. At the time of writing, Netflix's *The Stranger* (2020) featured a corrupt policeman named Patrick Katz, played by Jewish actor Paul Kaye.

## References

Aaronovitch, D. (2018), 'The BBC's Jewish Gangsters Aren't All Bad News', *thejc.com*, 25 January. Available online: https://www.thejc.com/comment/columnists/the-bbc-s-jewish-gangsters-aren-t-all-bad-news-1.457419 (accessed October 2019).

Abrams, N. (2012), *The New Jew in Film: Exploring Jews and Jewishness in Contemporary Cinema*. London: I.B. Tauris.

*The Apprentice* (2005–), [TV programme] BBC One.

Arendt, H. (1944), 'The Jew as Pariah: A Hidden Tradition', *Jewish Social Studies*, 6 (2): 99–122.

Brodkin, K. (1998), *How Jews Became White Folks: And What That Says about Race in America*, New York: Rutgers University Press.

'Countering the Smears' (2007), *British National Party*, 3 December. Available online: https://web.archive.org/web/20090131093708/ http://bnp.org.uk/2007/12/countering-the-smears/ (accessed March 2020).

*The Crown* (2016–), [TV programme] Netflix.

*The Dark Knight Rises* (2012), [Film] Dir. Christopher Nolan, USA: Warner Bros. Pictures.

*Downton Abbey* (2010–15), [TV programme] ITV.

*The Fall* (2013–16), [TV programme] BBC.

Frazer, J. (2020), 'Want a New Job? Join the Police', *The JC*, 3 January. Available online: https://www.thejc.com/lifestyle/features/want-a-new-job-join-the-police-1.494889 (accessed February 2020).
*Friday Night Dinner* (2011–), [TV programme] Channel 4.
Gilman, S. (1991), *The Jew's Body*, New York: Routledge.
*Giri/Haji* (2019–), [TV programme] BBC Two.
*Grandma's House* (2010–12), [TV programme] BBC Two.
Harpin, L. (2018), 'BBC's New Drama *McMafia* under Fire for Anti-Israel Tropes', *The JC*, 2 January. Available online: https://www.thejc.com/news/uk-news/bbc-s-new-drama-mcmafia-under-fire-for-anti-jewish-tropes-1.451333 (accessed January 2020).
*Hebburn* (2012–13), [TV programme] BBC Two.
Jacobson, H. (2007), 'There Is an Obduracy in Anti-Semitism', *The New Humanist*, 31 May. Available online: https://newhumanist.org.uk/articles/723/there-is-an-obduracy-in-anti-semitism (accessed January 2020).
*Jewish Mum of the Year* (2012–13), [TV programme] Channel 4.
*Jews* (2008), [TV programme] BBC Four.
*Jews at Ten* (2012), [TV programme] Channel 4.
Kraft, D. (2018), 'Is New BBC Hit TV Show "McMafia" Anti-Semitic and Anti-Israeli? Its Writer Fights Back', *Ha'aretz*, 9 January. Available online: https://www.haaretz.com/life/.premium-is-mcmafia-anti-semitic-and-anti-israeli-its-writer-fights-back-1.5730028 (accessed December 2019).
Margolyes, M. et al. (2019), 'Open Letter', *The Stage*, 22 August. Available online: https://www.thestage.co.uk/opinion/letters/2019/jewish-theatremakers-speak-out-against-cultural-appropriation-on-stage-your-views-august-22/ (accessed December 2019).
*McMafia* (2018), [TV programme] BBC.
Moloney, D. (2014), Personal communication to author, 10 September.
*Peaky Blinders* (2013–), [TV programme] BBC.
Round, S. (2014), 'Alfie Solomons, a Gangster Who Reached His Peak', *The JC*, 30 October. Available online: https://www.thejc.com/news/uk-news/alfie-solomons-a-gangster-who-reached-his-peak-1.60183 (accessed December 2019)
Spiro, A. (2018), 'Global Crime with a Local Flavor: Israeli Actress Yuval Scharf Stars in the BBC's "McMafia," Which Has Been Criticized for Its Portrayal of Organized Crime in the Jewish state', *Jerusalem Post*, 7 January. Available online: https://www.jpost.com/Israel-News/Culture/Global-crime-with-a-local-flavor-533070 (accessed December 2019).
Stratton, J. (2000), *Coming Out Jewish: Constructing Ambivalent Identities*, London and New York: Routledge.
Stratton, J. (2008), *Jewish Identity in Western Pop Culture: The Holocaust and Trauma through Modernity*, Basingstoke and New York: Palgrave Macmillan.
Stratton, J. (2009), *Jews, Race, and Popular Music*, Farnham, UK: Ashgate.
*Strictly Kosher* (2011–12), [TV programme] ITV.

*Two Jews on a Cruise* (2013), [TV programme] BBC Two.
*WPC 56* (2013–15), [TV programme] BBC One.
Yaffe, J. (1990), 'Is This Any Job for a Nice Jewish Boy?' in J. L. Breen and M. H. Greenberg (eds), *Synod of Sleuths: Essays on Judeo-Christian Detective Fiction*, 19–55, Metuchen, NJ and London: The Scarecrow Press.

Part Five

# Interviews with Contemporary British-Jewish Theatre Artists (2017–2018)

# 14

# Nicholas Hytner

This interview took place on 30 March 2017, in London.

**Jeanette Malkin (JM):** I understand you grew up in Manchester, in a very Jewish environment.

**Nicholas Hytner (NH):** It was Jewish but it wasn't religious. Until I had my bar mitzvah I attended the Reform congregation, although my father's side was Orthodox. My upbringing was less Jewish than a lot of the people you're going to talk to.

**JM:** I don't define Jewishness by any connection with ritual.

**NH:** I agree with that. I can only speak personally and from observation. From my tiny corner of experience. But I think that the British-Jewish experience is entirely different from the American-Jewish experience, and obviously entirely different from the German-Jewish or French-Jewish experience. In a way, the British-Jewish community is very protected. I think British-Jewish communities – for the first time in my experience – and I'm sixty – are justifiably and genuinely terrified by antisemitism. But I think French Jews never lost their fear, and you know, German Jews obviously. French and German Jews have the living memory – even middle-aged German and French Jews – of slaughter; whereas with British Jews it's not so.

The really strange difference to me – I will start with a small anecdote which I think is quite revealing. When I commissioned Mike Leigh to make a play at the National, I just said, 'Make a play,' and Mike said to me, 'I'm not going to tell you anything about it,' which is always the deal with Mike. 'You give me sixteen weeks and you come to see the first run through.' And then he said, 'But I think I will tell you that I want to make something about what we have in common.' I said, 'That's great,' and we laughed a lot. And we do laugh about common roots. He then had to find eight Jewish actors, because Mike's plays are all improvised collaboratively. He knew he wanted to make a play about an Orthodox Jewish family or a kind of lapsed Orthodox Jewish family. And I'm sure even then he knew the catalyst of the play was going to be the son's rediscovery of ultra-

Orthodoxy because that's a kind of nightmare of assimilated London Jews. But he knew that every single one of his actors had to be Jewish, and not just Jewish but Jewish enough to be able to improvise freely from the basis of quite intense Jewish experience and upbringing. That meant in turn that the casting director of the National had to call all the prominent London agents and say: 'Mike Leigh is doing a play, could you tell me which of your clients are Jewish?' And all the Jewish agents, and there are lots, said, 'Here is the list.' Every non-Jewish agent said something like, 'Well, I don't know who's Jewish, how would I know?' And that is inconceivable in America. In New York that would not be the case. First of all, most of the agents are Jewish, and even the non-Jewish ones – because New York in general and Broadway in particular is so very Jewish – are familiar with Jewish culture, are familiar with who's Jewish. That in its turn says something about the way British Jews stay under the radar.

**JM:** They're not open about being Jewish.

**NH:** It's not that they're not open, because I've always been very happy, rather proud to tell people I'm Jewish. It's just something that they tend to keep separate from, very definitely, their professional lives. A lot of the Jews I know – not in the theatre, but a lot of the Jews I know in London – their social lives are almost entirely Jewish. But their professional lives may be predominantly non-Jewish. I know lots of Jewish professional people, lawyers, financiers, a number of artists, for whom their Jewishness plays no part in their careers and in their non-family life, but whose social lives may be mainly Jewish.

London has changed since I first arrived. A large percentage weren't born here. That's always been the case, of course. London is a great immigrant city so it always changes, and most of London is completely relaxed about being part of a vibrantly multicultural cosmopolitan city. Manchester has changed too. When I was growing up, every British school day started with a religious assembly. At my high school, Jewish boys went off to Jewish prayers and the majority went off to Christian prayers. And now, in that same school there are Muslim prayers and Hindu prayers. There weren't when I was a kid, because those communities had yet to develop.

**Eckart Voigts (EV):** Julia Pascal has said that there is a constant low-level antisemitism in England. In a way you're being ... careful.

**NH:** Everything here is 'Don't make an exhibition of yourself'. I would say, until the last few horrible years, really quite a low level of antisemitism. Speaking as a sixty-year-old gay man: it was agony in the sixties and the seventies to grow up then and try to come to terms with being gay. That was awful. Being Jewish? It didn't matter as much. Really, truly. Being gay was tough; being Jewish was not tough. That was my experience. It's hard to come to terms with the current legitimization of antisemitism, particularly on the Left. I'd expect if from the populist Right. It never went away on the far-Right. But the current state of the British Labour Party horrifies me.

**JM:** Where did your parents come from?

**NH:** My parents were both born here.

**JM:** And their parents?

**NH:** My father's father was a Galitzianer (from eastern Poland). His mother was born here, her parents born in Warsaw. My mother's mother was born here; her father was born in South Africa very shortly after his family first left Kovna, Lithuania. So it's all over the place. But I felt my experience growing up in Manchester was only partially about being Jewish, it was as much about other things.

**EV:** What are the funding situations here? That's something that I'm also interested in. It's probably the case, if you're doing 'Black-British Theatre' or something, you would seek Arts Council funding.

**NH:** Really interesting. I'm not aware of any Jewish theatre groups that have sought funding. Is it because we've kept our heads below the parapet? And maybe we thought that other minorities in some way needed the funding more than we did. Or – and this is a depressing thought and plays to what Julia Pascal said – maybe we thought we wouldn't get it if we applied. Now, I'm not so sure. I'm aware of young Jewish theatre-makers who very much want to make theatre that expresses their identity. I think they deserve funding the same as everyone else. I also think they'd find it hard in the current climate to make the case for it.

**EV:** Where are these British-Jewish plays being produced? Obviously, Hampstead Theatre.

**NH:** Hampstead has a large Jewish community, so I'd say Hampstead for many years had the most Jewish repertoire in the country, yes.

**JM:** If you were looking at the question of British-Jewish theatre, would you tend to approach it by generation? I mean we have Pinter, Kops, Wesker, Berkoff – we have a generation of important Jewish theatre people who were very aware of being Jews.

**NH:** So interesting! There'd be a lot of people who would go 'Pinter, Jewish? I didn't know.' I would say that generations of students and theatre goers, do not approach his plays through …

**JM:** Oh, absolutely.

**NH:** Even Wesker: when *Roots*[1] was revived three or four years ago, I don't think it was received as a Jewish play. I think it was received as an East End play. Watching *Roots* so beautifully revived, I thought that the London Jewish community is more confident than the Manchester one. And I was very moved by it. I thought then that things have kind of taken a turn – in one way for the better, in that the majority just don't know what a Jew is and don't care. Really don't care. It's horrible that antisemitism has found a new voice in the very political circles that used to be the natural home for people like me who work in the theatre. I was slow to wake up to it. It's unavoidable now.

**EV:** Can I ask you about your plans for the new theatre?

**NH:** Yeah, it opens in October [2017]. We're starting with a play by Richard Bean, a very funny play, the kind of a play that would be so inconceivable in the German theatre because bringing in the laughs is high up his agenda. It's about, I would say, the most influential of all Jewish immigrants to London: Karl Marx[2]. But who in this country knows that Karl Marx was Jewish? Very few. And to be honest, his relationship with his own Jewishness did him no credit. And when he arrived in London, he was fleeing political, not religious, persecution. Yet, in Highgate cemetery, there he is, along with many other irreligious British Jews, buried alongside the grandees of Victorian London.

## Notes

1   Wesker, A. (2001), *Wesker Plays 1*, London: Methuen.
2   Referring to the play *Young Marx* – Bean, R. and C. Coleman (2017), *Young Marx*, London: Oberon Books.

# 15

# Julia Pascal

This interview took place on 28 March 2018, in London.

**Eckart Voigts (EV):** Your *Shylock Play*[1] was staged at the Arcola Theatre, wasn't it? The casting was very interesting with Ruth Posner [as actress and Holocaust survivor] as the main character. How did that come about? I know it was a long time ago.

**Julia Pascal (JP):** It was 2003, I think. I guess when you live in Britain and when anyone talks about the Jews, they always talk about *The Merchant of Venice*. It becomes a weight and you either ignore it or you do something with it. For a very long time I ignored it and then I thought I want to do something with it. And because of Ruth Posner, because she was an actor, and someone who escaped the Warsaw Ghetto, she carried in her body a certain atmosphere of Poland, and in her voice. To juxtapose that presence against the Shakespeare play became a challenge and an interest to me. So I asked myself, 'What would happen if this time it was framed not as a full production, but as a dress rehearsal, so that Sarah (the 'witness' character) can break in and out of it?' I had a certain leeway with it as a director and a writer. To reframe it within a Jewish perspective that was also a woman's perspective.

**Jeanette Malkin (JM):** It's really interesting the way the character of Sarah, played by Ruth Posner, concentrates on trying to save Jessica, whereas Shylock is fairly hopeless. Jewish women are often a potential either for conversion to Christianity, or to be saved through marriage, in much of British literature.

**JP:** That's right. I don't think the audience knew what I was doing because that Jewish perspective is not known here. Shakespeare is always seen through a Christian perspective, and seen as a noble play, and I wanted to upend that, by adding a spectacular conversion of Shylock. The forced conversion and the importance of the Inquisition.

**JM:** I see the play-within-the-play, the satire and the grotesque happenings. Can you discuss these things? What's their role? Visual?

**JP:** I had to think about the Catholic Church, and why it was appealing, and why it might have been appealing to Jews who converted to it willingly rather than having to submit to it or die. The very theatricality of it, the imagery, the music, the beauty of theatre that the Catholic Church has embraced and has used to sell its message, I put that into the play, because the play is a piece of theatre about theatre, and about the Catholic Church as theatre and the attraction of that. Sarah is attracted by the celebration of the Mass, the joy and celebration; the Catholic Church has a way of sucking people in. It's a play about theatre, and the theatre of religion, and how attractive that could be.

**EV:** I thought it was fascinating that Sarah had escaped from the Ghetto by having a fake conversion … she parades as a Catholic.

**JP:** Which is based on the truth. Based on Ruth's actual situation. I wasn't inventing anything. The production reflects the historical subtext because Ruth, as a child who hid from the Nazis, only survived by pretending to be a Catholic. And in the production, she is a living witness to the way the central myth of Jews as Christ-killers is a narrative promulgated by the Catholic Church and the Inquisition. In her own life Ruth had to embrace the enemy and its culture in order to survive. Yes, it gave her another level, and because it was true, it gave me another level because she didn't need to act it. So the actor speaking those lines is speaking her own life. It gives her an authenticity. If I had cast an actor without that history, then it would have been merely an acting job rather than a visceral representation of a person's own life. These unspoken layers for me were very important. What language does the human body speak when that body has known Shoah? That is the question posed by Ruth's living presence in this new look at this troublesome play.

**EV:** I was also wondering about Portia. I haven't seen the production, but she doesn't come across as a very endearing character.

**JP:** No. That was interesting to me. Something I had never read about her, which I discovered when producing the play, was that Portia is seen as an impartial lawyer and yet she is a woman acting out of her own interest. Because she is defending her fiancé's friend, she's not impartial and yet she's always presented as this neutral figure, putting the world to right with her quality of mercy and displacing Jewish greed. I tried to present her as part of that antisemitic, self-serving society rather than the Christian angel. In my production Portia and Nerissa go into the Venice Ghetto and are disgusted by it. So that you see the antisemitism of Portia. That's an addition, obviously.

**EV:** We've been interviewing people who identify as British-Jewish and we'd like to be clear as to what that is. Where are the boundaries? I think there is no real group identity, is there? The 'We are the British-Jewish or the Anglo-Jewish playwrights'.

**JP:** No. There is no collaboration among us. Sadly. I think it has to do with being a Jew in Britain. We are not at all secure. We are a tiny group within the country's population and, as writers writing on Jewish issues, we are miniscule. We are all aware that the atmosphere is highly charged when the word 'Jew' or 'Jewish' is spoken … It's compounded by Israel. The Left, who run the arts and the theatre, is profoundly anti-Israel, therefore anything a writer produces or anything that is said in public, any petition that is signed or not signed, or whether support is given or not given to BDS [Boycott, Divestment and Sanctions campaign], affects whether work is commissioned. Many British Jews are frightened. To be a Jew in England has always been, and is, a state of low-level anxiety. Therefore there is always an inner fracture. Being a Jew does not place a person in a fashionable minority. I often feel that when I say I am a Jew there is a pause of embarrassment from the host community. I realize I am saying 'host' community as if we are guests. But in fact, we are not legally here. The 1290 deportation of the Jews was never rescinded. Our history in England is hardly discussed. If you go to the Arts Council to put on a play that touches Jewish history in any complex way, you're very unlikely to get support because Jews are perceived to be rich and can look after themselves.

**JM:** But take someone like Patrick Marber, who's very successful, and, if I understand correctly, has only one play with a Jewish theme [*Howard Katz*[2]]. It doesn't seem to affect Jewish playwrights as such.

**JP:** If you don't come out, if you're not writing Jewish themes particularly, you can assimilate and be absorbed and that's fine. You can 'pass'. See, I don't sign petitions against Israel, people don't quite know what I am. They don't know how to place me. Because I'm not writing *Seven Jewish Children*.[3] I'll never get a play in the Royal Court or the National, because even the plays of the National are either about Jewish victimhood or they're anti-Zionist. Paradoxically, my published dramas are stocked in the National Theatre Bookshop.

**Sarah Ablett (SA):** How much difference is there do you think between being a Jewish woman or being a Jewish man?

**JP:** I think it's all about class in this country. If you're a certain class, the gender isn't that important. And if you're a Jew, you have to be the 'right kind of Jew', who says Israel is terrible, Palestine is a good idea. The Jewish state should be dismantled. When I use the word 'Zionism', I'm aware of what it means. To those liberal thinkers who declare themselves anti-Zionist it means that Israel is a rogue state. They believe that it should be dismantled, like Yugoslavia or South Africa. That's the base line. There are two issues on the table here, certainly class is important, those from a certain class tend to give commissions to younger versions of themselves or to those who are already serving the establishment ... When it comes to writing about Israel, evidence reveals that only the anti-Zionist writer is commissioned and produced on mainstream subsidized British stages. Anything with nuance or complex historical interrogation will end up on the fringe. The binary and the easy option have dominated the Royal Court Theatre and the National Theatre output.

**JM:** When I think of American-Jewish plays, I can't think of any written about Israel. Here we have plays that take place in Gaza.

**JP:** It could have to do with the British Mandate. There is more of a connection between Britain and Israel.

**JM:** Yes, that is a possibility.

**JP:** I've interviewed many Jews for different projects, I think many of them have a mental suitcase packed.

**JM:** In Britain?

**JP:** Yes, dig a little bit and you'll get it. The Brexit story for example. I already made sure I have a French passport. I married a French man and had a French passport. But when Brexit happened I still felt very shaken and it was something Jewish inside me that made me feel disturbed. I don't think Jews in Britain ever feel really comfortable. Yes, those of a certain class try to hide it and assimilate. The Pinter experience seems to me as one of those. To be fashionably anti-Israel means that you are loved by the establishment. So your political opinions affect your artistic career, that's for sure.

I'm a secular Jew, I married out, I don't have Jewish children, and yet what I mostly write about is Jewish culture. Well, 95 per cent. I think it's got to do with my grandparents having brought me up; they were Romanian Jews. I heard Yiddish and I'm sure that's what that's about. It's the European experience.

**JM:** When did your grandparent arrive in England?

**JP:** In 1910. They remembered pogroms. That's what my grandparents were talking about when they came to England from Romania. They fled after the 1903 Kishinev pogrom, which their parents may have experienced as they came from Ukraine. All these waves of suppressed trauma remain. My grandparents kept kosher and did not turn on the light on Sabbath but it was their foreignness, their sense of danger and their difference that formed my sense of being other. I knew no girls at school with grandparents like mine.

**EV:** There was this commotion about your play *Crossing Jerusalem*[4] in Miami.[5]

**JP:** Yes, it was taken off!

**EV:** Because it was seen as antisemitic?

**JP:** I was accused of being an anti-Zionist, an antisemitic, a self-hating Jew. I had a good laugh, because sometimes here I am seen as the Zionist-Jewish woman warrior. I couldn't be offended by it, but it taught me something about conservative Jews in Miami.

**JM:** You could be very successful in the States.

**JP:** I'd love to be! I feel my work is more connected to that Yiddish-American world than the English one. This is because the rhythms of Yiddish lie underneath American-English. I hear it in New York. I never hear it in English society. This means that I have two 'English' languages, the English that I speak to English people who are Christian-based and then I have a place where I relax with Jews. With them I don't need to censor my thinking. I can say 'I schlepped here' or I can use the word *chutzpah* without having to explain it.

**SA:** How would you say that these feature aesthetically within your work? These different languages, the Yiddish you know. Do you speak Romanian?

**JP:** No. I speak French and a little German. It affects the aesthetics of my works profoundly. Certainly that of my more experimental plays, which are my instinctual way of writing. *Theresa*, *The Dybbuk*,[6] *The Golem*,[7] *Dead Woman on Holiday*,[8] they are scattered, they use many different traditions. It is a kind of jumping from Yiddish to English, to hearing my grandparents speaking other languages, it's that scattering of having to adapt in a multi-faceted way that has made my aesthetic mirror that volatile inner-landscape.

**EV:** But doesn't the British theatre system foster very different kinds of plays? Plays like *Crossing Jerusalem* that are topical and debate topical issues, rather than have a poetic-lyrical style?

**JP:** Yes. When *Crossing Jerusalem* was commissioned I thought, 'I have to write a straight play,' so it was a challenge, just to write these scenes, 'and then this will happen', and 'this will be the trajectory'. As a writer, to answer your question, the impulse is to push yourself to try and make every play different. To give it its own language, a vocabulary, a theatrical aesthetic. I quite enjoy that challenge.

**EV:** Did you notice a difference when working in the US, as opposed to the UK?

**JP:** Yes, I did the *Dybbuk* in New York after being invited to stage it in Theatre for the New City's Dream Up Festival in 2010. I just took the production over with European actors.

It was my first time producing anything in the USA. I felt I was jumping over the mountain. I had absolutely no idea, I didn't know anybody. It did extremely well, and all sorts of people came to see it. Not only Jews. There was a group from India who wanted to ask me all sorts of questions about it. I believe that the overlap between the mystical and the political interested them and many others. They got the multiple levels. My version of the *Dybbuk* is not naturalistic in form, as the Ansky version is. I use fragmentation and Rough Theatre techniques; it is inspired by Brecht, by Expressionism, by Yiddish Theatre. In New York's Lower East Side, it sat so comfortably. We were full and had to turn away audiences. The management asked us to extend the run. I feel totally comfortable in New York. I often feel like I'm in the wrong country. Why the hell did my grandparents not go to America?! Why did they get off the boat so early?

**Ido Telem (IT):** Do you think if there was less antisemitism, you would move to other subjects? Is it an interest of yours?

**JP:** Exile and difference is always my subject. It does not always have to be about Jews. It is just that my sense of 'other' comes from my experience of living as a Jew and looking 'different'. My life influences my writing and my interest in the 'other' is enormous. I'm writing a modern *Medea*. It's based on a woman I met who is a Kurdish fighter against the Turks. She came here as an asylum seeker. Her English was terrible, but I got enough and I've put it together with other research I've done on the Kurds. It's about the Kurdish struggle for independence but I think it also reflects debates I've heard all my life about the arguments for and against a Jewish state. It's about culture; it's about religion, about women fighting. Certainly, it also has a strong feminist narrative. I probably will be able to get that on. Because no one will understand what I'm doing, they'll think it's all about fashionable minorities.

**IT:** Little will they know that it's actually Jewish.

**EV:** That's one of our assumptions, that artists tend to address their Judaism covertly.

**JP:** I think you cannot help it. In this case I think about Abraham and Sarah being Kurds as they came from Ur. Nowadays this is Kurdistan. Also, we are genetically very close. As we are with Palestinians.

My Medea, for example, is a Kurd of Muslim background and her Jason is of Iraqi Muslim background. They are both Muslims but utterly different. Jason's Iraqi father tells his son that he must leave his Kurdish beloved because she's the wrong kind of Muslim. He has to get rid of her and marry his cousin. Of course, the play critiques the dominance of family tradition over individual choice. The criticism of patriarchal values is there. However, the play is not didactic. It expresses an understanding of the push-pull dynamic. It acknowledges the dilemma of a daughter who disobeys her mother to become a Kurdish fighter and a son who unwillingly obeys his father to conform to patriarchal values.

**JM:** I'm interested in how Jewish culture feeds into a type of theatre language, not directly translated as themes or characters.

**JP:** It's in *Dead Woman on Holiday*, the continual interrogation of language. The way Jews of my grandmother's generation carried several languages in their heads and everyday vocabulary. This is set in the Nuremberg Trials and the central characters are interpreters there. This choice of work is no accident. It allows a constant questioning of language. *Woman on the Bridge*[9] is perhaps also interesting in that way. It's Jewish but it's not Jewish. The narrative is about a secular Jewish English journalist, Judith, who goes to New York to reconnaissance for a BBC Radio job but also to meet her great-aunt. Through her, she learns of her grandmother's suicide and gradually we witness Judith's own suicidal tendencies. This is about a generational rift between great-aunt and great-niece. Both are outsiders to their (Jewish) society and both suffer the fragmentation of the psyche provoked by exile. Their conflict dramatizes

Jews of two different generations who have both absorbed several cultures and are rooted in none. It is also about the Jewish woman who has no worth in the traditional family unless she is a wife and mother.

**EV:** We do indeed find there is a lot of Jewish influence in the British theatre scene, but nobody would, like you, become part of the new aesthetic identity. Overtly.

**JP:** It can seem parochial, it seems narrowing, not being universal, not being very important.

**JM:** We need a television series here.

**JP:** Yes, we do, but who would do it?

**EV:** Television certainly has an influence on the theatre; there was, for instance, the influential Jack Rosenthal.

**JP:** Yes, Jack's work was great. In the sixties, it was all right to be Jewish, in a way. It was cool to be Jewish as it was seen as liberal. Now this is not the case.

**IT:** If you had to speculate about the future of Jewish theatre or identity in the UK, would you say it's a slow fade, or do you think this is the *zeitgeist* and something might change?

**JP:** It depends on what happens globally and what happens with Israel. You can't separate these because theatre is profoundly political, although you can write a play and divorce it from what's happening. Were there to be a terrible tragedy in Israel, then the mood might change.

**JM:** Or were there to be political sanity in Israel, that could also change things?

**JP:** Yes. It's very hard to write about Jews, because you can't write about Jews in a vacuum. Israel has become such an important part of our lives. You can't divorce the two, being a Jew and an Israeli – as a writer, it's difficult.

## Notes

1   Pascal, J. (2007), *The Shylock Play*, London: Oberon Books.
2   Marber, P. (2001), *Howard Katz*, New York: Grove Press.

3 Churchill, C. (2009), *Seven Jewish Children*, London: Nick Hern Books.
4 Pascal, J. ([2003] 2017), *Crossing Jerusalem and Other Plays*, London: Oberon.
5 *Crossing Jerusalem* was shown at the Jewish Community Centre in Miami. After four performances, it was cancelled, responding to criticism of audience members that it was anti-Israeli 'in order to avoid any further pain and to engage in rigorous, vibrant conversation that advances our community' (JCC President Gary Bomzer). See the report online in the *Times of Israel* (19 February 2016), https://www.timesofisrael.com/miami-jewish-center-cancels-play-criticized-as-anti-israel/ (accessed 20 August 2019).
6 Pascal, J. (2000), *Pascal: The Holocaust Trilogy: Theresa; A Dead Woman on Holiday; The Dybbuk*, London: Oberon Books.
7 Pascal, J. (2003), *Pascal: Crossing Jerusalem and Other Plays*, London: Oberon Books.
8 Pascal, J. (2000), *Pascal: The Holocaust Trilogy: Theresa; A Dead Woman on Holiday; The Dybbuk*, London: Oberon Books.
9 Pascal, J. (2013), *Political Plays: Honeypot, Broken English, Ninevah, Woman on the Bridge*, London: Oberon Books.

# 16

# Patrick Marber

This interview took place on 16 May 2018, in London.

**Jeanette Malkin (JM):** A year and a half ago we wrote you a letter asking you about your relationship with Shylock. You wrote many things, but at the end of the letter you wrote, 'I'm a writer and a Jew and an Englishman and a European and a husband, son, father etc. But I was a Jew before I was a writer and I feel a belonging with a particular tradition and a particular way of perceiving the world.' Did this sense of Jewishness stem from your childhood? Could we begin with your parents? Where they come from?

**Patrick Marber (PM):** Both my parents are Jewish. They're both still alive.[1] My father's father was Belgian. Born in Antwerp. There's a whole branch of the family from there.

**JM:** Belgian Orthodox?

**PM:** Yes. My father is a member of the West London Synagogue which is Orthodox. He's very conscious of his Judaism, always has been. He's very ill, he's dying. I'm the *kaddishel* (the son who will say the mourning prayer). I'll be saying the prayer. My father's great friend Henri sent me a phonetic text nearly twenty years ago when I was writing a *kaddish* scene in my play *Howard Katz*.[2] I kept it on my pin board. I knew I'd need it one day. I haven't read Hebrew since my bar mitzvah. But I'm very glad I had one despite being less keen at the time. My mother is a Jewess, both her parents are Jewish.

**JM:** Where did her people come from?

**PM:** East End and North London. Before that, I don't know. Two or three generations back there's Polish blood on my father's side. I didn't like, as a boy, going to all these Jewish events and religious services – I found it oppressive. Which I don't like to admit. Now I find it comforting – somewhere in the back of my mind I'm looking to join a *shul*. Not as a true believer but as a Jew checking back in. But when I was growing up, teenage years and twenties, I didn't feel the sense of belonging I feel so strongly now. Back then I felt deep feelings for writer Jews. *Shraybers* [writers in Yiddish]. This was a tradition of Judaism and belonging I loved. Arnold Wesker, Harold Pinter, Philip Roth, Arthur Miller. And comedians too of course. The Marx Brothers, Woody Allen, Mel Brooks.

**JM:** Mamet.

**PM:** Mamet for sure and Mike Nichols, Billy Wilder and so on – these were the Jews I followed and admired.

**JM:** Did you have holidays at home?

**PM:** We did Friday night dinner. Every Friday night we'd all be in, my mother would light the candles, my father would bless my brother and I – it moves me to remember this – we'd say prayers for bread and wine, so that's the only Hebrew I can still speak.

**JM:** That's a very good base.

**PM:** Yes, it is. My father would drag me to synagogue on various Jewish holidays, and I would go, reluctantly ... So when I discovered Cultural Judaism, that was something I could celebrate. I didn't want to *not* be a Jew, but I wanted to find a version of it that I could relate to, and that had meaning for me. When I found the writers, the filmmakers, the comedians, I felt much more comfortable as a Jew and could embrace that.

**JM:** You grew up in Wimbledon?

**PM:** Yes, in a small house. It's a little suburb of London, famous really for the tennis, we lived quite close to the courts. Then we moved around a bit, so I grew up in some other houses, but the first six or seven years of my life were in a little 1960s new-build detached house, a four-bedroom house. Quite small but nice, in a cul-de-sac. And we had a back garden which I loved.

**JM:** Did you grow up with Jewish friends?

**PM:** Yes, a few, not many. I was at a school where there were maybe twenty Jews in a school of four hundred boys. I was conscious that I could be bullied for being a Jew. I was worried about it. I wouldn't say I ever experienced extreme antisemitism, but you know, comments. Things overheard for sure.

I knew I was different and to an extent I identified with other boys who were different; the Indian and Pakistani kids. There was a small group of those boys too. So I kind of felt that I was a bit like them. Later, at boarding school, I had to go to Christian prayers, chapel, and I didn't like that.

**PM:** It was a Christian school?

**PM:** Yes. I remember protesting about enforced Christianity to the headmaster who responded, 'If you don't like the club, don't join the club.' This was in 1979. So my Judaism was always present and potent and meaningful to me.

**JM:** As difference?

**PM:** As difference. Absolutely.

**JM:** And today?

**PM:** Now, I have a circle of Jewish friends. Writers, comedians, actors. And I love my Jewish friends and I feel identification with them and a love for them that is slightly different from my friendships with gentiles. It's not very different, but it's a tiny bit different. We've been through something similar.

**JM:** So you really did experience a sense of being different, a sense of being an outsider.

**PM:** Not completely an outsider. A little bit. It's only a little but it's significant to me. I remember when I was thirteen or fourteen and learning about the Second World War – really learning about it. A feeling of anxiety when we were learning about the Nazis and the Holocaust, and being the only Jew in the classroom, and feeling it differently from the other kids. Feeling the horror of it, I guess, personally. Because this was a generation ago, and I'd heard my parents talking about it, and we had relatives who were murdered by the Nazis and I knew people who knew people who died in the camps. It was shocking and it was very painful. It still is. I take it personally. I remain offended. Who wouldn't? That feeling never left me – the horror, the injustice, the cataclysm of it. It affected my view of humanity, and what people could do. How could it not?

**JM:** If I look at *Dealer's Choice*,[3] for example, which is more or less your first play …

**PM:** It is.

**JM:** It's revealing, I assume, of people you met in London during your early London period? Or are these voices you bring with you from …

**PM:** Well, the father is sort of my father, and I'm sort of the son, and I played a lot of poker, and I knew these guys. So they are all combinations of people, but the core of the play is a Jewish father-son relationship. It's not declared that they're Jews, but I made sure they had names that could be Jewish or gentile.

**JM:** Stephen and Carl.

**PM:** They can be played as Jews or not. But the guy – Nigel Lindsay – who created the role of Mugsy is a Jew. And so the first Mugsy was a Jew. To a small extent I feel it's a Jewish play, a Jewish family drama, or a workplace drama. It doesn't declare itself overtly as such, but it is. That said, I've seen it performed in many different countries and cultures over close to a quarter of a century since it was premiered and it doesn't really matter. It's a play about men in a particular world but it seems to travel well. It's been a very lucky play for me and I'm extremely grateful to it.

**JM:** Are there any markers in other play that might suggest Jewish themes or context, any cloaked markers?

**PM:** Well, look at *Closer*.[4] One of the characters is called Daniel Woolf. He's obviously a Jew. For me he's a Jew, but I don't want to limit who can act this part. Both in England and globally. So, he's called Daniel Woolf. If you've got some great Jewish actor who can play him, fabulous. If you haven't – doesn't matter. So is *Closer* a Jewish play? Of course it is, it's written by a Jew. *Howard Katz* is a declared Jewish play. *Closer* is an undeclared Jewish play.

**JM:** So the question 'what's a Jewish play,' for you, would include plays written by Jews that don't necessarily include Jewish themes or explicit Jewish markers? Such as, for example, the Austrian-Jewish playwright Arthur Schnitzler, most of whose plays have no explicit Jewish themes or characters, but whose Viennese world was, for the most part, Viennese-Jewish?

**PM:** It's a good question and a very difficult question to answer! And I don't think I can answer it.

**JM:** *Closer* and *Dealer's Choice* were great successes. Everybody talks about your talent, how you have an innate sense of form. And everything you've adapted, many plays which were great dramatic successes, everything is so perfectly structured, and then we come to a declared Jewish play …

**PM:** And it's a messy play. It was necessary for me to write a messy play, after the structural coherence of *Dealer's Choice* and *Closer*. It was a conscious choice to write a different kind of play. I wanted to write a play with a big company of actors in it. I wanted to write a play with a declared protagonist, because I hadn't done that before. And I wanted to write a play that was more of a collage rather than a finely structured piece. These were all conscious decisions, and I knew my protagonist before I knew the play. I wanted to write for this voice. And remember: I was writing as a young man about a middle-aged man; at the time it was guesswork. But I wanted to write about this guy, who I thought, in another life, I could become.

**JM:** What? A failure?

**PM:** A sort of failure, yes. Well, he had a successful career that meant nothing to him. And a man who'd never taken the time to extract any meaning from his life. A lost soul. A wandering Jew. The director of the New York production – very good guy called Doug Hughes – he described the play as being like watching a man falling through a tree clinging to branches. And it was a very important play for me to write. And I've rewritten it, periodically. I've done a new draft; someone might revive it next year, or the year after.

**JM:** Will it be republished?

**PM:** Yes, I'll republish it. Faber are going to bring out two anthologies of my work next year, and there will be a new *Howard Katz* in that. But the DNA of the play remains the same, and people who like it love it, and people who don't – hate it. And there it is.

**JM:** You know, I specialize in German Expressionism, and I couldn't help feeling that *Katz* is really an expressionist play.

**PM:** Yes, well, it comes from *Woyzeck*,[5] via *Edmund*; those are its two source plays. A drifty play, where a guy goes through the mill, comes out the other side burnished.

**JM:** But the mill is seen through his eyes. Subjectivity, a very expressionistic characteristic. I could almost see it being directed in a warped way, because it's all through Katz's eyes.

**PM:** Yes, the potentially great production of *Howard Katz* would be experimental, hallucinatory, dreamlike. A Paul Klee. Which I wasn't able to deliver because I was too close to it, maybe too young and definitely too busy rewriting the damn thing in rehearsals – an extremely tolerant, talented and beautiful company of actors went through a lot on that one! But one day someone, hopefully, will, as you say, direct it as a piece of subjective expressionism. Its production will be much stranger and more haunting than the production I delivered. And it needs some very talented person to really go to town with it. I hope it happens one day, ideally in my lifetime, but who knows.

**JM:** It also seems to me that it's just more difficult to write an overtly Jewish play. Emotionally, I would think.

**PM:** Not for me. I didn't find it difficult. I loved writing that play. I loved being able to say some things that, as a Jew, amused me to say. There were jokes in it, or characters in it, that just made me cackle with laughter. In a way that was funny to me, but probably only to me and maybe other Jews.

**JM:** It *is* a funny play. And your conversations with god are especially intriguing. The ending of *Howard Katz* is wonderful.

**PM:** *Howard Katz* was going to kill himself, and the person who said, 'Don't kill him' was Stoppard. He read the play, made me lunch and gave me some notes. He said, 'I have one suggestion for you. Don't kill him. Make him live.' I think it's a play that will have its day one day. I still think it's good. I think it's got flaws, but all plays are flawed. But it was, you know, even at the time, 2001, it was a hard sell. A play about a middle-aged man having a crisis – who cares. People don't care about that subject. I do, though. And other men and women of around fifty. I think what got me into it was directing *The Old Neighborhood* by Mamet.[6] I so loved directing that play. I thought, 'Yes, I'll write a Jewish play.'

**JM:** Mamet, yes. Though all of Mamet's plays are undeclared.

**PM:** Except *The Old Neighborhood*.

**JM:** Yes! It seems to me that what Mamet has, and what you and Pinter have, is a voice. Mamet's comes from a Chicago Jewish background. It's a somewhat similar voice to Pinter's, in the sense that it's curt, and a little scary. A threatening type of voice. They both claim it comes from their surroundings when growing up – I don't know if their people spoke like that, or always feeling threatened a bit, is part of how they felt. And you have that too. You have that voice.

**PM:** I do. I felt threatened by my father. My father is bipolar, and for the first ten years of my life he was undiagnosed. And he was this raging, frightening, strange man, who could flip from being hilarious, and making funny voices and being the warmest and the most loving man to being this red-faced fury who I was terrified of. Even though I had a traumatic time with my father, he's the one I most identify with. He's both the enemy and the person I feel I've come from. So it's a very complicated set of things. The complicated father–son relationship repeats endlessly in my work. Fathers are always being killed or dying. Have you read *The Red Lion*?[7] It's a complete dramatization of various father–son relationships in play. Sons looking for fathers, fathers accepting them and fathers rejecting them, and so on and so forth. Even in *Don Juan in Soho*,[8] the father–son relationship is very strong. The son just lies to the father to get what he wants from him. Totally exploits him. But the father loves the son, even though the son is no good. It's always present. To me, it's the core of life. How what happened to you – you know, Freudian things. What happened to you as a kid is everything. How you were with your parents, how they were with you, it's the beginning.

**JM:** 'Jewish' plays in Britain, I find, from what I've read, are mostly about families who just happen to be Jewish. There are very few plays that really have a Jewish factor.

**PM:** Yes. I think that's true to a degree. I think we English Jews don't want to make too much noise. We're doing okay, we're tolerated. To a minor extent embraced. We're doing quite well here and we just want to keep our heads down, and just not make too much noise.

**JM:** No hubris.

**PM:** Then we'll get away with it, and then we can pass as English people, which we sort of are. You know, it's a predicament. We are not fully declared. Which is why it's so strange when you see the Hasidic Jews in London, the Jewish cowboys with all the gear. And you think, guiltily, 'Don't make a big thing out of it.' That's where the antisemitism is. It's not directed so much at the liberal Jews, like me, it's directed at the religious …

**JM:** You're also a director and worked as a director from the start of your career. How is that different from being a playwright, for you?

**PM:** I love doing both. I enjoy my writing time when it's limited due to directing work. And I find that directing, being with actors, designers, the whole life of the theatre inspires me to return to my desk. For a long period, I made a conscious decision to stop directing; from 2007 to 2014 I didn't direct. I thought I'd get more writing done. In fact, this period turned out to be incredibly unproductive for me as a writer. I seem to need both elements in my life to be creative.

**JM:** At the moment you're doing quite a bit of directing; are you also writing something new?

**PM:** I'm always writing something. It's always new to me. And unknown and unknowable. And it always feels like starting from scratch. I've spent the last twenty-five years feeling like a beginner.

## Notes

1 Patrick Marber's father died on 9 June 2018.
2 Marber, P. (2001), *Howard Katz*, New York: Grove Press.
3 Marber, P. (1995), *Dealer's Choice*, London: Methuen.
4 *Closer* will be published in Marber, P. (forthcoming), *Patrick Marber: Plays*, London: Faber and Faber.
5 Written by Karl Georg Büchner and published posthumously in 1879 after it was completed by various artists after his death.
6 Mamet, D. (1998), *The Old Neighborhood – Three Plays*, USA: Vintage Books.
7 Written by Patrick Marber, the script was published by Samuel French Limited in 2018.
8 Marber, P. (2017), *Don Juan in Soho, After Molière*, London: Faber and Faber.

## 17

# Ryan Craig

These interviews took place in 2017 and 2018, in London.

**Jeanette Malkin (JM):** I think you are the (male) contemporary British-Jewish playwright with the most produced 'Jewish' plays – i.e., plays with Jewish characters; six by my count.

**Ryan Craig (RC):** It's true I've written a lot but I don't know about 'the most'. I've been fortunate that they've been produced at some high-profile venues. The National and Hampstead and so on.

**JM:** We saw *Filthy Business* the other night at the Hampstead Theatre. I loved it – and it has received mostly excellent reviews. We interviewed Nick Hytner who spoke very highly of the play. You spent more than a year as a writer-in-residence at the National Theatre?

**RC:** Yes, which is where I wrote the play. Hytner read about four or five early drafts. And we did a couple of workshops. So the DNA was there, most of the characters, Yetta ...

**JM:** Sarah Kestelman was wonderful as Yetta!

**RC:** She's fantastic. Full disclosure though, the original character was a man. He was based on my father's *zeyde* (grandfather), my great-grandfather, who started the business and whom my father constantly impersonated when I was growing up. He and his wife were Polish and they had that tough, unsentimental immigrant drive and dynamism. The first drafts of the play though had all the energy sucked into this one massive central self-obsessed figure and the other characters weren't allowed space to breathe. I thought making the central figure a woman would allow me to bring the notion of family more centrally into the play because Yetta wouldn't separate her role as a mother and grandmother from her stewardship of the business.

**JM:** Yes, the big mother, Mother Courage.

**RC:** I remember seeing Diana Rigg play Mother Courage at the National when I was a student. It was one of the productions that had an impact on me, lives with me, but I maintain it was *not* a conscious decision to reflect Brecht's play. Very little of this play was a conscious act. That's why it took so long to write. I wanted it to be as primal as possible. Built from the ground up.

**JM:** So it's more autobiographical than your other plays?

**RC:** Very much so. I wanted to tell that story, the immigrant story about the families, these characters – the successes and challenges of the immigrant.

**JM:** Could you tell me a bit about your family, growing up.

**RC:** Well, my family is very mixed. My dad's mum was an Irish Catholic and converted to Judaism (not an orthodox conversion) during the war, when she married my grandfather. I remember my father felt very warmly towards the Irish side. There were lots of them, lots of uncles and aunts and cousins. My maternal Grandmother's side was also large. They were Dutch Sephardic Jews, quite religious, but family lore has it that when my great-grandmother Betsy De Hond lost two of her sons during the war, she announced that the family would no longer be religious. She was cancelling religion. I put a version of that event in *Filthy Business*, when Yetta declares at the end of Act One: '[T]here is no God, there is no humanity, there is only family.' The strong women were a feature of both sides of my family and heavily influenced the character of Yetta. But my maternal grandfather was also a huge figure: a professional gambler, Lew Saltsman probably stemmed from Polish/Russian Jews, but, again mixed, I believe his mother was from French Huguenots. My parents brought my brother and myself up as deeply culturally Jewish, emotionally Jewish, through a combination of food and attitude – but not religiously. I had a bar mitzvah, I did that, but I was never forced to go to *shul* after that and we never ate kosher.

**JM:** Through your plays we understand that you identify with a certain group of people who happen to be Jews. However, as a professional strategy, wouldn't it have been better to write the same plays but make the characters, say, Irish?

**RC:** That's an excellent point, I must say. Every time I start a new play, I say 'no more Jews', enough with the Jews. I can't do it anymore because it makes it so hard to break through, professionally. But then what happens is that I start writing and the ghosts start taking over the characters, they're still here, there are voices that are still here. Don't know why, and I can't explain it. I mean, I was told to keep quiet about it when I was younger. Not necessarily to hide it, but just not to go around shouting about it, which is advice I've clearly ignored my entire career. I don't know why.

**JM:** The voice of the character Monty [in *Filthy Business*[1]] reminded me of Pinter. There's something so ambivalent about him.

**RC:** Well, Pinter is a big influence; you can't get away from that. My father and grandfather – if you sat and listened to them talking, they sounded like Pinter characters. For me, his writing is hyper-naturalistic. When he's writing *The Caretaker* or *The Dumb Waiter*[2] or *The Homecoming*[3] you can see that the play is affected by his life, he's writing about the places he's from. Those people are very familiar to me. They're the people I grew up with.

**JM:** A lot of dangerous crooks?

**RC:** They're tough. I wouldn't say they were crooks, but they were always ready to be violent if it was absolutely necessary, let's put it like that. They had a way of speaking that had this inbuilt menace, but also a mocking, piss-taking thing. Very tough people who use language as a weapon. And to mark out their territory. The way they speak in Pinter is very familiar to me.

**Ido Telem (IT):** Where does this menace come from? This weaponized language?

**RC:** I think there was a sense of being constantly under threat. Not just of violent attack as they were in Cable Street, but of marginalization. Of being rejected culturally by the host nation.

**JM:** Was it difficult for that generation, the combination of being Jewish and English?

**RC:** I think they wore their Jewishness very easily in spite of this, yes. The dual identity, very easily in spite of the outsider status, or maybe because of it, they were able to be absolutely themselves. All the ones I remember had incredibly strong individual personalities and quirks.

**JM:** And does your generation wear it, perhaps, less easily?

**RC:** Sometimes. The Jewish personality, if you can call it that, doesn't compliment the English personality. The English are reserved, don't really talk about themselves too much. They don't like to brag or push themselves forward. When I was growing up, my father always said, 'Don't be a *shtummer*' [silent one, in Yiddish]. That's terrible advice in England. It's good to know when to hang back here, how to read the subtle undercurrents. If there is such a thing as a Jewish personality, it's probably more forthright, so it rubs up against the English one.

**JM:** You know, Pinter and Miller have called themselves 'Jews who write'. Jews who write, not Jewish writers – that is, not Jewish writers whose Jewishness is central to their art. Now, you've written far more plays with Jewish characters than most British-Jewish (male) playwrights.[4] Where do you see yourself between being a Jew who writes and a Jewish writer?

**RC:** Well, you'd have to define for me the difference.

**JM:** A Jew who writes, like Pinter, means I'm not denying that I'm Jewish, but my writing ...

**RC:** ... is something else.

**JM:** Is something else ...

**RC:** As I've said before I don't believe the writing process is wholly conscious activity, so I don't think you make that choice. All kinds of things impact on your writing: background, education, experience, environment, cultural climate, the list goes on. I think all I've done differently is choose to be explicit for various reasons about the cultural and religious context in which the play is set. The idea is to find the universal through the specific, which I think is quite the opposite to being a niche writer. Arnold Wesker wrote to me after he saw *The Holy Rosenbergs*[5] at the National and said that we had been compared as writers, but that he thought the comparison was too easy and superficial and it was only made because we'd written about people from similar backgrounds and place. I think I'd agree with that.

**IT:** I'd like to ask you about *What We Did to Weinstein*.[6] The play ends with the son, who left England for Israel, being rejected by Israel, saying, '[T]he officer told me, I don't think you should be in the army.'

**RC:** It's kind of a key moment in the play. I guess what I'm saying is – we (diaspora Jews) can be in a lot of places, we have the freedom to be here in the

UK, to live in America, in Israel. But we are nowhere. We feel like we belong nowhere.

**JM:** I liked *Weinstein*'s mixture of realism and an open stage which allowed, for example, for the prison and hospital to appear simultaneously.

**RC:** *Weinstein* plays with form and time and space. What I was trying to do was to reveal something about the theme of the play through its structure, to show that memory sometimes deceives the person remembering. Also, the idea that memories – even of the same event – clash; I wanted the structure to reveal that. I thought that both the father, the writer Max, and the son – who left England for Israel: that both figures were after some kind of connection to their identity, which had eluded them in England. They had both felt English and not English, Jewish and not Jewish. And they had gone seeking a sort of … rooted identity, a sense of place and purpose of belonging – Josh to his Jewishness in Israel and Max to a sort of internationalist, literary world. Identity is a work in progress. I don't think anyone goes, 'This is who I am, end of story, let's draw a line,' unless they're incredibly …

**JM:** … uninteresting. Has *Weinstein* been done professionally in England since 2005? Because it's a really good play.

**RC:** Thank you. 'No' is the answer. I think there are reasons for that, political reasons, I should imagine. You know, you write something like this and you don't come down on one side or the other … You're asking for trouble. Because you're not on a team, you're taking that perilous lonely road. But, to me, that's absolutely the job of the playwright. There were several off-Broadway readings in New York, and Habima[7] did a workshop production of it – and apparently it was done in India, which I found fascinating.

**JM:** What about *The Holy Rosenbergs*? Did that have a similar trajectory?

**RC:** Yes. It's been done once; it attracted a vast audience – for a play like this, you know. Again it's had interest from New York.

**JM:** *Holy Rosenbergs* has a bit of Arthur Miller in it, doesn't it? You've in fact often been compared to Arthur Miller – as a Jew whose plays have an ethical backbone. We could also speak of Ibsen, whose 'problem plays' are socially as well as ethically engaged, like yours.

**RC:** *Rosenbergs* is actually a loose template of *All My Sons*.[8] If you follow it, it's not exactly the same, but it has a similar arc … I wrote it really quickly.

**JM:** And was it a success?

**RC:** It was certainly a box office success. It was packed, and I would say critically ... some people really liked it, really liked it, and some people really didn't like it. Up until *Filthy Business*, that happened with everything I'd done. Even though I've touched the same subject of Jewish identity, British-Jewish identity, in many of my plays, I write different mood plays every time. If it were up to me, and I had a proper strategy, I would do something more like Pinter or Mamet, which is you get a really strong style, everyone knows that's you, and then you write whatever the hell you want. I've done exactly the opposite. It's pushing boulders up a hill.

**JM:** It was done at the National, which is incredible.

**RC:** Yes, but that came about, you know ... I had done *Our Class*,[9] and it was a very happy experience. A great thing to be involved in.

**JM:** I understand it was very successful, and visually stunning.

**RC:** It's a Polish play about the Holocaust – well, it touches on themes of genocide and war and segregation and nationalism that had never been performed. Not in Tadesuz's native country, not anywhere. It was deemed too politically sensitive because it suggested that some Poles murdered their Jewish classmates during the war by locking them in a barn and setting it alight. Our production was the first, meaning part of my job was to help knock it into some sort of stage-worthy shape. But I didn't really know what we had on our hands. I remember the first preview. The first act ended with the barn burning and the audience, instead of clapping or going to the bar, sat, completely still. Completely silent. 'I thought, Oh God, they hate it.' But I realized they were in a sort of cosmic shock. Subsequently, there've been productions all over the world, particularly in America. It had a big (joint) production in the Camari and Habima [theatres in Tel Aviv]. Nick was very affected by that play. After he said, 'Okay, well, what do you want to write next?' I had a couple of ideas. I was watching Jeremy Bowen on BBC news – he was a BBC Middle East correspondent – and he was talking about the Goldstone Committee.

**JM:** Yes, I remember.

**RC:** And about this religious Jewish South African judge, Goldstone, who was charged with leading a human rights investigation for the ICC. And I just thought, hey, that's sort of interesting territory. Immediately my brain goes: what happens when he goes home for Friday night dinner? Are they going to discuss that? It just seemed obvious to me that there was something rich there for me to explore. And from there I just went in the next day and said, 'What about this?' And they went, 'Do that.' But the whole point of that play was – and in a way, I did the scenes similarly with Weinstein – that there was a constant push and pull. Here were people who are as close to each other as they can be, related – father/daughter, father/son, wife/husband. How do they deal with a disagreement on such a profound level? She can't stop being his daughter. He can't not be her father.

**JM:** Interesting ... Push and pull. Your plays often put people in a position where they must choose, make a moral choice – or not. This is also true for *Filthy Business* I think. Hampstead is considered a sort of 'Jewish' theatre, isn't it?

**RC:** It has a large Jewish audience. But until *Filthy Business* it hadn't done a play with a Jewish theme in about six years.

**JM:** Really?

**RC:** I did a play there ten years ago called *The Glass Room*. That was very hard. I knew it would be.[10] Sian Thomas, who played the denier, was incredibly brave, going out in front of that audience. That first Saturday night, a surprising proportion of the audience had *kippot* (traditional head coverings worn mainly by Jewish men). You could feel the hostility. I mean, they knew she was acting, but the hostility! It's a brave person who's prepared to play that part. But it's a cracking part.

**JM:** That must have been a really difficult play to write!

**RC:** It was not an easy year. But I had to do it. I researched it a lot and then just went for it. I wrote it quickly again in a sort of frenzy. I really wanted to climb into the mind of someone I thought I could never understand. Why would they pit themselves against the mainstream so extremely, deny something as recent and as enormous and as well documented as the genocide of six million people? What would drive another human being to do that? It was cathartic. But you're really on an uphill battle with a play like that. I'm not sure I'd write a play like that now. As a young man, my instinct was to be bold. It gets you into trouble, but that's my job. To get into trouble.

## Notes

1 Craig, R. (2017), *Filthy Business*, London: Oberon Books.
2 *The Caretaker* and *The Dumb Waiter* were published in Pinter, H. (1991), *Harold Pinter: Plays 1*, London: Faber and Faber.
3 Pinter, H. (1991), *The Homecoming*, London: Faber and Faber.
4 Playwrights Julia Pascal and Gail Louw have more Jewish-themed plays. See Chapter 9 in this volume by Eckart Voigts and Sarah Jane Ablett.
5 Craig, R. (2011), *The Holy Rosenbergs*, London: Oberon Books.
6 Craig, R. (2005), *What We Did to Weinstein*, London: Oberon Books.
7 Habima is Israel's national theatre, located in Tel Aviv.
8 Miller, A. (1947), *All My Sons*, USA: Reynal & Hitchcock.
9 Slobodzianek, T. (2009), *Our Class*, trans. R. Craig, London: Oberon Books.
10 Craig, R. (2006), *The Glass Room*, London: Oberon Books. *The Glass Room* is about the trial of a Holocaust denier and her Jewish lawyer.

# John Nathan

This interview took place on 31 March 2018, in London.

**Eckart Voigts (EV):**   We are interested in the connection between writers, how their plays were received, and plays inflected with some kind of Jewishness.

**John Nathan (JN):**   A play that could be described as 'Jewish' is a description I have always found difficult and elusive. When I think about what we cover for *The Jewish Chronicle*, I think in terms of plays that have Jewish *interest*. In most circumstances, you don't have to be shackled by a definition of what makes a Jewish play – like who it has to be written by, and what the subject has to be, because Jewish interest is broad. I think that playwrights who have written plays of Jewish interest don't necessarily have to be Jewish.

**Jeanette Malkin (JM):**   Let me bring up somebody like Ryan Craig, who has written two plays, at least, in which, within the same family, you have a son fighting *for* Israel, and a father, or a sister, who has problems with Israel – for example *What We Did to Weinstein*,[1] or *The Holy Rosenbergs*,[2] where the sister is a lawyer working to condemn Israel for Human Rights' abuses. I find that a much more interesting way to approach the complexities within the British-Jewish public.

**JN:**   I think British Jews are still handicapped by the fear of being too visible as a subject.

**Ido Telem (IT):**   Still? This is what we hear a lot about the older generation.

**JN:**   There is still a lot of that older generation. If you look at the post-war generation, even baby-boomers, there are still people who, perhaps in a diluted sense, have the sensibility that visibility can invite problems. The defence mechanism has often been to be as insular as possible, as invisible as possible. Just the act of visibility increases the sense of vulnerability.

**JM:** If we go back to Craig for a moment, do you think that his plays – *Weinstein*, *The Holy Rosenbergs*, *The Glass Room*,[3] even *Filthy Business*,[4] which was just out last year – are limited to a Jewish audience? Do you think the world is not interested in his subjects? We spoke with Sir Nicholas Hytner, who had Craig's English version of Tadeusz Slobodzianek's *Our Class* (2009) and *The Holy Rosenbergs* (2011) performed in his National Theatre.

**JN:** Hytner, in a planned way or not, presided over a period of Jewish theatre at the National. He will say that programming the National is a process which involves lots of other people – and, certainly, many of whom are not Jewish. He never programmed anything against their opinion or had to fight for it on the grounds that it was Jewish. Yet there are plays which I think it is fair to say would probably not have been programmed had Nick Hytner either not been the artistic director or had he not been Jewish. I think *Travelling Light*[5] is a really good example. In terms of what we define as a Jewish play, you could not ask for a more Jewish subject. Yet Nicholas Wright, who wrote it, is not Jewish.

**EV:** Richard Bean is not Jewish either, as far as I know, but his plays have a dimension of East End history.

**JN:** Well, Richard Bean is a really interesting example in this because he collaborates with Nicholas Hytner quite a lot. I think Richard Bean is a supremely accomplished comedy writer, but with political heft to him, as well, so he can do those things. They revived *London Assurance*[6] by Boucicault at the National – and I will not go into the plot, but it involves a sort of mythical offstage character who is Jewish and who is the object of quite a few antisemitic jokes. And Nick Hytner, being Nick Hytner, wanted to do the play, and got Richard Bean to rewrite it. He turned jokes *by* Victorian antisemites into jokes *about* Victorian antisemitism. He completely subverted it, and we were, in the end, just laughing at *them* instead of their jokes. The way he did it was brilliant, because you are supposed to have this hook-nosed Jew coming onto stage, having been talked about in terms of Jewish stereotypes, while the word 'Jew' is never mentioned – and then on comes a Chinese man ...

**IT:** That's kind of playing with the audience's expectations.

**JN:** ... and being an expert gag-writer, he stoked up our expectation and then completely undercut it. Who are the inheritors of Pinter and the great Jewish figures? You could probably build a case that if there is a Golden Era of theatre over the last couple of decades, the key would be the works presented by three artistic directors rather than playwrights. Three Jews.

**JM:** Who?

**JN:** That would be Nicholas Hytner at the National, Dominic Cooke at the Royal Court and David Lan at the Young Vic.

**JM:** The idea that you have a period with three directors who are in some way responsible for a Golden Age of British theatre is in itself interesting.

**EV:** This was a pivotal time that Lan brought in. Not necessarily Jewish – he brought in European influences.

**JN:** As far as playwrights are concerned – and you would never blame them for this – what Jewish playwright would want to be known as a *Jewish* playwright?

**JM:** Craig. Craig is the only one who said, 'I can't *not* write about the people I know.'

**EV:** Nina Raine is one of those cases you would think is not particularly Jewish, although she is Jewish. She has done *Tribes*,[7] which is about a Jewish family.

**JN:** I think that maybe the problem – especially of post-war artists like Mike Leigh – is the fear of being pigeonholed. There are Jewish playwrights who fear that it is restrictive, that it restricts the way you are thought about and what you are expected to write about.

**JM:** Patrick Marber, whom I'm very interested in, proclaimed in an interview that he is a Jew first, a Brit second: 'I'm a Jew. Proud. That's what I am.' How do we view him? As a Jewish playwright? Not as a Jewish playwright? Obviously Jewish, because he defines himself that way.

**JN:** Well, I think, probably in a similar way you would with Pinter; you can see influences. He is much quicker than Pinter ever was to talk about his Jewishness. I think you could probably look at a play like *Dealer's Choice*[8] and identify a Jewish culture running through that.

**JM:** Do you mean the type of talking?

**JN:** The kind of talking, the rhythm … Even the act of playing poker – which is by no means exclusively Jewish but … It's a milieu he is interested in.

**JM:** Marber has said - and we can see - that he is influenced by Mamet. I want to put forward the thesis that both Pinter and Mamet are imitating the rhythm of Jewish English in Chicago and the lower East Side. Not *imitating* it but taking the *rhythm* of it.

**JN:** Well, I hear it more in Marber and Mamet than I do in Pinter, actually.

**JM:** Craig has said that when he reads Pinter, it is hyper-realism for him, that it is exactly his family in the East End.

**JN:** I can see a link between Mamet and Marber, and I can also see that link with Nina Raine. In that rhythm, in those speech patterns, in just the thrilling energy of the language and how thrillingly articulate it is. Let me tell you something about *Tribes*. I remember going to see it and thinking, this is really interesting. I don't think I knew Nina Raine was Jewish. I think I assumed she wasn't for some reason - and there is that opening scene.

**EV:** At the dinner table - the pasta is 'like being fucked in the face by a crab'. I just love that joke. It's aggressive, highly articulate, sophisticated.

**JN:** My note was: 'this is really interesting, a non-Jewish family speaking like Jews.' There is a combativeness to the discourse around the table, and everything that every member of that family is saying is being probed by another member of the family for weakness.

**EV:** Yes, but then Christopher - the Dad - is the most aggressive and he is the non-Jewish character. He is modelled on Craig Raine, the father who is not Jewish, but who fits into that scenario so well, and so presides over his half-Jewish kids.

**JN:** But the family is then outed - despite Craig Raine being the model for the father- as being Jewish. And then I had to cross out that note, about the non-Jewish family speaking like Jews.

**EV:** It's interesting that Nina isn't perceived as a Jewish playwright - because of the Dad, probably. Nina Raine is Craig Raine's daughter, and Craig Raine is not Jewish.

**JN:** Annie Baker, who is a Jewish-American playwright, has written a masterpiece in her play *John*. There is a moment quite early on, when there's a couple whose relationship is in trouble. There's an exchange, something like - from her: 'Why do we always end up having an argument?' and he says, 'But that wasn't an argument.' And I thought, 'Okay, he is Jewish, she is not.' I was pleased with myself, because it emerged that he was Jewish and she wasn't, and that dynamic between people for whom the definition of arguing is very different speaks of two different cultures coming together really beautifully.

**IT:** You make the case that the three major players in the shaping of the golden age of the British theatre are Jewish. Is that a coincidence? Are they simultaneously insiders with an outsider's perspective, so they know the ins and outs of the British theatre?

**JN:** I am not sure I can say that it's more significant than the fact that, to my mind, theatre is almost a form of Jewish expression. It is not exclusively a Jewish expression, of course, but theatre as an art form is very well populated by Jews. As all producers know, whether they are producing Jewish work or not, Jews go to the theatre and they don't only go to Jewish theatre or plays of Jewish interest.

**JM:** I just want to say that the academic argument for this is that Modernism was an opening, not only nationally – and this is especially true for Germany, but also for America and, perhaps, for England. Wherever anything new opened, Jews jumped in, because they usually weren't allowed to compete in traditional theatre. German and American cinema are largely Jewish, because it was completely new. So there is a thing about *openings* – where there are openings, Jews came in, because they weren't allowed into the old things. Jews and Theatre came together in the Western world in and through Modernism, where they were allowed to partake, as artists and as an *audience*.

**JN:** Well, I'm not sure there is one unifying argument, because theatre is such a diverse art form. You could, perhaps, say that theatre is a sort of citadel of argument. And if argument is, as we already discussed, a particularly Jewish characteristic, then you can bring those characteristics to the stage, and it must feel very natural to hear it. Because drama is about conflict, of course. There is not a play that's written; there is not a dramaturge that looks at a piece of work and doesn't ask where the conflict is, unless it's completely experimental. But whether, as I say, there is a unifying argument that can also encompass Jewish input in musical theatres, I don't know. Probably not.

**JM:** Well, music is also very Jewish in other ways. Jews, not being pictorial, went more for the abstract, like music.

**EV:** What about the links to American playwrights? Tony Kushner is an American-Jewish playwright but resonates very well in the London scene. There has also been the David Mamet/Harold Pinter connection.

**JN:** There is a relationship between American writers speaking to British audiences, but doing so – in those two instances of Kushner and Mamet – through Jewish characters who seem to be quicker to be embraced by British audiences. Arthur Miller is another writer whose career has been embraced.

**EV:** I am also looking for contemporary Jewish-themed plays that would address the communities that exist in Golders Green, and there is a lack of that, truly. Orthodox communities, coming in and out of these scenarios ...

**IT:** It has been addressed in literature and even film.

**EV:** Yes, it's been addressed in fiction, but where is the play that really addresses this? We've seen one play by Stewart Permutt at the Park Theatre. I can't think of any other plays that engage with orthodoxy or fundamentalism of any kind. It certainly makes an interesting cultural clash.

**JN:** Again, this is probably a question for artistic directors, as well. Is that something they have tried to commission and have only had *drek* (Yiddish: rubbish) come back? I think there is a weakness to the argument that all theatres have to be universal, but of course theatre needs to speak outside the *shtetel* or the context in which the action takes place, no matter what it is. Maybe there is an expectation, an unfair association, which speaks of that fear – that a Jewish writer is more concerned to be categorized as a Jewish writer than, say, a Black writer might be, because there is a view that it is a particularly narrow world. And so, if that is the case, then maybe that view translates into the way artistic directors think about Jewish community plays.

**IT:** We were just talking about how all these American-Jewish plays appeal to the London audience.

**JN:** The fact that you have American writers who feel uninhibited about writing on these themes maybe speaks of the culture in which they are brought up. Howard Jacobson and David Baddiel are two relatively rare examples of British Jews who feel utterly uninhibited about expressing, offering their art as unambiguously Jewish.

**JM:** And as worthy of contemplation by the world.

**JN:** Yes, exactly. And as valid as any other kind of art.

**IT:** Jacobson is very American.

**JN:** Well, you know, you think of him as very American because he is …

**JM:** Because he is outspoken.

**IT:** So Britishness is about not being able to speak to it directly?

**JN:** I think there is a still an inhibition. Although I really do hesitate to be a sort of psychologist for the Jewish community here.

**IT:** I was reading the history of the Board of Deputies of British Jews and this was the agenda: 'Don't stand out. Keep your Jewishness indoors and be British. Stay out of the political.'[9]

**JN:** That is certainly a characteristic of British Jewry, I would say, but also you asked quite rightly, does this still apply to the younger generation? I would guess less so.

**JM:** Do you see a change?

**JN:** I think so. But the reason I'm slightly hesitant is that if I suggest that I can see a change in terms of drama, I would like to be able to give more examples.

**EV:** Ryan Craig can be one example of someone who is not afraid to say, 'This is my *shtick* and these are my people, and these are my scenarios.'

**JN:** What he has created in *Filthy Business* is a fantastic antidote, in many ways, to the Jewish mother stereotype. Yetta, played by Sara Kestelman, is the anti-Jewish mother. She is motivated by a kind of personal ambition, or an ambition for her family, and she is prepared, in many ways, to sacrifice her children on that altar to keep her vision of the family going. The extent to which she would personally damage the people around her in order to sustain her vision of the way the family should continue was not something that I had ever seen so vividly. It has potency because it subverts the sort of Jewish stereotype of the over-protective Jewish mother, but it also subverts stereotypes of the mother.

**JM:** And it doesn't have to be Jewish. It's immigrant, mainly.

**EV:** I think that was also the reason why *Filthy Business* was produced in this way – as an immigration story that would resonate with maybe other ethnic groups, as well.

**JN:** Maybe in answer to your earlier question: could that particular Jewish play in fact be interpreted outside of the community as an immigrant story? I would say that there was a fear that it might be applied to Jewish stories more than to other ethnic stories.

**JM:** A fear of what? You can certainly talk about the Jewish contribution. Certainly, to the extent that Nick Hytner has had a huge influence on British theatre that was associated, whether he meant it to be or not, with a blossoming, if you like, of Jewish theatre within the National. Whether that translated and had a knock-on effect outside the National would take some research.

**EV:** The fact that you are hesitating suggests that it hasn't. If it had, you would be aware of it.

**JN:** And it also suggests that Nicholas Hytner's Jewishness did have, perhaps, a bigger effect on his programming than he might have initially acknowledged.

**JM:** But if we were to talk about a contribution to British culture, what would that be?

**JN:** The first thing that flicks into my mind is the stereotype. It has been a long complaint by Jewish actors that they have been directed by often non-Jewish directors in Jewish roles and told to behave in a certain way, in order to appease the preconceptions of non-Jewish audiences as to how a Jew behaves on a stage. And I think that maybe because Jewish directors are so conspicuous in the theatre culture, a degree of sophistication has at last been brought to the presentation of Jews on stage in Jewish stories. While I might be onto something, when I say that argument is a reason why there are Jews in theatre and why Jews are attracted to theatre, I am not so sure I can come up with one observation of what all of those Jews have brought to theatre that other non-Jewish practitioners haven't brought.

**IT:** Ironically, one of the answers we found to this is that Jews brought a great European influence into British theatre. Pinter for example brought an existentialist, modernist European heritage to the British theatre.

**EV:** Maybe that only applies to that generation and doesn't apply to someone like Ryan Craig.

**JM:** Another thing that was put forward is that many Jewish plays deal with ethical questions. A lot of Marber's plays, and Craig's, a lot of the plays we've read seem to deal with inner-family, ethical questions.

**JN:** I think it is fair to say that. It certainly ties in the observation about argument as a Jewish characteristic in British theatre because you cannot address these questions without argument.

## Notes

1. Craig, R. (2005), *What We Did to Weinstein*, London: Oberon Books.
2. Craig, R. (1991), *The Holy Rosenbergs*, London: Oberon Books.
3. Craig, R. (2006), *The Glass Room*, London: Oberon Books.
4. Craig, R. (2017), *Filthy Business*, London: Oberon Books.
5. Wright, N. (2012), *Travelling Light*, London: Nick Hern Books.
6. Boucicault, D. (1984), *London Assurance*, London: A & C Black.
7. Raine, N. (2013 [2010]), *Tribes*, New York: Nick Hern Books.
8. Marber, P. (1995), *Dealer's Choice*, London: Methuen.
9. According to JLAC, the Jewish Leadership Council website, 'The Board of Deputies of British Jews exists to promote and defend the religious and civil liberties of British Jewry. For over 250 years the Board of Deputies of British Jews has been at the forefront of safeguarding Jewish life in the UK.' Available online: https://www.thejlc.org/the_board_of_deputies_of_british_jews (accessed 23 March 2020).

# Index

the absurd 56–8, 71, 158, 193
Alderman, Naomi 15, 125, 135, 181, 210
Alfreds, Mike 12–14, 144
Almeida Theatre 4, 144
American-Jewish 6, 11, 32, 144, 217, 224, 250, 251
Amstell, Simon 189–93, 202
Anglo-Jewish 7, 52, 100, 101, 147, 174, 181, 200, 223. *See also* British-Jewish
antisemitism 3, 4, 5, 6, 8, 12, 13, 15, 17, 18, 20, 21, 22, 31, 40, 44, 46, 48, 50, 68, 72, 97, 100, 104–17, 121, 125, 134, 135, 162, 165, 167, 168, 174, 179, 181, 197, 209, 217, 218, 219, 220, 223, 231, 236, 247
Aramaic 17
Arcola Theatre (London) 14, 145, 221
Arts Council 11–13, 142, 177, 219, 223
Ashcroft, Peggy 22, 202
Ashkenazi 5, 9, 79, 147, 208
assimilation 5, 8, 9, 14, 17, 18, 128, 159, 198
Aukin, David 12, 13, 14
Azouz, Josh 15, 16

Baddiel, David 22, 206, 210, 211, 251
Baraitser, Marion 145, 146
Barnes, Peter 12, 19, 52
Baron Cohen, Sacha 6, 202
Baum, Devorah 141, 147, 148, 150
BBC. *See* British Broadcasting Corporation
Berkoff, Stephen 4, 5, 12, 15, 18, 21, 44–54, 105–16, 145, 220
Berman, Ed 6, 144

Billington, Michael 2, 10, 11, 53, 61, 68, 70, 79, 107, 115, 142, 146, 158, 159, 168, 174
blood libel 20, 104–17
Bonham Carter, Helena 6, 202
Boycott, Divestment, Sanctions (BDS) movement 22, 223
Brenton, Howard 4, 32
Bridge Theatre (London) 12, 21, 182
Britain 4–22, 33, 38, 44, 52, 67, 70, 85, 86, 90, 104, 105, 106, 108, 109, 121, 122, 135, 141, 142, 146, 154, 164, 174, 176, 177, 179, 180, 189, 201, 203, 208, 210, 211, 221, 223, 224, 236
British Broadcasting Corporation (BBC) 4, 66, 116, 158–61, 175, 188, 198, 199, 203–11, 227, 243
British-Jewish
history 7, 45, 46, 48, 49, 79, 86, 108, 25, 143, 146, 155–60, 178, 181, 189, 195, 197, 207, 223, 247, 252
identity 1 2, 5, 8, 9, 10, 13, 17, 20, 21, 57–9, 61, 62, 67, 71–3, 85–7, 89, 104, 107, 108, 121, 124, 126–35, 141, 142, 146, 148, 150, 151, 154, 155, 162, 165, 166, 168, 177, 179, 212, 219, 223, 228, 240–3
population 7, 8, 70, 76, 174, 202, 208, 223
theatre venues 14, 19–21, 125, 143–5, 154, 172–80, 238
Britishness 1, 133, 173–7, 198, 252
Brook, Peter 4, 5, 6, 9, 10, 12, 174, 231
Brookner, Anita 12

Bush Theatre (London) 4, 16, 116, 143
Butler, Judith 10

Cassenbaum, Nick 16
Chaikin, Joe 6, 144
Christianity 1, 9–11, 22, 40–2, 63, 79, 91, 105, 109, 115, 116, 131–3, 218, 221–5, 232
Churchill, Caryl 17, 21, 32, 63, 122, 143, 155, 176, 178
   *Seven Jewish Children* 17, 21, 122, 130, 178, 223
Cooke, Dominic 14, 172, 173, 174, 176, 178, 180, 182n10, 189, 248
Coon, Suzette 146
Craig, Ryan 1, 6, 8, 14–18, 21, 22, 32, 123–6, 132–5, 154, 155, 164–6, 178, 238–44, 252–4
   *Filthy Business* 18, 167, 168, 178, 238–40, 243, 244, 252
   *The Holy Rosenbergs* 125, 129, 155, 167, 169, 178, 241, 242, 246, 247
   *What We Did to Weinstein* 125–9, 155, 164–8, 241, 246
criminals 70, 76, 206
Czechoslovakia 2, 156–8

Day-Lewis, Daniel 6
diaspora. *See* Jewish diaspora
didacticism 18, 31, 40, 42, 64, 106, 130, 227
directing 5, 6, 12, 14, 22, 57, 142–4, 151, 154, 172–6, 180–2, 212, 235, 236–7, 248, 251–3
Diski, Jenny 12
Dodgson, Elyse 6, 144, 174
Donmar Warehouse (London theatre) 174, 175

East End (London) 14, 44–55, 67, 75, 145, 164, 173, 179, 181, 195, 220, 247, 248, 249

Eilenberg, Charlotte 86, 146, 178
Ellis, Samantha 2, 9, 14–16, 21, 145, 146, 151
Elton, Ben 22
Europe 2, 3, 4, 5, 6, 8, 9, 10, 17, 18, 33, 44, 56, 58, 75, 85, 86, 108, 109, 143, 147, 154–9, 202, 209, 210, 224, 226, 230, 248, 253
exile 10, 86, 87, 146, 154, 167, 191, 226, 227

feminism 142–6, 227
food 50, 133, 147–9, 189–91, 239
Frears, Stephen 6
Friedman, Sonia 22, 145
fringe theatre 4, 6, 14, 144, 145, 151, 154, 224
Fry, Stephen 12, 22, 202

gangsters 206–11
gender 13, 104, 141, 142, 146, 187, 192, 193, 198, 224
genocide 85, 89–93, 243, 244
German-Jewish 11, 58, 169, 203, 217
'Good Jew' 34, 38–41, 62, 64
Goodman, Henry 22, 202
Grant, Linda 1, 9, 10, 210

Hackney (London) 16, 53, 59, 66, 68, 79, 80
Hall, Ed (Edward) 14, 144
Hampstead Theatre 143–6, 151, 164, 166, 168, 178, 219
Hare, David 4, 32, 132, 144, 169, 174
Haredi 8, 15, 122, 146
Harris, Eve 15
Harwood, Sir Ronald 3, 9, 12, 76, 77, 101, 172
Hebrew 7, 17, 50, 54, 67, 71, 96, 148, 149, 164, 190, 19, 196, 197, 230, 231
history 4, 7, 12, 38, 45, 46, 48, 49, 53, 54, 78, 79, 86–97, 108, 125, 143, 146, 147, 154–60, 163, 165, 174,

## Index

178, 187, 189, 195, 197, 207–11, 222, 223, 247, 252
Hoffman, Eva 20, 85–101, 182
Holocaust 19, 20, 31, 35, 36, 42, 52, 56, 57, 59–61, 66, 69–71, 74–8, 85–101, 105, 106, 109, 110, 113, 146, 154, 159, 166, 171, 178, 179, 201, 204, 209, 221, 229, 232, 243, 245
Hugh of Lincoln 108, 110
Hungary 6, 41, 54
Hytner, Nicholas (Nick) 4, 7, 12–14, 22, 169, 173–7, 180–4, 217–20, 238, 247, 248, 253

Israel 5, 6, 8, 9, 13, 17, 18, 21, 22, 36, 37, 40, 41, 50, 52, 79, 100, 104–7, 121–37, 146–8, 154, 157, 165–8, 179, 188, 190, 206, 207, 211, 223–5, 228, 229, 241, 242, 245

Jacobson, Howard 12, 125, 208, 210, 251–2
Jays, David 10, 11, 14, 164, 176
Jerusalem 6, 21, 31, 34, 36, 40, 42, 43, 105, 122, 124, 130–4, 174, 225, 226
Jewish diaspora 8, 9, 17, 104, 121, 122, 135, 147, 166, 241
Jewish identity 1, 2, 8–10, 13, 17, 21, 57, 59, 61, 62, 67, 70, 73, 104, 121, 124, 126–9, 134–6, 141, 142, 151, 154, 155, 162, 165, 156, 169, 177–9, 241–3
Jewish theatre 1–6, 9–18, 21, 22, 52, 53, 105, 123, 134, 141–5, 154, 164, 172, 173, 177, 179, 180, 182, 219, 220, 247, 250, 253
Jewishness 1–5, 7–11, 13, 14, 17–9, 21–3, 50, 56, 57, 59, 62, 63, 67, 72, 73, 106–8, 125–7, 129, 133, 141, 146, 147, 150, 151, 159, 172–7, 180, 182, 195, 201, 204, 207, 209–12, 217, 218, 220, 230, 240–2, 246, 248–49, 252, 253

Judaism 2, 4, 22, 41, 67, 74, 108, 109, 162, 164, 165, 187, 191, 193, 195, 198, 210, 211, 227, 230, 232, 239
JW3 (Jewish Arts Centre, London) 14, 20, 21, 89, 101, 178–83

Kanaber, Daniel 15
Kendal, Felicity 22
Kerbel, Lucy 146
Kiln Theatre 15, 145, 180. *See also* Tricycle Theatre
Kops, Bernard 4, 5, 12, 18, 23, 42, 44–8, 50–4, 145, 220
Kushner, Tony 6, 250, 251
Kwei-Armah, Kwame 14, 174, 182

Ladino 17
Lan, David 12, 14, 174, 176, 181, 248
Laughton, Stephen 6, 9, 15, 17, 20, 104, 105, 108, 115, 116, 121–3, 174
Leigh, Mike 1–4, 9, 14, 15, 18, 21, 32, 47, 123–31, 135, 136, 145, 167, 173, 174, 178, 182, 217, 218, 248
Levi, Primo 19, 70, 86
Levy, Deborah 8, 141–3, 145, 164
Lewenstein, Oscar 22, 145
Lipman, Maureen 22, 190, 202
Louw, Gail 9, 15, 19, 131, 141, 146, 147, 151, 245
Lustgarten, Anders 6

Mamet, David 6, 162, 231, 235, 243, 249–51
Mandatory Palestine 3, 6, 108, 124, 224. *See also* Palestine
Marber, Patrick 154, 155, 160–3, 165, 167–9, 172, 223, 228, 230–7, 248, 249, 253, 254
  *Closer* 7, 14, 21, 154, 161–3, 233, 234, 237
  *Dealer's Choice* 7, 161–3, 232, 234, 237, 248, 254

*Howard Katz* 7, 155, 161–3, 165, 167, 223, 228, 230, 233–5, 237
Margolyes, Miriam 9, 202, 210, 211
Marowitz, Charles 6, 22, 123, 124
masculinity 129, 134, 187, 189, 191, 194
Meckler, Nancy 6, 14, 22, 143, 144, 151
Mendes, Sam 6, 12, 174–6, 180
messianism 3, 31, 34, 36, 40–2
Miller, Arthur 6, 16, 162, 167, 174, 231, 241, 242, 245
Miller, Jay 16
Miller, Jonathan 4, 9, 12
minority 7, 8, 11, 13, 151, 166, 168, 174, 177, 178, 209, 210, 219, 223, 227
Mizrahi 9, 210
Morgan, Peter 3, 4
multiculturalism 8, 14–17, 49, 86, 94, 176, 208, 210, 218
Muslim-Jewish Theatre Company (MUJU) 16, 178

Nathan, John 7, 10, 14, 22, 122, 134, 155, 159, 160, 162, 167, 177, 178, 246–54
National Socialism 3, 4, 19, 20, 35, 59–61, 70, 76, 77, 85, 100, 141, 146, 156, 163, 164, 170, 197, 204, 205, 222, 232
National Theatre (London) 4, 7, 12, 14, 19, 21, 125, 142–4, 154, 155, 161, 163, 164, 168, 169, 172–4, 176, 181, 224, 238, 245, 247

Oberman, Tracy Ann 14, 144, 146, 151
Okonedo, Sophie 22, 202
Old Vic Theatre (London) 12, 80
Open Space Theatre (London) 6
Orthodox Jewry. *See* Haredi
Osborne, John 2, 31, 32, 66, 105

Palestine 3, 6, 14, 17, 18, 79, 108, 121–5, 127–34, 144, 224
Park Theatre (London) 14, 15, 131, 145, 251

Parry, Natasha 9
Pascal, Julia 8, 11, 13, 14, 20–2, 46, 86, 100, 122–4, 130–2, 141–7, 151, 172, 177, 218, 219, 221–9, 245
  *Crossing Jerusalem* 21, 124, 130–2, 134, 226, 229
  *Dead Woman on Holiday* 225, 227
  *The Shylock Play* 46, 221
  *Theresa* 20, 86, 225
Permutt, Stewart 15, 251
Pinter, Harold
  *Ashes to Ashes* 2, 19, 56, 58–60, 62, 64, 77, 78
  *The Birthday Party* 18, 32, 56, 59, 60, 62, 72, 76
  *The Room* 18, 57, 71, 73
  screenplays 61, 63, 76, 77, 80
Pip Simmons Theatre Group 6
Poland 53, 86–91, 95, 97, 162–4, 169, 219, 231
Poliakoff, Stephen 3, 4, 12
police 61, 67, 68, 79, 181, 203–6, 211, 212
politics 8, 21, 33, 63, 64, 68, 69, 100, 122, 127, 134, 146, 173, 175, 179
Popper, Robert 189, 195, 196
Power, Ben 12

Radcliffe, Daniel 6, 202
Raine, Nina 141, 144, 147, 149–52, 248–9
ritual murder 8, 105, 108–14
Rosenthal, Jack 187–97, 228
Royal Court Theatre 4, 12, 16, 18, 143, 144, 149, 172–6, 178, 223, 224, 248
Royal Shakespeare Company (RSC) 4, 6, 12, 145, 175
Russia, Russian 4, 9, 50, 51, 131, 144, 155, 162, 163, 203, 206, 207, 211, 239

Samuels, Diane 8, 11, 14, 19–21, 86, 141, 145–7, 151
Schechner, Richard 6, 144
Self, Will 12
Sephardic 9, 14, 67, 164, 239
Shaffer, Peter, 3, 4, 12, 52, 141
Shaffer, Anthony 3, 4
Shakespeare, William 6, 34, 46, 53, 58, 106, 114, 123, 221
Shared Experience (theatre company) 12, 14, 144
Sher, Antony 7, 9, 12, 19, 86
Sherman, Martin 6, 19
Shoah 17–20, 35, 85, 86, 99, 209, 222. *See also* Holocaust
Shylock 6, 11, 34, 40, 42, 46, 106, 114, 124, 164, 202, 221, 230
Silas, Shelley 9, 14, 21, 123, 124, 132, 133, 141, 147–9, 151
Sinclair, Clive 12
Slovo, Gillian 9, 146
stereotypes 1, 11, 97, 131, 133, 142, 148, 175, 179, 201, 202, 207–11, 247, 252, 253
Stoppard, Tom 2, 5, 8, 9, 11, 15, 19, 21, 141, 146, 154–63, 165, 168, 172, 173, 235
  *Every Good Boy Deserves Favour* 158
  *The Invention of Love* 157
  *Leopoldstadt* 2, 9, 15, 19, 21, 154–8, 163
  *Professional Foul* 158
  *Rock'n'Roll* 158, 169
  *Travesties* 163

Taylor, C. P. 19, 52
television 12, 71, 110, 161, 175, 201, 211, 228
  television drama 158, 188, 189, 194, 195, 197, 201, 203–5
Tempest, Kate 146
Thomas of Monmouth 111, 115
Topper, Jenny 14, 143
tribalism 5, 49, 149, 154, 206
Tricycle Theatre 14–16, 21, 130, 145, 172–5, 178
TV drama. *See* television, television drama

Utopia 2, 3, 18, 31–42

Wanamaker, Sam 6, 174
Wandor, Michelene 141, 142, 145, 151, 177
Warner, David 22
Watford Palace Theatre 14, 15, 145
Weisz, Rachel 6, 202
Wesker, Arnold 2–7, 12, 18, 20, 21, 31–42, 44, 46, 52, 53, 73–6, 104–16, 141, 146, 164, 172, 178, 220, 231, 241
  *Blood Libel* 20, 104, 105, 107–16
  *The Kitchen* 18, 31, 34, 36, 39–42, 106
  *The Merchant* (renamed *Shylock*) 5, 34, 40, 46, 106
White, Michael 22
William of Norwich 110, 111
Wright, Nicholas 6, 178, 247

Yard Theatre (London) 16, 145
Yiddish 2, 17, 39, 46, 50, 53, 73, 155, 165, 168, 173, 179, 192, 196, 203, 205, 208, 224–6, 231, 241, 251
Young Vic Theatre (London) 12, 14, 21, 144, 174, 176, 178, 181, 248

Zangwill, Israel 17, 52, 146
Zegerman, Alexis 14, 15, 144, 145, 151, 178
Zionism 10, 107, 108, 122, 125, 127, 131, 224

www.ingramcontent.com/pod-product-compliance
Lightning Source LLC
Chambersburg PA
CBHW072135290426
44111CB00012B/1881